Emancipation through Muscles

Emancipation through Muscles

Jews and Sports
in Europe

Edited by Michael Brenner
and Gideon Reuveni

UNIVERSITY OF NEBRASKA PRESS
LINCOLN AND LONDON

This publication was made possible by the generous support
of the Alfried Krupp von Bohlen und Halbach-Stiftung, Essen and
the UNL Harris Center for Judaic Studies, Lincoln, Nebraska
Chapter 10, by Rudolf Oswald, originally appeared as
"Ein Gift mit echt jüdischer Geschicklichkeit ins Volk gespritzt
(Guido von Mengden): Nationalsozialistische Judenverfolgung und
das Ende des mitteleuropäischen Profifußballes, 1938–1941"
(" 'A Poison Injected with True Jewish Cunning)'
[Guido von Mengen]: The Nazi Persecution of the Jews and the
End of Central European Professional Soccer, 1938–1941")
in SportZeiten 2 (2002): 2.
Chapter 13, by Victor Karady and Miklós Hadas, originally appeared as
"Football et antisémitisme en Hongrie"
("Soccer and Antisemitism in Hungary") in
Actes de la recherche en sciences sociales 103 (June 1994): 90–101.
⊗
Library of Congress Cataloging-in-Publication Data
Emancipation through muscles: Jews and sports in Europe /
edited by Michael Brenner and Gideon Reuveni.
p.   cm.
Includes bibliographical references and index.
Proceedings of a conference organized in May 2002 by the Lehrstuhl für
Jüdische Geschichte und Kultur, Universität München and the Merkaz
Kobner le-historyah Germanit, Universitah ha-'Ivrit bi-Yerushalayim.
ISBN-13: 978-0-8032-1355-5 (cloth: alk. paper)
ISBN-10: 0-8032-1355-7 (cloth: alk. paper)
1. Jews—Sports—History—Congresses.
2. Jewish athletes—History—Congresses.   I. Brenner, Michael.
II. Reuveni, Gideon.   III. Universität München. Institute of Jewish History.
IV. Universitah ha-'Ivrit bi-Yerushalayim. Merkaz Kobner le-historyah Germanit.
GV709.6.E53   2006
796.089'924—dc22
2005032319

Set in Quadraat by Bob Reitz.
Designed by R. W. Boeche.

Contents

Illustrations

Acknowledgments

This book is based on a conference organized in May 2002 by the Institute of Jewish History and Culture at the University of Munich and the Richard Koebner Center for German History at the Hebrew University, Jerusalem. Our thanks are due to the assistance we received for both the conference and the editing of this volume by our graduate students Jens Kugele and David Rees. Without the enormous help of Dr. Ernst-Peter Wieckenberg this volume would not have come into existence.

The Alfried Krupp von Bohlen und Halbach-Stiftung gave generous financial support for the conference and the translation of several articles for this volume. The Norman and Bernice Harris Center for Judaic Studies at the University of Nebraska–Lincoln generously supported the publication of this volume. Our final thanks are due to Robert J. Taylor and Sara Springsteen of the University of Nebraska Press, and to our copyeditor, Sue Breckenridge, for handling this manuscript with extraordinary care and enthusiasm.

Emancipation through Muscles

Introduction

Why Jews and Sports

Michael Brenner

J EWS AND SPORTS? We all know how much Jews contributed to the cultural heritage of humankind, from Freud in the realm of psychology and
Einstein in the natural sciences all the way to Marx in politics, Kafka in
literature, and Schönberg in modern music. But Jews and sports? Do the two
really go together? Just as one knows that all Jews are smart and business-
minded, one is certain of the fact that they are inept in sports. Sure, there
was Mark Spitz, who saved "Jewish pride" with seven gold medals in the
1972 Munich Olympics, or the famous left-handed baseball pitcher Sandy
Koufax, but they seem to be the famous exceptions to the rule. And then
there were numerous Jewish sports world champions—in chess. But here
again, we are back to the realm of mental, not physical exercise. Thus, when
we announced a conference on the topic of Jews and sports in Munich, the
usual response we encountered was: "Oh, this is certainly going to be a brief
meeting."

If you were to ask a central European Jew around 1930 about Jews and
sports, his response would have been very different from what we expect
today. A German Jew might have remembered Alfred and Felix Flatow, the
first German Jewish athletes to win gold medals in the modern Olympic
Games. An Austrian would have answered immediately that Hakoah Vienna, a Jewish, even a Zionist club, received the most prestigious national
sport trophy, the Austrian soccer championship, in 1925. If that Austrian
were really into Jewish sports, he might have added that in the same year
Hakoah also became Austrian champions in field hockey, wrestling, and
swimming. A Hungarian would not have hesitated to name all the Jewish Olympic fencers who secured Hungarian medals, and a Czech would
have recalled the water polo team of Hagibor Prague, which gained the
Czechoslovak championship in 1928. One of its players was the well-known
writer Friedrich Torberg, the author of what was likely the only water polo
novel ever produced. Torberg became more famous for other parts of his
literary oeuvre, but he later wrote about his success with the water polo
team: "This was, I believe, the most beautiful day of my life."[1]

A Polish Jew around 1930 probably would not have talked about the success of other teams but of his own involvement in one of the numerous Jewish sports clubs active between the two world wars. The club in which one played usually also stood for one's political orientation: the right-wing Zionists gathered around Betar, the mainstream Zionists assembled around Maccabi, Socialist-oriented Zionists founded the Hapoel sports movement, and the Socialist (anti-Zionist) Bundists were active in the Morgnshtern teams, which Jack Jacobs analyzes systematically in this volume.

In the Europe between the world wars one knew that Jews could win Nobel Prizes—what was the big fuss about that? But that in 1925 a Jewish soccer team like Hakoah Vienna could beat the best European team, West Ham United, 5–0 on their London home grounds was a real source of honor and pride. Thus, today it is perhaps the lack of interest in sports, and particularly European sports, among intellectuals, and mainly among American intellectuals, that has made this a non-topic of historiography so far.[2] The present volume tries to balance this view with respect to the European Jewish experience in the twentieth century. It is based on the assumption that the way in which a society defines sports and the body is a reflection of how its members define themselves. The essays in *Emancipation through Muscles* explore the different meanings and functions of the "muscles" in the construction, dissemination, and perpetuation of Jewish identity in twentieth-century Europe. The outcome is a work that illuminates a side of both Jewish and sports history that so far has been almost entirely neglected.

Sports served both as a means of inclusion and as a way of exclusion, and Jews used sports as vehicles for emancipation at both the individual and collective level. Jews could show that they belonged to the surrounding society by participating in the sports associations of their neighborhood, while in other instances they were not allowed to join, either by being officially barred or prevented simply by a prevailing antisemitic atmosphere, as described for Austria and Britain by Michael John and Tony Collins. As a result they would often found their own sports associations.

In both instances—inclusion and exclusion—athletic activity was more than a marginal addition to their lives. The interwar period was not only a time of rising antisemitism, but also a high tide for sports enthusiasm. In his *History of a German*, Sebastian Haffner dedicated a whole chapter to "the sports craze that took possession of the youth in Germany." Haffner emphasized the political dimension of sports and observed that during the 1920s and '30s the membership of sports clubs and the number of participants in sporting events increased tenfold: "It was the last German mass mania to which I myself succumbed," Haffner admitted. Like Haffner himself, millions of Germans took part in this craze, usually without noticing in it the pseudo war-play it often manifested. Even the political left

> regarded sport as a splendid invitation by which we would hence-
> forth be able to vent our warlike instincts harmlessly and peacefully.
> The peace of the world was, they felt, assured. It did not strike them
> that the "German champions," without exception, wore little black,
> white and red ribbons in their buttonholes, the colors of the prewar
> Reich, while the colors of the republic were black, red, and gold. It
> did not occur to them that through sports, the lure of the war game,
> the old thrilling magic of national rivalry, was being exercised and
> maintained and that this was not some harmless venting of belli-
> cose instinct.[3]

Were Jews part of this enthusiasm? Of course, the seeming contradiction between Judaism and sports is not entirely without ground. In Jewish tradition, learning always played a central role, and every other activity was considered a waste of time. Moreover, in Greek and Roman times, sports were associated with idol worship, and the gymnasium was a place to perform in the nude. Still, physical activities were not absent from Jewish history even in premodern times. There are some reports of Talmudic sages being active in physical activities, such as Rabbi Simeon b. Lakish ("Resh Lakish"), who was a professional gladiator. In the Middle Ages, there are more reports of Jews in diverse sporting activities, including ball games. Thus, we also possess rabbinical responsa relating to the question of whether ball games were permitted in sixteenth- and seventeenth-century societies. In contrast to the strict objection expressed by the author of the *shulkhan arukh*, Rabbi Yosef Caro of Palestine, his colleague Moses Isserles of Cracow allowed ball games in public with reference to their enormous popularity.[4]

We also know some details of how those games worked in early modern Europe. In a rabbinical responsum around 1560, Rabbi Moses Provenzal of Mantua explained two versions of a kind of premodern tennis game (one with racket, the other without), which included betting on the winner. His responsum made clear that on Shabbat one was prohibited from playing for money and should distribute the gains in the form of food products. He also forbade the use of rackets, since they could break and one would be tempted to repair them on Shabbat. Of course, Rabbi Provenzal emphasized, one was not to play during the time of the synagogue sermon. Otherwise he did not

3

object to the game.[5] In nineteenth-century Central Europe when enthusiasts gathered around the "father" of the gymnastics movement, Turnvater Jahn, Jews were rarely among its pioneers. It wasn't easy for them, either, to participate in a physical exercise closely tied with nationalist romantic notions, which often included a good dose of antisemitism. By the end of the nineteenth century many gymnastics and sports associations made it clear that they would not welcome Jewish members, and thus they stood in line with student associations and parts of the youth movement. The image of the "Jewish body," which was not considered equal with the "Aryan body," began to play an ever-larger role in the minds of antisemites. The contributions in this volume by Moshe Zimmermann and Daniel Wildmann illuminate the rise of the "muscle Jew" phenomenon from different angles. This athletic image of the muscle Jew was, as for its general counterparts in European society, mainly a male image. As Gideon Reuveni makes clear, it was closely related to military training and early plans to transform Jews to soldiers. No one expressed this image in interwar Europe better than Sigmund Breitbart. In her essay, Sharon Gillerman analyzes the different perceptions of Europe's Jewish strongman. Women only played a minor role in the early efforts of transforming the Jewish body. Only in the interwar years did Jewish women become more active in athletics, with some of them rising to fame on the national and international scene. The most popular team sports, first and foremost soccer, however, remained a predominantly male issue, which is reflected in most contributions to this volume as well.

It was the young Zionist movement, which around the turn of the century took up most fiercely the fight for the equalization of the Jewish body. Zionism not only rose in order to make Europe's Jews resettle in their old home of Palestine, but also to create a "new Jew." In Theodor Herzl's words that meant "aus Judenjungen junge Juden zu machen" (to form young Jews out of Jewish lads). In this respect, the Zionists demanded a completion of emancipation, not just in a mental, but also in a physical sense, thus responding to the earliest calls heard in the fight for emancipation. The demand for transforming the Jewish body was already present in the title of the prize-winning 1788 essay of Abbé Grégoire, "The Physical, Moral, and Political Regeneration of the Jews."[6]

Herzl's second man, the extremely popular writer Max Nordau, expressed the Zionist longing for the physical transformation of the Jew bluntly, when he stated in a committee meeting at the Second Zionist Congress in 1898: "We have to think of how to recreate a muscle Jewry [Muskelju-

dentum]." [7] Two years later he returned to this thought in the *Jüdische Turn-Zeitung,* the journal of Jewish gymnasts: "In no other nation does gymnastics play such an important role as with us Jews. It is supposed to make our bodies and our character straight. It shall provide us with self-confidence." [8] And during the Zionist Congress in 1901 Nordau integrated the demand for a *Muskeljudentum* into his often quoted speech to the congress. Thus, the motto of the Jewish sports movement, which makes one smile today, was born.

Some Zionists derided the idea of muscle Jewry even back then. The later founder of the academic study of Jewish mysticism, Gershom (then still Gerhard) Scholem was a famous example. His father was a member of the athletic association Berliner Turnerschaft, which after 1890 became more and more open to antisemitic influences. Scholem père was also the author of a booklet for gymnasts, *Allerlei für Deutschlands Turner,* which had appeared in 1887. Gerhard felt a close relation to his uncle Theobald, a cofounder of the Zionist sports club Bar Kochba in Berlin, named after the heroic Jewish fighter against Roman rule in second-century Palestine. Scholem, however, had little sympathy for Jewish—or any other—sports activities. As much as he liked his uncle Theobald, he could not share the uncle's sports enthusiasm: "In the gymnastics association, which was supposed to give concrete expression to the 'Judaism of muscles,' Max Nordau's dreadful formula for the physical regeneration of the Jews, this man, who represented nothing of the sort, found a relaxation that was rather incomprehensible to me. The formula bothered me from the beginning, and although my uncle kept inviting me to join once I had shown an interest in Zionism, I could never bring myself to satisfy my Jewish enthusiasm, which thirsted for knowledge and insight, with gymnastics." [9]

At the time of Nordau's congress speech in 1901, Jewish sportsmen and sportswomen had already shown considerable success. They had received six gold medals at the first modern Olympics in Athens in 1896. By 1901, there were thirteen Jewish gymnastics and sports clubs in Central Europe—a number that would rise quickly and soon include non-Zionist clubs as well. Thus, the Reichsbund jüdischer Frontsoldaten, the association of World War I veterans, established the Schild (shield) movement. Sports clubs were part of a milieu building both among the Catholics and the working class. Likewise, for many Jews, sports served on the one hand as an important element of strengthening their collective identity as a minority (especially for Zionists who organized in their separate clubs) and on the

5

other hand as a means of integrating into society (for the more assimilationist element among European Jewry). In this book Jacob Borut examines the two different affiliations—with Jewish and non-Jewish clubs—from the perspective of interwar Central Europe. The most vivid description of the different milieus into which Jews integrated concerning their respective attitudes toward Judaism stems from the pen of the writer—and water polo champion—Friedrich Torberg. Describing the situation in Vienna, he distinguished between the various popular soccer clubs: Hakoah attracted those sympathetic to Zionism, Austria (then still called Amateure) drew the assimilated Jews, while Rapid, as the club of workers and the petite bourgeoisie, remained virtually closed to Jews. In a remarkable essay, Torberg recalled how once, when he watched a game by Hakoah, the supporters of the opposing team did not break out into their usual antisemitic "Sau-jud" slogans, but respectfully applauded one of their players with the call: "Hoppauf, Herr Jud!" The Hakoah stadium was, as Torberg noted, one of the rare places where Gentiles expressed unreserved respect for Jews in interwar Vienna.[10]

Even those Jews who were far removed from Judaism and Jewish communal life were often attracted by the success of this Zionist team. Thus, the historian Eric Hobsbawm, who defined himself a "non-Jewish Jew," recalled first and foremost the presence of Hakoah when he wrote about Jews and antisemitism in interwar Vienna: "There was no way of overlooking the existence either of antisemites or of the blue-white football club Hakoah, which faced my father and Uncle Sydney with a problem of loyalties when it played the visiting team Bolton Wanderers."[11] Likewise, the historian Susanne Miller recalled that the only thing Jewish she identified with from her childhood in Vienna was her enthusiasm for Hakoah Vienna.[12] In his essay here, John Bunzl further explores the legends built around Hakoah.

We should keep in mind that Hakoah was exceptional not only in its success but also in terms of its ability to attract assimilated Jews. Otherwise, in Central Europe, most of them were active in general teams, not in Jewish sports clubs. It may be psychologically telling that, in an age of rapidly increasing antisemitism, the greatest success of the Jewish sports clubs in Germany was in defensive sports, such as jujitsu, and in sprinting. Otherwise, most German Jews were members or supporters of the big clubs of the cities in which they lived. Historian Peter Gay, then called Peter Fröhlich, was—like many Berlin Jews—a fan of the popular soccer club Hertha BSC. Together with his father, who was subscribing not just to one but to two soccer journals, he listened to the radio whenever Hertha played or attended their games. More than half a century later he still knows by heart the formation of Hertha's championship-winning team of 1930, just as Henry Kissinger still follows the results of the soccer team dear to him from his native Fürth.

In Peter Gay's description of his childhood years, another aspect of identifying with sports becomes clear, however. Sports also served as a means of comfort in difficult times: "With its regular weekly rhythms, the soccer season provided a certain continuity at a time when we lived, as it were, from day to day, Nazi decree by Nazi decree. That sports brought me even closer to my father only added to its charms. 'Ha! Ho! He! Hertha B.S.C.!' It almost seemed something to live for."[13]

Jews were soon ousted both as players and fans from the soccer stadiums of Nazi Germany. More than that, Nazi ideology developed a particular identification of German soccer as a clean amateur sport, while in neighboring Austria and Hungary, in the view of antisemites, the all-too intrusive Jewish spirit was made responsible for its professionalization. Drawing upon new and original source material, Rudolf Oswald in this volume juxtaposes the different brands of central European soccer under the influence of Nazi ideology in the late 1930s.

Many emigrants expressed their longing for home through the familiar ways of playing sports. The nostalgic feelings seemed the more necessary the more exotic their surroundings. Thus, as Albert Lichtblau makes clear in his contribution, for Jewish refugees in Shanghai soccer was a means of surviving as Europeans in a foreign culture. The few Holocaust survivors may have had similar reasons when they established sports associations as one of their first acts in the postwar Displaced Persons Camps of Central Europe. They preserved at least the appearance of normality and continuation of prewar life. As Philipp Grammes describes for the first time in this volume, boxing fights, soccer matches, and ping-pong tournaments soon became a part of the day-to-day life in the DP camps. Teams with strangely sounding names in small places in the Bavarian province that had never before harbored Jewish communities, such as Maccabi Marktredwitz and Hapoel Neunburg vorm Wald, now played against each other in a variety of soccer leagues.

Not far away, in the Bavarian capital of Munich, a prewar Jewish hero had returned to lead his team again to the road of success. Kurt Landauer, president of Bayern Munich for most of the interwar period, had left his

Swiss exile and was re-elected president of the club in 1947. Fifteen years earlier he had presided over the first championship of Bayern, which much later would become the most successful club in German soccer history. Only a few years after his greatest success he found himself in the Dachau concentration camp, just outside the gates of Munich. It seems that the Bayern team remained somewhat loyal to their former president even after he emigrated to Switzerland. There are reports of players visiting him while on a friendly away game in Geneva during the Second World War. Indeed, the team never found sympathies with the ruling Nazi party. One of the reasons may be that Bayern was sometimes designated the "Jew team" long before 1933, perhaps due to their president, but also to the substantial support they received from Jewish fans. In contrast to their local rival 1860 Munich, which switched from a "red" working class team to a "brown" club, supportive of the new Nazi regime, Bayern was always regarded as a bourgeois club, with no clear neighborhood association.

In this respect, Bayern shared its reputation with other significant European clubs. In contrast to the German case, this association lasts until today in many European countries. The supporters of Holland's most successful team, Ajax Amsterdam, swing flags with the Star of David, while antisemitic Hungarians still get upset about the success of "Jewish" MTK Budapest, as is shown here by Viktor Karady and Miklós Hadas. In his essay, John Efron explores why first-time visitors of White Heart Lane, the home of London's Tottenham Hotspur, might be surprised to hear their non-Jewish supporters roar: "We are the Yids."

While those cases of identification with imaginary Jews may be part of a growing phenomenon described by journalist Ruth Gruber as "virtual Judaism," the opposite phenomenon of antisemitism in Europe's soccer stadiums from Rostock to Rotterdam to Rome is certainly more typical.[14] To give but one example: In April 2002, a news report read: "In the vicinity of Paris, ten Jewish soccer players were attacked by unidentified people while training, and part of them were injured. As the police reported, the fifteen masked attackers entered the training grounds in Bondy with clubs, irons and lead balls. The goalkeeper of Maccabi Bondy had to be hospitalized with a head injury."[15]

So why, then, Jews and sports? Because, contrary to common opinion, Jewish history cannot be reduced to intellectual history. Jews had bodies as well as minds. European Jewry comprised fencers and boxers, soccer and athletic teams, just as they counted rabbis and philosophers, lawyers and businessmen among their ranks. For many Jews in interwar Europe, sports was more than just an occasional pastime. Sports served as a weapon in their various fights. For some, Jewish teams like Hakoah Vienna demonstrated that Zionism could breed a "new Jew." For others, participation in non-Jewish soccer or athletic teams was a vehicle for their acceptance in general society. They all used their muscles as well as their minds in their respective fights for the Jewish national cause and for individual emancipation.

Notes

1. Friedrich Torberg, "Warum ich stolz darauf bin," *Wien oder der Unterschied* (Munich, 1998), p. 16.
2. This holds true mainly for English-language publications. One recent exception is the highly reliable account on European soccer by the American journalist Franklin Foer, *How Soccer Explains the World: An Unlikely Theory of Globalization* (New York, 2004). Most Jewish histories do not even mention the realm of sports. See for example the four-volume *German-Jewish History in Modern Times*, ed. by Michael A. Meyer (New York, 1996–1998); the follow-up *Geschichte des jüdischen Alltags in Deutschland: Vom 17. Jahrhundert bis 1945*, ed. by Marion Kaplan (Munich, 2003); and the more general *A History of the Jewish People*, edited by Haim H. Ben-Sasson, 2nd ed. (Cambridge MA, 1976).
3. Sebastian Haffner, *Defying Hitler: A Memoir*, trans. by Oliver Pretzel (New York, 2002), pp. 71–74.
4. See "Sports," in *Encyclopedia Judaica*, vol. 15 (Jerusalem, 1972), pp. 291–92.
5. Cecil Roth, *The Jews in the Renaissance* (Philadelphia, 1959), p. 28.
6. See John M. Efron, *Defenders of the Race: Jewish Doctors and Race Science in Fin-de-Siècle Europe* (New Haven, 1994), p. 6.
7. Max Nordau *Zionistische Schriften* (Cologne, 1909), p. 380.
8. Nordau, "Muskeljudentum," *Jüdische Turn-Zeitung*, June 1900; reprinted in *Zionistische Schriften* (Berlin, 1923), p. 425.
9. Gershom Scholem, *From Berlin to Jerusalem: Memories of My Youth*, trans. Harry Zohn (New York, 1980), p. 24.
10. Torberg, "Warum ich stolz darauf bin," pp. 15–23.
11. Eric Hobsbawm, *Interesting Times: A Twentieth-Century Life* (New York, 2002), p. 23.
12. Personal remark by Susanne Miller to the author.
13. Peter Gay, *My German Question: Growing Up in Nazi Berlin* (New Haven, 1998), p. 107.
14. Ruth Ellen Gruber, *Virtually Jewish: Reinventing Jewish Culture in Europe* (Berkeley CA, 2002).
15. *Frankfurter Allgemeine Zeitung*, April 12, 2002.

From "Talmud Jews"
to "Muscle Jews"

1. Muscle Jews versus Nervous Jews

Moshe Zimmermann

WHAT IS THE antonym for "muscular Judaism" (*Muskeljudentum*)? The term commonly used in German is either "spiritual Judaism" (*geistiges Judentum*) or "Talmudic Judaism" (*Talmudjudentum*). "Muscular Judaism" is always associated with the opposite of the typical Galut (diaspora) Jew: weak, frail, despised, doing his *Luftgeschäfte* (unproductive business). Max Nordau, the man who invented both the idea and term of "muscular Judaism," emphasized this juxtaposition from the early days of the Zionist movement. He wrote in 1898 that he expected that Zionism would revolutionize the Jewish image, creating the "new Jew": "Zionism regenerates the Jewish body through the physical education of the young generation, which will regenerate the long-lost muscular Judaism."[1] Twenty years later, in 1922, a representative of the German Jewish student movement wrote, "With us, the idea of sports is closely connected with, and deeply embedded in Zionism. . . . The feeble *Jeschivebocher* (Talmud student) has served long enough as a stigma of our banning."[2] Or in the same spirit: "The sportsman . . . is the most capable of all to dedicate himself totally to Zionism."[3] The most radical remark was made in 1920 by yet another Zionist of the first generation, the physician Theodor Zlocisti: "Turnen [Gymnastics] and Zion are only different expressions of one and the same necessity: the physical and spiritual regeneration of our people," a remedy to the "curse of the galut."[4] The founding fathers of Zionism thus raised gymnastics (and later sports in general) together with the ideal of "muscular Judaism" to the level of Zion itself in their solution of the "Jewish problem."

Max Nordau and Theodor Zlocisti were authentic representatives of fin-de-siècle central European society who had no difficulty introducing this message into Jewish society and its national movement. Nordau, who wrote his famous book *Degeneration* (*Entartung*) in 1892, was not only well acquainted with the relevant terminology and with the reciprocity of the physical and the spiritual, but also contributed decisively to this ongoing debate.

Two characteristic components of this nineteenth-century debate deserve the historian's attention. First, we can recognize clear parallels between the goals of the German and the Jewish gymnastics and sports movements. A short time after the beginning of the century, Napoleon and his "Grand nation," by defeating the German states on the battlefield, triggered a national German reaction. Out of this defeat came the idea of gymnastics as a national remedy, propagated by Turnvater (Gymnastics Father) Jahn, and its channeling into the gymnastics movement. The basic idea was that a healthy nation needs men and women with "mens sana in corpore sano," or a healthy mind in a healthy body. Jahn's social criticism was directed mainly at the German bourgeoisie, who, according to him, lacked the necessary physical health and thus had dragged the nation into defeat. This idea of gymnastics, which became popular not only in Germany but also in other parts of Central Europe (e.g., the Sokol movements in Bohemia and Poland) eventually found its way into the late-nineteenth-century Jewish national movement. In 1897, in a meeting of the delegates of German Zionism that took place shortly after the first Zionist congress, delegate Fabius Schach from Cologne tried to convince his listeners: "The creation of pro-Zionist gymnastics associations is needed in order to turn the Jews from bookworms into men capable of fighting the war of survival." Such associations would enhance "the moral power and the spiritual alertness of men. Gymnastics is of far-reaching importance for the national future of our people."[5] Thanks to Nordau's speech about "muscular Jews" in the following year before the delegates of the Second Zionist Congress, the idea became a platform for the whole Jewish national movement: "For no other people does Gymnastics have such an important educational role as with us Jews."[6] From the start, Nordau's endeavor was supported by Prof. Max Mandelstamm, an east European Zionist leader who got to know the gymnastics association while a student in Germany and prepared an analysis of the physical conditions of east European Jewry.

Less than five years after the First Zionist Congress, Hermann Jalowicz could summarize the achievements as follows: "Curiously enough, a process very similar to the one we observed while following the efforts of the German nation toward unity is taking place in the history of the Jewish people: it also started with a national gymnastics movement."[7] This observation remained valid even twenty years later: "The Jewish gymnastics movement took upon itself the same task as the German gymnastics movement did more than a hundred years ago: preparing the people for national revival!"[8] Nordau, in his call for a "muscular Judaism," followed in Jahn's footsteps so far as to express his hope for the regeneration of an "arms-loving Judaism" (waffenfrohes Judentum)[9] like in the times of Bar Kochba's rebellion against the Romans (132–35 CE). No wonder that the first national Jewish gymnastics association in Germany (1898) called itself Bar Kochba, the Jewish version of Hermann the German, the war leader who defeated the ancient Romans.

The second characteristic component in the national or *völkisch* context of the time was just the other side of the coin: it was the conviction that peoples, rather than just being aggregates of individuals, are large organisms. This conviction eventually led to the pessimistic conclusion that peoples, like individuals, could deteriorate and degenerate. This conclusion guided those who looked for a solution to the "Jewish problem." When Nordau suggested that "each local Zionist association should open a department for gymnastics," [10] his explanation theoretically combined both components we consider here: "The nineteenth century was the epoch of the organic disintegration (*Zersetzung*) of Judaism." [11]

Indeed, the terms Nordau used—degeneration (*Entartung*) and biological disintegration (*Zersetzung*)—in order to illustrate the general state of society became fundamental concepts for Jewish gymnasts and sportsmen when it came to criticizing Jewish society. [12] Nordau and his followers were not satisfied with these terms alone. For example, when he explained their background, Nordau made early marriage responsible for this decay, since "it hampers physical development and lays the seeds for later sickliness [*Siechtum*] of the organism." [13] It remained an open question whether the problem was only an east European one (while west and central European Jews should be considered as halfway regenerated), [14] a general Jewish one, or a specific problem of the Jewish bourgeoisie. Be it a general or a specific problem, the function of "muscular Judaism" was understood as "curbing the already radicalized process of physical degeneration of the Jewish race." This, at least, was the argument proclaimed during the first meeting of Jewish gymnasts during the Sixth Zionist congress in 1903. [15] A statement made later by a representative of the student movement called it "exercising the physical regeneration," [16] or "the physical renaissance of the Jews." [17] That is to say, even if one defines the Jews as a race, they are not inherently inferior, but rather only degenerate, and are capable of starting a process of regeneration and rejuvenation.

These statements were truly representative for their time. They did not ask for regeneration of the individual Jew alone, but for the regeneration of the Jewish people, the nation as an organic unit, using the word "sickliness" to illustrate the state and behavior of a people. "We know that most modern information provided by psychology of peoples (*Völkerpsychologie*) and ethnology teaches us that every people should, like every individual, live its life based on its specific organic nature . . . and reject any attempt to languish (*verkümmern*) as a result of pressure, scorn, or enmity."[18] Yet these very terms used by Nordau, the psychiatrist, in this speech of 1907, demonstrate clearly that the opposites are not only "muscle" and "spirit," that is, power versus powerlessness, but also health and mental sickness. Talking about "the generational malady," as early as 1882 Nordau specified: "Some call it nervosity, some call it pessimism. Others refer to it as skepticism. But the multiplicity of the definitions refers to one and the same malady."[19] Contemporary observers referred to it as a mass sickness, even an epidemic. The author of the book *Die geistigen Epidemien* (1906; The Mental Epidemics), Willy Hellpach, described "the millions to whom one refers as 'nervous,' 'inferior,' 'degenerate,' 'perverse,' or otherwise."[20] In his memoirs, Nordau mentioned the most common of all such illnesses: "In the year 1887, my two-volume novel *The Malady of the Century* appeared. It was a study of the mentality of the pessimist, the man devoid of will and energy, the prototype of 'fin de siècle.' . . . The hero of *The Malady of the Century* is a neurasthenic, degenerate person."[21] For Nordau, the source of the illness did not lay in the muscles but in "the centers of control of movement in the brain," that is, in the nervous system.[22] Indeed, the notion of degeneration that became the title of Nordau's famous book was connected from the time of its inception in 1857 to a disruption of the nervous system caused by alcohol, drugs, and so forth.[23]

In sum, Nordau and the other spokesmen for "muscular Judaism" who looked for a collective remedy to the "generational malady" and its most popular expression (as we shall see later), did not confine themselves to an abstract discussion of body and spirit, but used concepts and theories derived from new and innovative sciences—psychology, psychology of peoples, eugenics, medicine, hygiene, and so on—and referred to the collectivity of the nation. "During the centuries of their extreme misery, the Jews experienced a peculiar state of hallucinatory dream" (*halluzinatorischer Traumzustand*).[24] In other words, the definitive antonym of the "muscular Jew" was neither the "*Luftmensch*" nor the "spiritual Jew" (*geistiges Judentum*), but rather the Jew of "pondering and anxiety, of nervous thought and timid wavering,"[25] in short, the nervous Jew. *Nervenjudentum* was the problem that Zionism had to solve. *Nervenjudentum* was the challenge for Jewish gymnasts and sportsmen.

Shortly after the Jewish gymnasts' monthly *Jüdische Turn-Zeitung* (hereafter

jtz) began to appear, it raised the argument that the activity of the Jewish gymnastics movement was a reaction to "the symptoms of degeneration . . . the amazing increase in nervousness and insanity" among Jews.[26]
Professor Max Mandelstamm recommended the improvement of the physical conditions of the Jews against the background of "overstrain and fatigue
of the Jewish brain and his entire nervous system."[27] A year later, jtz's editor, Hermann Jalowicz, an enthusiastic supporter of gymnastics and sports
as a part of the Zionist enterprise, explained how important sports were
for Zionism: "No wonder that under such lamentable circumstances [life
in the ghetto] which are the fostering soil for physical degeneration . . .
a lamentable human type emerged with deranged nerves and a weakened
body. . . . Zionism is the healing serum against these miasmas of the pesti-
lent ghetto air."[28] In the eyes of Zionists, it was not ghetto life alone but also
Jewish emancipation that contributed to the creation of this very syndrome.
"Emancipation was advantageous for German Jews . . . but it distorted the
physiognomy of the Jewish soul."[29] Thus, they went so far as to call the
gymnastics association "defense association [Abwehrverein] against intellectualism."[30]

From an early stage of Zionism, the contrast between "muscular Judaism" and "nervous Judaism" was present. Overcoming the neuroses so
characteristic of the Jewish image became one of the aims of Zionism.[31]
No wonder that the physician Moritz Jastrowitz gave one of the articles he
published in jtz in 1909 the very title "Muskeljuden und Nervenjuden."[32]
There he declared his allegiance to Nordau's slogan of "muscular Judaism,"
but added, "there is no use in strengthening the muscles without improving
the nervous system." This was meant as a warning to those who automatically suggested physical exercise as the sole answer to the Jewish problem;
"neurasthenia can put even the athlete out of action." Gymnastics as a remedy must therefore pay attention to nerves too, not just to muscles. Five years
earlier, another Jewish gymnast published an article in the same journal
on the relation between Jahn's remedy for national illness—gymnastics—
and the nervous system. "The healing influence of gymnastics is especially
adequate for the nervous species of our age," he wrote.[33] Gymnastics were
intended to overcome the unceasing irritation of the nerves and the "poison
to the nerves called coffee shops and pubs." Even after World War I, one of
the leaders of the Jewish gymnasts had no doubt that "the founders of the
gymnastics movement considered 'the physical regeneration of the Jews'

as their main aim. . . . Investing in 'muscular Judaism' as against the over-spiritualized 'nervous Judaism' seemed to be especially useful."[34]

This contrast received much attention during the first phase of Zionism, partly because of the "popularity" of neurasthenia at the time—feebleness of the nervous system and chronic fatigue. The term neurasthenia, which had been invented in 1880 by the New York physician George Beard, was used by Nordau just seven years later. Contemporary literature tells us how widespread the term neurasthenia became in the medical and psychological discourse of bourgeois society. [35] In Germany, this disease gained special popularity. Freud remarked in 1887 that it "is the most widespread [disease] in our society."[36] The existence and ubiquity of neurasthenia was interpreted as a result of capitalism, the industrial revolution, and accelerated urbanization—in other words, of modernization[37] and the nature of a "restless age . . . the age of nervousness."[38] In Germany, the appearance of neurasthenia coincided with the end of the liberal era and the rise of modern antisemitism (around 1880). Willy Hellpach, a physician and democratic politician around 1900, the author of many contributions on nervosity, paid much attention to this correlation. From the discussion of the interrelation between modernity and nationalism in Germany there arose also the discussion of this very topic in the Jewish, especially Jewish-national context.

There was no unanimity concerning collective inclinations of peoples and nations to neuroticism or neurasthenia. In any case, those who believed in a susceptibility of certain nations to neurasthenia did not necessarily include the Germans. The German tradition, to which Nordau belonged, was considered to be one of gemütlichkeit, of easy going and good nature, with "Michel," a figure representing the good-natured German, as its prototype. If neurosis and neuroticism were to be attributed to any national population, it was the French.[39] But in any case, what the historian Joachim Radkau called "neurologic nationalism" was not considered by scientists a serious matter. Yet there was one exception: the assumption that the Jews as a community were especially prone to nervousness was widespread.

Radkau, the author of Das Zeitalter der Nervosität (The Age of Nervousness, no doubt thus adopting the term coined by Willy Hellpach in 1906), quotes quite a number of contemporary experts who believed that Jews were typical carriers of nervous and mental diseases. At the same time, he found out that this conclusion was not followed in the scientific literature by antisemitic innuendos. After all, a number of reputable Jewish physicists and experts shared this belief. Rafael Becker, who had published two relevant lectures

by the end of World War I, put it bluntly: "Nervousness was common espe-
cially among Jews. . . . Every second Jew is believed to be neurasthenic." [40]
This belief was shared by many. [41] Sander Gilman, the expert on "the Jewish
body," agrees with Radkau's conclusion, basing his judgment on Maurice
Fishberg's observation of 1911: "Every physician is aware of the fact that Jews
especially suffer from functional disorders of the nervous system." [42] But
Gilman, like historian George Mosse, argued retrospectively, contrary to
Radkau, that attributing to the Jews a special susceptibility to nervousness,
mainly identified with hysteria, led to their stigmatization, and that it was
not accidental that the early era of neurasthenia coincided with the beginning of the new antisemitic movement, the early 1880s. According to their
view, those who wanted to reinstate old-time, premodern gemütlichkeit in
Germany could translate their efforts into a war against the Jews, the alleged
carriers of this disease that was a symptom of harmful modernity. [43] But
despite the common belief that Jews were more susceptible than others
to mental disease and nervousness, the identification of neurasthenia as
typically Jewish did not remain unquestioned. Ignaz Zollschan, the early-
twentieth-century Jewish expert on questions of the Jewish race, claimed
on the one hand that during the nineteenth century "the Jews have become
more nervous and irritable." But on the other hand, he stressed that "the
Jew, although his nervous system is especially delicate and sensitive, does
not necessarily turn neurasthenic." [44] To this he added a demographic observation: "Compared to the Jews, the other people have an advantage . . .
because they can replace the exhausted nerve power (Nervenkraft) of their
city-dwellers thanks to the steady and rejuvenating stream of people from
the country whose nerve power has not yet been wasted." Neurasthenic or
just nervous—according to Zollschan the Jewish race was in danger, "and
without Zionism there are only two alternatives: dissolution of the [Jew-
ish] race or physical degeneration." [45] Since both the expert and his readers
rejected these alternatives, the only solution to widespread nervousness or
neurasthenia of the Jews was Zionism.

As did many people in his circles, Zollschan drew a connection between
the disease, be it neurasthenia or sheer nervousness, and urban life in the
age of industrialization. Indeed, the Jews were especially vulnerable in this
respect, both in the eastern European Shtetl and in already emancipated
Central and Western Europe. Whereas Mandelstamm believed that mainly
the east European ghetto was to be blamed, others, like Martin Engländer,
stressed the fact that western Jews had moved out of the ghetto: "Consider-

ing the behavior of western Jews we must pay attention primarily to the process of degeneration of the nervous system." Among western, modernized Jews, "material capital was acquired at the cost of nervous capital."[46] More than one commentator described the connection between westernized urban life and neurasthenia in terms of "coffee-house Jews" (Kaffeehausjuden). The suggested remedy was gymnastics: "Gymnastics is the cure for rising neurasthenia within Judaism." In this spirit, the Jewish gymnastics movement was called on to promote gymnastics and hiking (wandern).[47]

Franz Oppenheimer, a Zionist close to Theodor Herzl and a physician by profession before he became a university professor of sociology, related to this connection in the following manner: "The professional disease of the upper-class workers of the brain, the neurasthenia, can be cured through physical activity in form of games, that is through sports." For this group, according to Oppenheimer, sports could even substitute for sleep as a way for the body to renew and regenerate itself. Oppenheimer's preference for sports instead of gymnastics was unusual at the time, among Germans and German Jews alike.[48] Hermann Jalowicz opposed sports because he believed that, contrary to gymnastics, it irritated the nerves.[49] But Oppenheimer was supported by another Zionist, Felix Theilhaber (well known because of his 1911 book The Downfall of German Jewry), who strongly opposed "one-sided gymnastics fanaticism" because it ignored some nerve-related questions: "Especially we Jews . . . who struggle against nervous restlessness . . . are less inclined to do gymnastics. . . . That's why we should create sports associations." While taking part in sport games, so he assumed, "the nervous Jew is doubly satisfied."[50]

There was one group that allegedly needed a special "medication" when it came to physical exercise. "Whereas the powerful man's body is ruled by the muscular system, the sensitive body of a woman is ruled by the nervous system . . . [A]bout 80 percent of highly situated German women suffer from nervous over-sensitivity. . . . Women's gymnastics should therefore include only exercises that do not burden the nervous system too much." This recommendation was brought to the attention of the national Jewish gymnasts in 1902.[51]

Looking for the causes of the illness among Jews—men or women—led not only to modern urban life but also to exile. "Two thousand years ago, the Jewish psyche was intact, but two thousand years [of exile] have made it sick. It has now become a characteristic of the Jewish race that the nervous system of the individual Jew is extremely sensitive and vulnerable."[52] The

Jewish nervous sensitivity is thus attributed to the condition of exile, to the "nerve-racking torture of never-ending persecution." Its effect was so crushing that even emancipation could not repair the damage "caused by inherited neurasthenia," either because the period of emancipation was too short compared to the previous period of persecution or because of emancipation's inability to change the notorious Jewish inclination for "intellectualism."[53] Rafael Becker, too, assumed that among modern Jews the lack of a healthy occupation, with agriculture on the one hand and the pressure to take up academic studies on the other hand, had a clearly negative effect on the nervous system. Thus, Becker rejected an explanation that admitted the inferiority of the Jewish race or even a special Jewish tendency to degenerate, and preferred an explanation that stressed Jewish social conditions or a Jewish inferiority complex. He, like many others, could therefore reach the conclusion that this nervousness was curable, mainly with the help of Zionism.[54] But on the same basis, antisemitic conclusions could also be reached, as George Mosse has demonstrated.[55] Some Jews reached a conclusion defined as self-hatred, according to which nervous diseases are "essentially Jewish." Nor did Zionists hesitate to adopt antisemitic approaches that seemingly supported their case. JTZ, the journal of Jewish gymnastics and sports, delightfully quoted an article written by a non-Jew in the journal *Kraft und Schönheit*, stating that "present cultural Judaism, *partly degenerated from the physical and nervous point of view* [my emphasis], should be considered a serious warning to the spiritually leading races not to push the culture of intelligence and learning beyond the limits of damage to the body."[56]

The confrontation between psychiatry and neurology led to the disappearance of the phenomenon called neurasthenia and the public debate around it during the third decade of the twentieth century. And yet because of World War I, which sharpened the awareness of the influence of psychological causes on human health (Alois Alzheimer published his book *Der Krieg und die Nerven* [The War and the Nerves] in 1915)[57] and made German Jews more aware of eastern European Jewry in the occupied territories, the internal Jewish and Zionist debate concerning Jewish nervousness received an additional incentive. Rafael Becker believed that nervousness was less an outcome of the war than one of its causes, and he offered a solution symptomatic of the national trend of the peace agreements: to create living conditions for the Jews similar to those of other nations, in order to overcome their overdose of nervousness.[58] This Zionist solution—considered by Becker as "radical therapy"—meant in practical terms the emigration to Palestine. There, "the Jewish people . . . will flourish also eugenically, i.e., will improve racially." Gymnastics exercises in the diaspora would serve as proper preparation.[59] Indeed, Zionists did let loose. "It is the curse of exile that we react like sick people, to the level of hysteria or . . . apathy," was Zlocisti's verdict, to which the cure was proposed, "Fresh air and physical activity, sports and games will provide the people with healthy senses and strong muscles and nerves. . . . We need healthy nerves. Then we could challenge fate, we will survive!"[60] The same idea appears in Siegfried Bernfeld's post–World War I utopia called Das jüdische Volk und seine Jugend (The Jewish People and Their Youth). There, this aim had already been achieved. "The Jewish people totally changed their nature: they became more active, happier, and self-confident. Hardly anything can remind us of the meaningless busybodyness, sad somberness, and depression of past exile days."[61]

Indeed, the post–World War I climate helped revive the relevant debate. Süssmann Muntner, a physician, an expert on Maimonides, and a prominent member of the national Jewish gymnastics and sports movement, still urged physical training as a means to "overcome nervous feebleness," but at the same time warned against excessive training which might cause "nervous irritation."[62] It seems that the awareness of the danger of overdoing gymnastics and sports grew, this time concerning not only women, and therefore a more cautious approach was recommended. "All those exercises that strain the nervous system should be practiced only occasionally."[63] It was this very need to react by way of sports and muscular activity to "nervous Judaism" that dictated cautiousness and restraint to those who prescribed the "medication." Ernst Jokl, one of the leaders of Jewish national sports in Weimar Germany, used the following distinction: "There are two types of sportsmen. The first type I called 'the unshakable.' . . . On the other hand, the other group I called 'sensitive.' To the latter belong people with a sensitive, delicate nervous system, where one concentrates on the one big performance. . . . The Jewish sportsman nearly always belongs to the second type. That is why boxing, which is a typical exercise in concentration for a very short time span, fits the Jews so well."[64] Those who know the history of Jewish boxing in the early-twentieth-century United States will surely appreciate this remark.

The progress of psychiatry and neurology during the twentieth century on the one hand and the way Zionism developed after World War II on the other have helped suppress and overcome the debate on this triangle of

The Jewish Gymnastics Association Bar Kochba,
Berlin, 1902. Courtesy of the Central Zionist Archives, Jerusalem.

nerves, muscles, and Jewish nationalism, but not the basic idea of "muscular Judaism." This term is still in use in Zionist discourse, now as a synonym for the lust for military power so symptomatic of Zionist politics since the beginning of the Middle East conflict. The debate has now become obsolete, but for the historian of Zionism, sports, or the social function of maladies, it remains significant. It discloses some of the issues that challenged early Zionism; it helps place this chapter of Jewish history in a broad, mainly German framework; and it helps explain what made "muscular Judaism" such a convincing and attractive argument in the eyes of many Jews and Zionists looking for new horizons for Jewish life.

Notes

1. Max Nordau, "Kongressrede," in *Stenographisches Protokoll des II. Zionisten Congress* (Vienna, 1898), p. 24.
2. Paul Hirsch, "Leibesübungen im K.J.V," *Der jüdische Student*, Sonderausgabe jüdische Jugend (1922), pp. 55–59.
3. Hirsch, "Turnen und Sport im K.J.V," *Der jüdische Student* 53, no. 2 (March 1921), p. 53.
4. Theodor Zlocisti, "Aufruf zum Werk," *Jüdische Turn- und Sportzeitung* (February 1920), pp. 3–4.
5. In Yehuda Eloni, *Zionismus in Deutschland von den Anfängen bis 1914* (Gerlingen, 1987), p. 97.
6. Max Nordau, "Muskeljudentum," *Jüdische Turn-Zeitung* (hereafter *JTZ*) no. 2 (June 1900), pp. 10–11; rpr., *Zionistische Schriften* (Berlin, 1923), p. 425.
7. Hermann Jalowicz, "Die körperliche Entartung der Juden, ihre Ursachen und ihre Bekämpfung," *JTZ* no. 4 (1902), p. 64.
8. Nathan Kaminski, "Regeneration oder Erziehung?" *Jüdische Monatshefte für Turnen und Sport* no. 5 (September 1918), p. 9.
9. Nordau, "Muskeljudentum," p. 425.
10. Nordau, "Kongressrede 1901," in *Zionistische Schriften*, pp. 132–33.
11. Nordau, "Das Judentum im 19. und 20. Jh.," 1909; rpr. in *Zionistische Schriften*, pp. 434–59, here 458.
12. Emanuel Edelstein, "Die Aufgabe der jüdischen Turner," *JTZ* no. 7 (November 1900), pp. 73–75; Arnold Kutzinski, "Über die jüdische Degeneration," *Jüdische Monatshefte für Turnen und Sport* no. 6 (1913), pp. 179–83. See also [Kutzinski], "Die Rassenmerkmale der Juden," *JTZ* no. 4 (1913), pp. 115–19.
13. Kongressrede 27.12.1901, in *Stenographisches Protokoll der Verhandlungen des V. Zionisten-Congress* (Vienna, 1901), pp. 99–115, 111; also relevant is the speech that follows, by Dr. Jeremias, pp. 115–22, in which he refers to the *Nervensystem* of the Jews (p. 120). See also Dr. Jeremias, "Turnen und Nervensystem," *JTZ* no. 9 (September 1904), pp. 154–56.
14. Jalowicz, "Die Körperliche Entartung," p. 64.
15. Jalowicz, "Der erste jüdische Turntag in Basel," *JTZ*, 1903, no. 9, p. 165.
16. Hirsch, "Turnen und Sport," p. 54.
17. Nathan Kaminski, "Regeneration oder Erziehung?" *Jüdische Monatshefte für Turnen und Sport* no. 5 (September 1918), p. 6.
18. Nordau, "Kongressrede 1907," in *Zionistische Schriften*, pp. 174–87, 176.
19. Nordau, *Die Conventionellen Lügen der Menschheit* (Leipzig, 1884), p. 34.
20. Willy Hellpach, *Die geistigen Epidemien* (Frankfurt am Main, 1906), p. 51.
21. Nordau, *Erinnerungen* (Leipzig, 1928), pp. 133–34.
22. Nordau, "Was bedeutet das Turnen für uns Juden?" in *Zionistische Schriften*, p. 430, originally published in *JTZ* no. 7 (July 1902), pp. 105–7.
23. George L. Mosse, "Max Nordau, Liberalism, and the New Jew," in *Journal of Contemporary History* 27, no. 2 (1992), pp. 565–81, esp. 566; Eric T. Carlson, "Medicine and Degeneration," in *Degeneration: The Dark Side of Progress*, J. E. Chamberlin and Sander L. Gilman, eds. (New York, 1985), pp. 121–41.

24. Nordau, *Das Judentum im 19. und 20. Jh.* (Cologne, 1908), rpr. in *Zionistische Schriften*, pp. 434–49, here 441.

25. Walter Littwitz, "Muskeljudentum?" *Jüdische Turn- und Sportzeitung*, May 1920, pp. 16–17.

26. Emanuel Edelstein, "Die Aufgabe der jüdischen Turner," *JTZ* no. 7 (November 1900), p. 74.

27. Max Mandelstamm, "Die Frage der körperlichen Hebung der osteuropäischen Juden," *JTZ* no. 6 (October 1900), p. 66. This was the title of his speech at the Fourth Zionist Congress.

28. Jalowicz, "Die körperliche Entartung," p. 65.

29. Max Jungmann, *Erinnerungen eines Zionisten* (Jerusalem, 1959), p. 32.

30. Dr. Moses, "Jüdische Erziehungsprobleme," *JTZ* no. 2 (February 1901), p. 17.

31. On Zionism and the notion of physical regeneration of the Jews, see John M. Efron, *Defenders of the Race: Jewish Doctors and Race Science in Fin-de-Siècle Europe* (New Haven CT, 1994); and Mitchell B. Hart, *Social Science and the Politics of Modern Jewish Identity* (Stanford CA, 2000).

32. Moritz Jastrowitz, "Muskeljuden und Nervenjuden" *JTZ* no. 3–4 (March-April 1909), p. 33–34.

33. Dr. Jeremias (Posen), "Turnen und Nervensystem," *JTZ* no. 9 (September 1904), p. 154–56.

34. Nathan Kaminski, "Die neue und die alte Richtung in der jüd. Turnerschaft," *Jüdische Turn- und Sportzeitung* (November 1920), pp. 16–18 [also Oct. 1918 and Nov. 1919].

35. E.g., Ru. Arndt, *Die Neurastenie* (Vienna, 1885); Alfred Baumgarten, *Die Neurasthenie* (Wörishofen, 1903).

36. Joachim Radkau, *Das Zeitalter der Nervosität* (Munich, 1998), p. 54.

37. Radkau, *Das Zeitalter der Nervosität*, pp. 173–261.

38. Hellpach, *Die geistigen Epidemien*, p. 63: "unser Zeitalter mit seiner Unrast"; "Man redet vom 'nervösen Zeitalter' "; Dr. Moses, "Jüdische Erziehungsprobleme," p. 17: "In unserem nervösen Zeitalter."

39. Radkau, *Das Zeitalter der Nervosität*, p. 329.

40. Rafael Becker, *Die Nervosität bei den Juden: Ein Beitrag zur Rassenpsychiatrie* (Zürich, 1919), p. 13; Georg Arndt, "Zur jüdischen Rassenfrage," *JTZ* no. 10 (October 1902), p. 163.

41. Martin Engländer, *Die auffallend häufigen Krankheitserscheinungen der jüdischen Rasse* (Vienna, 1902); Richard Blum, "Das Turnen der Mädchen und Frauen," *JTZ* no. 5 (May 1902), pp. 76–80; and no. 8 (August 1902), p. 139: "ausserordentliche hohe Anteilnahme der Juden an nervösen Erkrankungen;" Jastrowitz, "Muskeljuden und Nervenjuden," pp. 33–63.

42. Sander L. Gilman, *The Jew's Body* (New York, 1991), pp. 54, 63. He refers to M. Fishberg's *The Jews: A Study of Race and Environment* (New York, 1911).

43. Radkau, *Das Zeitalter der Nervosität*, pp. 329–33.

44. Ignaz Zollschan, *Das Rassenproblem* (Vienna, 1911), p. 268.

45. Zollschan, *Das Rassenproblem*, pp. 269–70.

46. Engländer, *Die auffallend häufigen Krankheitserscheinungen*, pp. 12, 16.

47. E. Burin, "Kaffeehausjudentum," in *Jüdischer Turner* (Juni 1910), p. 74. See also John M. Efron, "The 'Kaftanjude' and the 'Kaffeehausjude': Two Models of Jewish Insanity," *Leo Baeck Institute Yearbook* 37 (1992).

48. Franz Oppenheimer, "Sport," *Neue deutsche Rundschau* (1901), rpr. in *JTZ* no. 10–11 (October–November 1904), pp. 174–90.

49. Jalowicz, "Der Sport und die Gesellschaft," *JTZ* no. 9 (December 1900), pp. 88–89.

50. Felix Theilhaber, "Eine Stimme für den Sport," *JTZ* no. 4 (April 1907), pp. 56–58.

51. Blum, "Das Turnen der Mädchen," p. 138.

52. A. Nacht, "Sind wir berechtigt, von einer Degeneration des jüdischen Volkes zu sprechen?" *JTZ* no. 7 (July 1906), p. 119.

53. [Dr. Moses], "Jüdische Erziehungsprobleme," *JTZ* (January 1904), pp. 1, 5–8.

54. Becker, *Die jüdische Nervosität: Ihre Art, Entstehung und Bekämpfung* (Zürich, 1918), pp. 20–22, 24–27; Becker, *Nervosität der Juden*, pp. 21–25.

55. Mosse, "Max Nordau," pp. 565–81.

56. Karl Mann's article in *Kraft und Schönheit*, quoted in "Ein Nichtjude über die jüdische Turnerei," *JTZ* no. 4 (April 1902), pp. 67–69.

57. Alois Alzheimer, *Der Krieg und die Nerven* (Breslau, 1915). Robert Gaupp wrote an article on nervous collapse and revolution in 1919. See also Paul Lerner, *Hysterical Men: War Psychiatry and Politics of Trauma in Germany, 1850–1930* (Ithaca NY, 2003).

58. Becker, *Die jüdische Nervosität*; Becker, *Die Nervosität der Juden*.

59. Becker, *Die Nervosität der Juden*, p. 24.

60. Zlocisti, "Aufruf zum Werk," pp. 3–4.

61. Siegfried Bernfeld, *Das jüdische Volk und seine Jugend* (Vienna, 1920).

62. Süssmann Muntner, "Vom praktischen Turnen und Sport: Physiologisches vom Trainieren," *Jüdische Turn- und Sportzeitung* (July–August 1920), pp. 35–37.

63. Julius Hirsch, "Vom praktischen Turnen und Sport: Ratschläge für unsere Turnwarte und Vorturner," *Jüdische Turn- und Sportzeitung* (October 1920), p. 19.

64. Ernst Jokl, "Der Typ des jüdischen Sportsmannes," *Der Makkabi* (February 1929), p. 4.

2. Jewish Gymnasts and Their Corporeal Utopias in Imperial Germany

Daniel Wildmann

O N OCTOBER 22, 1898, forty-eight Jewish men, mostly aspiring academics, met in Berlin and founded the Bar Kochba Jewish Gymnastics Association of Berlin—the first such Jewish association in Imperial Germany. In the course of the following years, it would produce crucial organizational and ideological impulses for the development of a nascent Jewish gymnastics movement. [1] Five years later, in August 1903, the Berlin gymnasts formed another association, the League of Jewish Gymnasts (Jüdische Turnerschaft), meant to unify the scattered Jewish gymnastic groups that had emerged in the meantime throughout the German-speaking Jewish world. While the occasion for the league's founding was the Sixth Zionist Congress in Basel (August 23–28, 1903), [2] the league (officially founded on August 21) did not view itself as primarily Zionist, but rather as a grouping of "national Jewish" gymnast's associations. Its goals were described in the statutes as "the cultivation of gymnastics as a means for the physical elevation (Hebung) of the Jewish community of descent (jüdischer Stamm) in the sense of the national Jewish idea." [3] The league thus understood gymnastics as work on the body for the sake of a Jewish collective idea, its purpose being "uplifting" or "elevating" the "Jewish community of descent," or in short, its "renaissance." The statutes did not include any reference to the building of a national territory in Palestine. [4]

Over the following years, the league grew steadily. While eleven associations had banded together in 1903, by 1909 there were nineteen, and in 1914, just before the outbreak of the First World War, there were eighty-nine. The membership likewise increased, from approximately 1,500 in 1903, to 3,100 in 1909, and 9,300 in 1914. [5] From the original eleven associations in 1903, four were from Germany; in 1914, this was the case with only twenty-one of the eighty-nine. [6] The German associations nevertheless exercised a decisive influence on the league's fortunes, with Berlin constituting the organizational and intellectual center of the Jewish gymnastics movement. [7]

Vigorous Bodies

The same year as the Berlin Jewish gymnasts' tenth anniversary celebrations (1909) also marked the sixth anniversary of the League of Jewish Gymnasts—grounds for Bar Kochba and the league to jointly publish their programmatically entitled Festschrift. Alongside texts reviewing the recent history of both the league and association, the Festschrift also contains articles of more sweeping argumentative scope. Mainly written by medical doctors, these articles are meant to place the groups' actual activity, that is, gymnastics, in a comprehensive historical context. This is the case, for instance, in the essay by the Hamburg physician and gymnast Max Besser entitled "The Influence of the Economic Position of the German Jews on their Physical Constitution."[8] Besser begins his text with the observation that human beings can define their "physical features" as either markedly different or similar, and divide themselves into "peoples" (Völker) or "communities of descent" (Stämme) on that basis. The differences and similarities have, Besser argues, various sources; he distinguishes between anthropological, hence constant, features and those which are exclusively the result of historical processes. Besser indicates that the latter, historical varieties are themselves subject to transformations and might lead to an "enlargement" (Vergrößerung) of the anthropologically grounded physical differences between various "communities of descent" or peoples.[9]

In arguing for an inalterable anthropological body and a mutable historical body, Besser would appear to have been also arguing for the existence of an essential physical core to which an historically developed body is then attached. The appearance of the entire body is alterable because of this structure. A central thesis of Besser's essay is that on historical grounds, the physical condition of German Jews has been strongly altered—and this is, as he wrote, "in the sense of a degeneration" (im Sinne einer Degeneration). The purpose of gymnastics is thus to reverse these visible physical alterations.[10]

The Berlin physician Moritz Jastrowitz argues in similar fashion in an essay entitled "Muscle Jews and Nerve Jews."[11] Jastrowitz places special emphasis on the nondegenerative core of the German Jewish body: a body rendered invisible in the course of history, and whose positive qualities are meant to again be rendered visible: "If the latter [degenerative phenomena], with their disagreeable impression, vanish in a happier generation, then in and for itself, the purely Semitic type that remains can by no means have an unpleasant effect on the expert as well as every educated person who has ceased hating anything foreign [alles Fremdartige]. In its own way, this type is as beautiful and noble as the Germanic blond type, so beloved by Jewish women in the rich Western ghettos of our big cities, or the Slavic type, or any other."[12] The reemergence of an originary body is thus the central thrust of Jastrowitz's line of reasoning.

In their various articles, the Festschrift's authors underscore two reasons for the historically determined, hence changeable deformations of the Jewish body: on the one hand, a centuries-old history of persecution has resulted, it is suggested, in a professional focus on "trade," with professions linked to physical work remaining off-limits to Jews. On the other hand, German Judaism is defined as stamped by specific, negative consequences of emancipation and modernity—consequences reflected in Jastrowitz's "nerve Jews." The Mannheim doctor Julius Moses encapsulates these consequences under the rubric "brain Judaism"—*Gehirnjudentum*. [13] Besser, Jastrowitz, and Moses all lament a widespread "nervous" affliction among German Jews—its source being an overtaxing of the brain in day-to-day activities. In turn, such overtaxing is linked, on the one hand, to German Judaism's professional structure—too many academics and too few craftsmen—and, on the other hand, to a gravitation of Jews in Imperial Germany to the big cities, life there being understood as a fundamental threat to the individual's psyche and physis. [14] With the help of the terms "neurasthenia" and "nervous disposition," the Festschrift's authors thus formulate from both a medical and historical perspective an interpretive model for diagnosed physical inadequacies, and at the same time a critical analysis of contemporary Jewish life.

Jewish gymnasts held out the promise of counteracting such physical and mental inadequacies, which they classified as historical and hence as alterable. The Festschrift's editors spell out this promise by reprinting Bar Kochba Berlin's six-point program, which had appeared nine years earlier entitled "What we Want." The first of these points reads as follows: "We want to restore the elasticity lost to the Jewish body—to make it fresh and vigorous, agile and strong." [15] Put differently, through gymnastics, a body lost in the past is to be restored to the present. Working on the body is meant to check the process of degeneration, allowing the original anthropological body to reemerge on the scene.

It is clear that the Jewish gymnasts' arguments, demands, and goals constituted both a response to and reflection of prevailing antisemitic concepts of degeneration. [16] At the same time, they emerged from a crucial discourse within contemporary German Jewry. We thus find, for example, German Jewish physicians and statisticians intensively discussing the physical condition of Jews—or whether one could legitimately speak of a scientifically ascertainable, physically materialized Jewish entity (and if so, when).[17] But what renders the gymnasts unique within their particular intellectual context was an explicit linkage of their goals to the physical alteration and development of one's own body, and the creation of a specific organization for this work on the body.

Display of the Body

Already in 1901, Martin Buber had launched an appeal for a cultural renewal of Judaism—for, as he was first to put it, Judaism's "renaissance."[18] What Buber desired was a turn toward an authentic Jewish core, which he understood, in essentially mystic fashion, as manifest in "religiosity" and opposed to religion.[19] Reflecting a broader existential-vitalistic context, he similarly conceived experience aimed at "realization" (Verwirklichung) as the central element in an active process meant to lead to a renewed Jewish self-understanding.[20] It would seem that the League of Jewish Gymnasts itself shared this basic weltanschauung, describing the effect of the exposition staged in Basel on August 25, 1903, to mark the organization's founding in terms of an emotional communal experience. This emerges rhetorically, for instance, in the monthly periodical Jüdische Turn-Zeitung's (hereafter JTZ) description of the reaction on the part of spectators who were Eastern European delegates to the Sixth Zionist Congress: "They wept, wept authentic tears at the spectacle of young Jewish physical beauty and physical strength, offered them so directly amidst the excitement of the congress."[21]

This passage, however, underscores not only similarities, but also an obvious, decisive difference between Martin Buber's evolving, increasingly influential conceptual edifice and the gymnastic propensity. Here, the register involved in this search for the "realization" of a "renaissance" is not religious, but physical—the new inner experience, manifest in tears, being catalyzed by display of the exercising body.

Through both their newspaper and expositions, Jewish gymnasts consciously sought out and created a public. We thus find the Cologne gymnast Julius Berger arguing in a talk delivered at the Second Jewish Gymnasts' Convention, held in Berlin in 1905, as follows: "The more talk there is of Jewish gymnastics associations and Jewish gymnastics, the more people become aware they exist. Even polemics in the press are not to be avoided; they furnish us with the opportunity to answer and usually have the effect of an advertisement—with no need to pay."[22] A related spectacular awareness is manifest in the Festschrift, for instance in the description of the Basel exposition by Hermann Jalowicz and Theobald Scholem: "For the first time,

Jews from all over the world saw that efforts of their best men to produce a physical regeneration of our people had produced abundant success in a short time. The enthusiasm of the spectators was taken up by the gymnasts themselves, forming the backdrop from which, at the same time, the League of Jewish Gymnasts could be constructed."[23]

In paradigmatic fashion, the text by Jalowicz and Scholem reveals their belief in both the language of the body and its public forum. They interpret the exposition as a mode of visual and emotional communication capable of setting in play a creative process—the construction of the Jewish gymnasts' league. The Jewish public "sees" the gymnasts' bodies and reacts, and the gymnasts react to the public reaction. Jalowicz and Scholem continue: "Some may have wavered, viewed the work as premature, the number of associations and members as insufficient—the doubts sank into nothingness, flames of enthusiasm devoured all reservations. The League of Jewish Gymnasts came into being." [24] In public gymnastics expositions, the gymnastic collective—league or association—took center stage. On the one hand, this is grounded in the nature of gymnastics history: during this period, it had a more collective character than would be the case later on, when the emphasis would shift toward the individual gymnast. [25] On the other hand, precisely the appearance of an organized group of Jewish gymnasts embodied the league's or individual association's ideological program: the "renaissance" of the "Jewish community of descent."

One central task of the group expositions was synchronized exercise. Each gymnast had to follow all of the others' movements precisely, in order to execute identical movements simultaneously. The public could observe any deviations from the synchronous process—a process still in play when the gymnasts were standing still.

In 1907, the JTZ thus assessed the 130 gymnasts' static self-presentation, after their entrance on stage, in the inaugural exposition at the Third Jewish Gymnasts' Convention in Vienna: "Within the totality, the eye grasps the individual gymnast, evaluates the projecting rows with pleasure, eagerly seeks the befriended gymnast-countrymen, and rests with inner warmth on the mighty image that, in its entirety, has now fundamentally unfolded with historical effect [sic]." [26] But the consistent, harmonic totality depicted here, through all individual variations, was menaced. In 1909, the JTZ described the bearing demonstrated by "the majority" of gymnasts at the Fourth Jewish Gymnasts' Convention in Berlin, following their obligatory entry into the hall and concurrent with the usual ceremonial address, as "wanting."

The report then continued as follows: "No one demands that a crooked back, known to be made up for through enthusiasm, should suddenly be arrow-straight in the gymnastics exposition; but what anyone can do is avoid lolling about when a thousand eyes are aimed his way, indolently crossing his arms forward or backward, and proceeding with similar gymnastics. . . . These are small things that reveal the [level of] gymnastics training."[27]

With the quality of the corporeal movements standing for the success of the national Jewish gymnastics program, an important reason for publicly exhibiting the Jewish bodies was to determine the extent to which they were fulfilling their assigned tasks. Through their gymnastics, the gymnasts could demonstrate that they had regenerated their bodies. From their perspective and that of the public, the performance thus had the function of displaying and evaluating evidence.

Each gymnast trained and formed his own body. At the same time, he trained with others in a larger unit. His individual progress was thus credited to both himself and the collective, to which he was subsequently duty-bound. To be sure, this subordination to a gymnastic community was understood as the result of a voluntary decision.[28] But in the gymnastics' exposition, the gymnast was also understood as being tied to the "Jewish community of descent"—his individual body being the visual appendage of a Jewish collective body.

Body and Community of Descent

At the time of its founding in 1903, in the course of declaring its goal a regenerating of the "Jewish community of descent" in the sense of the Jewish national idea, the League of Jewish Gymnasts defined the concept of "national Judaism" as a "consciousness of belonging on the basis of common descent [Abstammung] and history as well as the desire to preserve the community of Jewish descent [Stammesgemeinschaft]."[29] In this regard, gymnastics was clearly not only meant to strengthen the physical substance of the "community of descent"—the bodies of Jewish men and women—but especially an awareness of its existence and a sense of belonging to it.

Beginning in the Germany of the 1880s, Jewish intellectuals of the most varied political provenance favored the concepts of Stamm (tribe) and Stammesgemeinschaft (community of descent). The main motive for this orientation was the desire to endow the minority Jewish collective's values with positive substance; the process involved a search for new ways to define that collective, extending or even dissolving the idea of Judaism as a *Glaubensgemeinschaft* (community of faith) without simultaneously having to call into question the affiliation of German Jews with the German state. In their reference to a society grounded in common origins and history, the concepts of *Stamm* and *Stammesgemeinschaft* reflected the prevalent political language of Imperial Germany, allowing a description of the German nation in terms of both unity and multiplicity—as composed of a variety of *Stämme*. [30]

Starting in the eighteenth century as a consequence of both the *haskalah* (the Jewish Enlightenment) and emancipation, generally binding Jewish religious interpretation and practice—religion as the determining factor in daily life—had gradually waned in the German-speaking realm. [31] On the one hand, this development was reflected in the emergence of two distinct directions in religious life: reform and orthodox Judaism. On the other hand, it was reflected in the emergence on the intellectual horizon of alternatives to religion, perhaps most significantly the alternative of history. [32]

The notion of history and descent as a unifying moment was reflected in the arguments of the gymnastics leagues' doctors and gymnasts. It found its expression in their postulation of both a mutable body and an immutable physical core in the course of history. Ideas from Imperial Germany's political vocabulary merged with neo-Lamarckian ideas of evolution and Jewish-national ideas concerning the purpose of gymnastics. The "physical elevation of the Jewish community of descent" stood for a politically legitimate and historically justified undertaking meant to give the Jewish collective back its own body.

The State and the Body

But precisely the required work on the body—the creation of one's own body, generating and visualizing affiliation—produced a basic problem: what sort of relationship did these gymnasts' bodies have with the German state? The League of Jewish Gymnasts found a solution in postulating two forms of affiliation for German Jews—with the Jewish "community of descent" and with the German state. Max Zirker thus spoke for the league in asserting in the Festschrift that "faithfulness to the state and faithfulness to the *Stamm* stand in no contradiction." [33]

For the national Jewish gymnasts, one important way of demonstrating that one was a good German citizen was by fulfilling universal military duty. But the gymnasts encountered barriers precisely in this regard: until the First World War it was practically impossible for Jews to become officers in Prussia. [34] The JTZ thus carried various texts concerned with the careers of Jewish officers in armies abroad. [35] There were also several articles concerned with one particular British Jewish organization, the Jewish Lads' Brigade (JLB), and the Festschrift itself contained three of the texts first printed in the JTZ, accompanied by photos. [36] In England in the 1880s, uniformed youth groups such as the Boys' Brigade and Church Lads' Brigade had emerged to promulgate Christian values; [37] in its military structure and appearance, the JLB was their Jewish counterpart: its members wore uniforms, enjoyed a sort of infantry training, and organized tent camps and maneuvers. British sports such as cricket and soccer, as well as (unspecified) "lectures," supplemented the military training. The brigade was founded in 1895 by Colonel Albert E. W. Goldsmid, a Jew whose main concern was easing the integration of young east European immigrants into British society. [38]

The League of Jewish Gymnasts interpreted the centrality of physical training in the execution of the brigade's goals as confirmation of their own bodywork. [39] But what the JTZ authors especially emphasized was the JLB's public reputation, especially in military circles, and the simple existence of Jewish officers. This was, in fact, a source of fascination. [40] In their periodical, the Jewish gymnasts only voiced the desire to see Jewish officers in Imperial Germany's armed forces in scattered fashion. [41] But the repeated discussions of the JLB as a civic institution and of its founder, Colonel Goldsmid, as a British Jewish officer can be read as a transparent pointer to an absence. The German Jewish gymnasts' wish to fill this absence points in turn to the question of the specific attributes of the national Jewish body they were preparing for public display. In their public discussions, there is frequent recourse to antonyms such as strong/weak, upright/crooked, and loose/taut. [42] The oppositional pairs at work here are applied to both collective and individual bodies—but also to individual parts of the body. [43] Within political debates over the body, the "loose/taut" pair was, predictably enough, a central category for the muscles, the visual attribution "taut" denoting a desirable aggregate condition of the muscle tissue, in turn standing metonymically for a vital, undamaged corporeal constitution. [44] This metonymic function is encapsulated in the term "muscle Jew" (Muskeljude), a term that Max Nordau had coined in an 1898 talk at the Second Zionist Congress in Basel. [45]

In the context of the gymnastics praxis, "muscle Jew" did not denote someone who had developed an extremely muscular body, but rather a smooth and balanced musculature meant to reflect a balanced physical and

34

psychic whole.[46] At play here were nineteenth- and early-twentieth-century ideas regarding corporeal aesthetics oriented above all toward the bourgeois reception of antiquity. The Jewish gymnasts thus chose their heroes from antiquity: Bar Kochba and the Maccabees.[47] If the contemporary followers of such Hebrew heroes—the gymnasts—were to be understood as "muscle Jews," this understanding was the result of an intellectual process, the conversion of specific bourgeois values into national Jewish values.

In Imperial Germany, the narrow-fitting clothing of the male gymnasts allowed a clear view of the protruding muscles—in contrast to the women's clothing, intended to obscure the female gymnasts' form. Furthermore, partial nakedness was becoming increasingly accepted as a representational medium for the ever-more popular photographic staging of exercising men.[48] In the context of such conventions it is understandable that the Festschrift's only muscle-revealing naked body is in fact a lithograph of the upper body of a man. In an echo of the name of Berlin's national Jewish gymnastics association at its tenth anniversary, the lithograph, created by Hermann Struck and inserted into the Festschrift, is entitled A Disciple of Bar Kochba (Ein Jünger Bar Kochbas).[49]

Nevertheless, the national Jewish collective was not only represented by male bodies. Starting in 1907, women were group participants in the gymnastics exposition, and the Festschrift does contain photos of clothed women, presented either as forming autonomous groups or as part of groups consisting of men and women. In any event, the exercises women could perform publicly were the subject of various debates within the Jewish gymnastics movement. They centered above all on the proper dress for female gymnasts and the substance of their performance. Were they to display dance-based movements, or, rather, classical exercises on the bar?[50] One source for such debates was presumably the fact that the bourgeois reception of antiquity furnished no images of exercising female bodies.[51]

Traveling Bodies

In 1912, three years after publication of the Festschrift, the League of Jewish Gymnasts injected a new element into their relationship with Palestine, Jewish gymnasts from Europe now being meant to present themselves there—a fact presumably linked in part to the election of younger gymnasts to the board.[52] In that year's July/August issue of the JTZ, Berlin dentist Henry Unna, editor of the journal and executive member of the board, confirmed plans that had been laid for the Fifth Jewish Gymnasts' Convention:

Gymnast brothers! . . . Palestine no longer lies in fog-land, in a mythic-obscure *aulam habo* [world to come]; it has moved tangibly near us. Palestine is no longer the land of the gray past, to which only old people and holy men wander in order to die at God-sanctified locations; for us it is the land of a present and future that wish to be tied to a beautiful past. For us it is the land of the budding and evolving in Judaism. Youth-land. And for that reason, our people's youth will move out to Palestine, in order to kiss the land in which our people's past and future extend a handshake.[53]

Unna brings Palestine in direct proximity to the association members, if only as a passing event: they must decide whether or not to undertake the trip. Unna also declares Palestine the locus in which Jews can find themselves: "Then we will smile over those 'halves' [*über jene Halben*] who struggle to define their Judaism, over the small ones who deny it. We will tell them 'go to Palestine, to the land of the Jews, and you will know who you are. For he who does not experience it will not comprehend it.' "[54]

The trip to Palestine took place between March 13 and April 27, 1913; there were forty-two participants.[55] It was organized in cooperation with Jewish student organizations.[56] Up to the war's onset in August 1914, a series of articles about this trip and about a second one planned and actually realized in the spring of 1914 appeared in the *JTZ*.[57] As apparent already in Unna's remarks in 1912, the trips represented both an emotional and physical experience, something reinforced in the appeal for future trips offered the following year by gymnast Theodor Zlocisti: "Wander with your own feet through the fields that made our ancestors strong for their grandchildren's will to creation, gaze with your own eyes at the young Unfolding [*sic*], hear with your own ears how the prophets' language brightly resounds, in order to awaken the spirit of the prophets! . . . Onward to pilgrimage—to the holy sanctuaries that once were, and are again unfolding!"[58] Like the gymnastic exercises, the trip to and wandering through Palestine was thus meant to catalyze a physical and—above all—sensory return to an origin, to a positive past of the "community of descent." Once they arrived at their destination, the German Jewish gymnasts practiced together with their counterparts in the local associations, and there was a mutual display of prowess.[59] As Zlocisti spelled out in his article, the entire experience was seen as having a powerfully rejuvenating effect: "Palestine has been made young through us, and we through Palestine."[60]

The turn to Palestine can be understood in the context of the Posen Resolution of 1912 by the Zionist Organization of Germany, a resolution to the effect that all Zionists should embrace a personal obligation to emigrate to Palestine. [61] That the demand was not adopted by the League of Jewish Gymnasts is suggested by its statutes remaining unaltered. But the new board's arrangement of trips to Palestine and their effort to make these an annual event would seem to reflect the resolution's impact; "national Jewish" gymnasts were now meant to draw close to a territory outside Germany. The same framework is apparent in Unna's explicit localizing, in 1912, of "national Jewish" youth in Palestine. [62] That the new focus on Palestine also involved a new focus on youth was made publicly visible in a change of the JTZ's subtitle in January, 1913, from Monatsschrift für die körperliche Hebung der Juden (Monthly for the Physical Elevation of the Jews) to Jüdische Monatshefte für Turnen und Sport. Organ der jüdischnationalen Jugendbewegung (Jewish Monthly for Gymnastics and Sports: Organ of the Jewish National Youth Movement). In addition, the JTZ's January edition was a special edition devoted to the planned Palestine trip.

In any event, these developments did not change anything basic in the League of Jewish Gymnasts' self-understanding: between 1914 and 1918, German Jewish male gymnasts, like many other of their German coreligionists, dutifully joined Imperial Germany's armed forces. The gymnasts' league drew concretely closer to the Posen Resolution after 1918, with the new founding in 1919 of the German Circle—the confederation of national Jewish gymnastics associations—after its wartime disintegration, and the new founding of the league in 1921 under the name Maccabi World Union (Maccabi Weltverband). The war experiences had led to a shift in the gymnasts' weltanschauung, and it was now possible for both gymnastics and sports in general to have the statutes-anchored goal of educating young people so they could help build up Palestine in situ. [63]

The League of Jewish Gymnasts presented itself as a collective moving toward a new, undamaged, anthropologically grounded, specifically Jewish entity. Through the body and work on the body, the gymnastics movement struggled to shed a past interpreted as a history of persecution, to establish affiliation and unity, and to define itself as an independent Jewish collective. The "Jewish renaissance" was itself rendered a performative act.

The authors of the Jewish gymnasts' movement translated Jewish history into Jewish bodies. If, from the perspective of the gymnasts, history had until now molded bodies, henceforth bodies were meant to mold history. Between 1898 and 1912, the body offered a new, third possibility for establishing and representing affiliation—an affiliation located between culture and religion, on the one hand, and territory on the other. But this positioning of the body was temporary. After 1912, Palestine—at first in the form of travel—increasingly became the gymnasts' physical and emotional point of reference for a "renaissance" of Jewish bodies.

Translated from the German by Joel Golb

Notes

1. The first Jewish gymnastics association, the Israelitischer Turnverein Constantinopel, was established in the Ottoman Empire's capital in January 1895 by German Jewish academics. Other such associations emerging before Bar Kochba were the Dutch Joodsche Gymnastiek—en Athletiekvereeniging Attila Groningen (April 1898) and the Bulgarian Zionistischer Turnverein Makabi Philippopel (June 1898). The Austro-Hungarian Jüdischer Turnverein Bielitz-Biala was formed in December 1898 and was thus only slightly younger than the Berlin association. But these associations did not play an important role in the development of the Jewish gymnastics movement. See Ernst Tuch, "Die jüdische Turnbewegung," *JTZ* no. 1 (1903), pp. 3–9, here 4; "Aus der jüdischen Turnwelt. Bielitz-Biala," *JTZ* no. 2 (1903), pp. 36–37; Joachim Doron, " 'Der Geist ist es, der sich den Körper schafft!' Soziale Probleme in der jüdischen Turnbewegung (1896–1914)," *Tel Aviver Jahrbuch für deutsche Geschichte*, 20 (1991), pp. 237–58, here 239–41; Arndt Krüger and Astrid Sanders, "Jewish Sports in the Netherlands and the Problems of Selective Memory," in "One Hundred Years of 'Muscular Judaism': Sport in Jewish History and Culture," special issue, *Journal of Sport History* 26, no. 2 (1999), pp. 271–86, here 272.

2. The founding gymnastics convention, called the Erster Jüdischer Turntag, took place between August 21 and 24, 1903; the actual founding was on August 21. M[ax] Z[irker], "Der erste Jüdische Turntag zu Basel," *JTZ*, no. 9–10 (1903), pp. 164–69.

3. *JTZ*, no. 9–10 (1903), p. 167 (*Statuten der Jüdischen Turnerschaft*).

4. The terms "national Jewish" and "Zionist" have a complex history. Until around 1890, *nationaljüdisch* designated various political streams viewing Palestine as the possible site of a Jewish future. Afterward, "Zionist" emerged for this purpose, *nationaljüdisch* now tending to signify other expressions of national consciousness, such as physical exercise. Doron, "Der Geist ist es," pp. 240–41; Heiko Haumann, "Zionismus und die Krise jüdischen Selbstverständnisses," in idem, ed., *Der Traum von Israel. Die Ursprünge des modernen Zionismus* (Weinheim, 1998), pp. 9–64, here 32–35.

5. "Allgemeiner Bericht," *JTZ* no. 6 (1907), pp. 95–97, here 95; "Geschäfts-und Finanzbericht," pp. 83–89, here 83–84; "Statistik der Jüdischen Turnerschaft," *JTZ* no. 6 (1912), p. 139; Daniel Wildmann, "Der Körper im Körper: Jüdische Turner und jüdische Turnvereine im Kaiserreich 1898–1914," in *Nation und jüdische Identität*, Peter Haber, Erik Petry, and Daniel Wildmann, eds. (Cologne, 2005).

6. In 1914, fifty-two associations were Austro-Hungarian, twenty-one German, one Romanian, one Turkish, and one Swiss; thirteen came from Palestine. Wildmann, "Der Körper im Körper"; "Aus dem deutschen Kreis. Turnstatistik," *JTZ* no. 7–8 (1912), p. 142; Tschechoslowakischer Makkabikreis, *Makkabi Handbuch*.

7. Berlin was already designated headquarters for the league in 1903; the city was also

home of the *jtz*. Zirker, "Der erste Jüdische Turntag," pp. 164–69. Moreover, the emergence and growth of Bar Kochba Berlin occurred in the context of the developing Jewish societies in Berlin. Cf. Reinhard Rürup, ed., *Jüdische Geschichte in Berlin. Essays und Studien*, (Berlin: Edition Hentrich, 1995); Barbara Schäfer, *Berliner Zionistenkreise. Eine vereinsgeschichtliche Studie* (Berlin, 2003).

8. Max Besser, "Der Einfluss der ökonomischen Stellung der deutschen Juden auf ihre physische Beschaffenheit," in Ausschuss der Jüdischen Turnerschaft, ed., *Körperliche Renaissance der Juden: Festschrift anlässlich des IV. Turntages der Jüdisches Turnerschaft und der Feier des 10-jährigen Bestehens des Jüdischen Turnvereins Bar Kochba–Berlin* (Berlin, 1909), pp. 7–9. A publicist and founding member of the Bar Kochba association, Besser (b. 1877) committed suicide in Hamburg in 1941 together with his wife.

9. Besser, "Der Einfluss der ökonomischen Stellung," p. 7.

10. Besser, "Der Einfluss der ökonomischen Stellung," pp. 7–9. See also the essay by Moshe Zimmermann in this volume.

11. Moritz Jastrowitz, "Muskeljuden und Nervenjuden," *Körperliche Renaissance der Juden* (Berlin, 1909), pp. 12–14. The article also appeared under the same title in *jtz* 3–4 (1909), pp. 33–36. The neurologist Moritz Jastrowitz was born in 1840 and died in 1912.

12. Jastrowitz in "Muskeljuden und Nervenjuden," p. 13.

13. Julius Moses, "Jüdische Erziehungsprobleme," in *Körperliche Renaissance der Juden* (Berlin, 1909), pp. 9–12, here 10. This text had already appeared twice under the same title in the *jtz*, the first appearance being in two installments: *jtz* no. 1 (1901), pp. 5–8, and no. 2 (1901), pp. 17–20 (longer version); no. 8 (1903), pp. 141–44 (shorter version). Moses was president of the Mannheim Jewish Community (1923–34).

14. Besser, "Der Einfluss der ökonomischen Stellung," pp. 7–8; Moses, "Jüdische Erziehungsprobleme," pp. 9–10; Jastrowitz, "Muskeljuden und Nervenjuden," p. 13.

15. Georg Arndt, "Die Jüdische Turnzeitung," in *Körperliche Renaissance der Juden* (Berlin, 1909), pp. 21–22, here 21; "Was wir wollen!," *jtz* no. 1 (1900), p. 1.

16. These concepts were, of course, embedded in a broader zeitgeist whose most popular expression was Max Nordau's highly influential *Entartung* ("degeneration"), first published in 1892 (vol. 1) and 1893 (vol. 2).

17. Cf. John M. Efron, *Defenders of the Race: Jewish Doctors and Race Science in Fin-de-Siècle Europe* (New Haven CT, 1994); Efron, *Medicine and the German Jews: A History* (New Haven CT, 2001), esp. pp. 105–50; Mitchell B. Hart, *Social Science and the Politics of Modern Jewish Identity* (Stanford CA, 2000).

18. Martin Buber, "Jüdische Renaissance," *Ost und West: Illustrierte Monatsschrift für modernes Judentum*, no. 1 (1901), cols. 7–10. Fifteen years later, Buber republished this essay in his programmatically oriented essay collection *Die jüdische Bewegung* (Berlin: 1916), pp. 7–16.

19. I would like to thank Astrid Deuber-Mankowsky and Martin Treml for insights gained from separate discussions with them about Buber's "Jewish renaissance."

20. Cf. Martin Buber, *Daniel: Gespräche von der Verwirklichung* (Leipzig, 1913).

21. Max Zirker, "Vom Basler Schauturnen," *jtz* no. 9 (1903), pp. 169–76, here 170. One of the founders of both the Bar Kochba association and the gymnasts' league, Zirker (1876–?), both a jurist and notary, emigrated to Palestine in 1936. In 1913, Austrian gymnast Siegmund Werner would use a similar diction in describing the emotional impact of the Viennese gymnastics exposition held for participants of the Eleventh

Zionist Congress: "the eyes of so many hundreds grew moist from deep inner joy at being able to share this sight." Siegmund Werner, "Unser Turnfest vor dem XI. Zionistenkongress in Wien," *JTZ* no. 7 (1913), pp. 197–99, here 198.

22. Julius Berger, "Referat über die äussere Propaganda des Verbandes," *JTZ* no. 5–6 (1905), pp. 105–10, here 109.

23. Hermann Jalowicz and Theobald Scholem, "Zehn Jahre Geschichte des Jüdischen Turnvereins 'Bar Kochba'-Berlin," in *Körperliche Renaissance der Juden*, pp. 17–21, here 19. Jalowicz (b. 1877) was a Berlin lawyer and notary and a founding member of the Bar Kochba association. A soldier in the First World War, Jalowicz remained in Germany after 1933 and was active as a jurist until 1938. He died in Berlin in 1941. Gershom Scholem's uncle, Theobald Scholem (1873–1943), was director of the Siegfried Scholem Press. He was a member of the Bar Kochba association and, between 1905 and 1907, chairman of the gymnasts' league. In 1938 he emigrated to Palestine.

24. Jalowicz and Scholem, "Zehn Jahre Geschichte des Jüdischen," p. 19.

25. On the collective nature of gymnastics in Imperial Germany, see Michael Krüger, *Körperkultur und Nationsbildung: Die Geschichte des Turnens in der Reichsgründungsära—eine Detailstudie über die Deutschen* (Schorndorf, 1996), pp. 287–346; Svenja Goltermann, *Körper der Nation: Habitusformierung und die Politik des Turnens 1860–1890* (Göttingen, 1998), pp. 151–81.

26. "Verbandsschauturnen," *JTZ* no. 6 (1907), pp. 102–5, here 102–3. The Third Jewish Gymnasts' Convention took place on May 20 and 21, 1907; the gymnasts' exposition was held on 20 May.

27. "Verbandschauturnen," *JTZ* nos. 6–7 (1909), pp. 105–8, here 106. The Fourth Jewish Gymnasts' Convention took place from May 30 to June 1, 1909; the gymnasts' exposition was held on May 30.

28. On the gymnasts' free choice and duty, see, for instance, Julius Heilbrunn, "Militärische und turnerische Erziehung," *JTZ* no. 6 (1903), pp. 97–101, here 101–2; Theobald Scholem, "Die Vorturnerstunde der Jüdischen Turnerschaft in Köln," *JTZ* no. 7 (1908), pp. 126–32, here 128.

29. Zirker, "Der erste Jüdische Turntag," p. 167.

30. Till van Rahden, *Juden und andere Breslauer: Die Beziehungen zwischen Juden, Protestanten und Katholiken in einer deutschen Grossstadt von 1860 bis 1925* (Göttingen, 2000), pp. 20–22; Till van Rahden, " 'Germans of the Jewish Stamm': Visions of Community between Nationalism and Particularism, 1850 to 1933," in Mark Roseman, Nils Roemer, and Neil Gregor, eds., *German History from the Margins* (Bloomington IN, 2006); cf. Andreas Reinke, "B'nai B'rith in Deutschland," in Andreas Gotzmann, Rainer Liedtke, and Till van Rahden, eds., *Juden, Bürger, Deutsche: Zur Geschichte von Vielfalt und Differenz 1800–1933* (Tübingen, 2001), pp. 315–40, here 322–25.

31. On the reorientation of the German Jews during the modernization process see esp. Shulamit Volkov, ed., *Deutsche Juden und die Moderne* (Munich, 1994).

32. Cf. Michael A. Meyer, *Response to Modernity: A History of the Reform Movement in Judaism* (Detroit, 1995); Shulamit Volkov, "Die Erfindung einer Tradition. Zur Entstehung des modernen Judentums in Deutschland," *Historische Zeitschrift* no. 253, (1991), 603–28; Ulrich Wyrwa, "Zur europäisch-jüdischen Geschichtsschreibung. Eine Einführung," in idem, ed., *Judentum und Historismus: Zur Entstehung der jüdischen Geschichtswissenschaft in Europa* (Frankfurt am Main, 2003), pp. 9–36.

33. Max Zirker, "Die jüdische Turnbewegung," in *Körperliche Renaissance der Juden*, pp. 2–5, here 2.
34. See Manfred Messerschmidt, "Juden im preussisch-deutschen Heer," in Militärgeschichtliches Forschungsamt Potsdam, ed., *Deutsche Jüdische Soldaten: Von der Epoche der Emanzipation bis zum Zeitalter der Weltkriege* (Berlin, 1996), pp. 39–62, here 45–54; Werner T. Angress, "Der jüdische Offizier in der neueren deutschen Geschichte, 1813–1918," in Ursula Breymayer, Bernd Ulrich, and Karin Wieland (eds.), *Willensmenschen: Über deutsche Offiziere* (Frankfurt am Main, 1999), pp. 67–78, here 72–74.
35. For example, "Zeitungsschau: Ein deutscher Jude als Oberst, JTZ no. 4 (1904), pp. 58–59; "Oberst Goldsmid" (obituary), JTZ no. 4 (1904), pp. 76–77.
36. "Leibesübungen unter den Juden Englands und Amerikas," JTZ no. 4 (1908), pp. 68–70; "Leibesübungen unter den Juden Englands und Amerikas: Jewish Lads [sic] Brigade (1. Fortsetzung)," JTZ no. 5 (1908), pp. 93–94; "Leibesübungen unter den Juden Englands und Amerikas: Jewish Lads [sic] Brigade (2. Fortsetzung)," JTZ no. 6 (1908), pp. 115–17. "Leibesübungen unter den Juden Englands und Amerikas," in *Körperliche Renaissance der Juden*, pp. 25–27. Other articles on the Brigade include Ernst Tuch, "Einiges über die Jewish Lad's brigade [sic]," JTZ no. 10 (1902), pp. 161–62; (no author), "Jewish Lads' [sic] Brigade," JTZ no. 12 (1903), pp. 215–16 (discussed below); "Die Jewish Lads Brigade," JTZ no. 8 (1904), pp. 136–37.
37. See Sharman Kadish, "*A Good Jew and a Good Englishman": The Jewish Lads' and Girls' Brigade, 1895–1995* (London, 1995), pp. 1–3.
38. "Leibesübungen," in *Körperliche Renaissance der Juden*, pp. 25–27; Sharman Kadish, " 'A Good Jew or a Good Englishman?': The Jewish Lads' Brigade and Anglo-Jewish Identity," in Anne J. Kershen, ed., *A Question of Identity* (Ashgate, 1998), pp. 77–93, here 77–82. Albert Goldsmid (1846–1904) was born in India to a British colonial officer. Having participated in the Boer War, he was awarded the Royal Victorian Order. In 1903, he took part in the Sixth Zionist Congress in Basel.
39. "Jewish Lads' Brigade," pp. 215–16; cf. "Oberst Goldsmid" (obituary). There was no female equivalent of the JLB in Britain; its exclusively male nature contrasts with the stated policies of the Jewish gymnastics associations. In 1963, the JLB decided to accept girls, changing its name to Jewish Lads' and Girls' Brigade. Kadish, *A Good Jew*, pp. 155–66.
40. "Jewish Lads' Brigade"; "Leibesübungen," in *Körperliche Renaissance der Juden*, pp. 25–27; see also Alfred Burin, "Eine militärische Chanukahfeier in England," JTZ no. 1 (1913), pp. 14–15.
41. For example "Zeitungsschau"; Burin, "Eine militärische Chanukahfeier."
42. This antonymic thinking is already present in Bar Kochba Berlin's reference in 1900 to an "elasticity lost to the Jewish body" needing restoration ("Was wir wollen!" p. 1).
43. See, for example, Jastrowitz, "Muskeljuden und Nervenjuden," p. 13.
44. See, for example, Jastrowitz, "Muskeljuden und Nervenjuden," pp. 12–14. On the visual staging of muscles, cf. Daniel Wildmann, *Begehrte Körper: Konstruktion und Inszenierung des "arischen" Männerkörpers im Dritten Reich* (Würzburg, 1998), pp. 76–79; on muscles as pars pro toto for the entire body, cf. Philipp Sarasin, *Reizbare Maschinen: Eine Geschichte des Körpers 1765–1914* (Frankfurt am Main, 2001), pp. 324–44.
45. "Rede von Max Nordau," *Stenographisches Protokoll der Verhandlungen des II. Zionisten-Congresses gehalten zu Basel vom 28. bis 31. August 1898* (Vienna, 1898), pp. 14–27, here 24–25. Nordau's reference to "muscle Judaism" (Muskeljudenthum) is brief; his talk

focused above all on the antisemitic campaigns in France in the wake of the Dreyfus Affair.

46. (Albert) Albu, "Turnen und Sport," in *Körperliche Renaissance der Juden*, pp. 14–16.

47. On the bourgeois reception of antiquity, see George L. Mosse, *Nationalism and Sexuality: Respectability and Abnormal Sexuality in Modern Europe* (New York, 1985); Klaus Wolbert, *Die Nackten und die Toten: Folgen einer politischen Geschichte des Körpers in der Plastik des deutschen Faschismus* (Giessen, 1982), pp. 126–47.

48. See, for example, the photos of a gymnast in "Fürs praktische Turnen: Mustergiltige [sic] Freiübungen," *JTZ* nos. 3–4 (1910), pp. 65–69; and Birgitte Werneburg, "Diverse Sprünge: Frauen, Sport und Fotografie," *Fotogeschichte: Beiträge zur Geschichte und Ästhetik der Fotographie*, no. 62 (1996), pp. 3–12; Thomas Reuter, "Kraft und Schönheit: Bildergeschichten," *Fotogeschichte: Beiträge zur Geschichte und Ästhetik der Fotographie*, no. 62 (1996), pp. 55–64.

49. The lithograph could also be purchased separately. Hermann Struck (1876–1944) was responsible for developing new engraving techniques and was a cofounder of Germany's Mizrahi movement of religious Zionists. He fought for Germany in the First World War and emigrated to Palestine in 1923.

50. See, for example, the photos on pp. 24 and 29 of *Körperliche Renaissance der Juden*. See also Gertrud Pfister and Toni Niewerth, "Jewish Women in Gymnastics and Sport in Germany 1898–1938," "One Hundred Years of 'Muscular Judaism': Sport in Jewish History and Culture," special issue, *Journal of Sport History* 26, no. 2 (1999), pp. 287–325, here 294–98; Gabriele Daum, "Die Frauen in der Jüdischen Turnbewegung von 1895–1918," unpublished MA thesis, Deutsche Sporthochschule Cologne, 1982, pp. 43–57.

51. On the representation of female bodies in nineteenth- and twentieth-century public space, see Wolbert, *Die Nakten und die Toten*; and Silke Wenk, *Versteinerte Weiblichkeit: Allegorien in der Skulptur der Moderne* (Cologne, 1996). On the specific case of the nudist cultural movement, see Maren Möhring, "Wie erarbeitet man sich einen natürlichen Körper? Körpernormalisierung in der deutschen Nacktkulturbewegung um 1900," *Zeitschrift für Sozialgeschichte des 20. und 21. Jahrhunderts*, no. 2 (1999), pp. 86–109; Möhring, "Ideale Nacktheit: Inszenierungen in der deutschen Nacktkultur 1893–1925," in Kerstin Gernig, ed., *Nacktheit: Ästhetische Inszenierungen im Kulturvergleich* (Cologne, 2002), pp. 91–109.

52. Hans-Jürgen König, *"Herr Jud' sollen Sie sagen!" Körperertüchtigung am Anfang des Zionismus* (St. Augustin, 1999), pp. 179, 233–35.

53. Henry Unna, "Unsere Palästinafahrt," *JTZ* nos. 7–8 (1912), pp. 139–40, here 139. A gymnastics tour in Palestine had already been proposed in *JTZ* in 1906 and 1909, but the call did not resonate. "Vermischtes: Eine jüdische Gesellschaftsreise nach Palästina," *JTZ* no. 9 (1906), p. 160; "Vermischtes: Turnen in Palästina," *JTZ* nos. 1–2 (1909), pp. 23–24. Unna (1888–1976) emigrated to Belgium in 1939, was interned in the French camps Gurs and Les Milles from 1940–1941, and successfully emigrated to the United States at the end of 1941.

54. Unna, "Unsere Palästinafahrt," p. 140.

55. Travel route in Theodor Zlocisti, "Zum Geleit," in Comité für Palästinafahrten jüdischer Turner und Studenten (eds.), *Bericht der ersten Palästinawanderfahrt zur Orientierung für die nächsten Fahrten. Mit einem Geleitwort von Dr. Theodor Zlocisti* (Berlin, 1913), pp. 15–20; list of participants, ibid., p. 5. Despite their interest, women were not allowed

to take part in the tour, as the men considered them physically too weak. For this reason, the female gymnasts planned their own tour for 1915, but it was scuttled by the outbreak of the First World War. "Ein Briefwechsel," JTZ no. 9–10 (1912), pp. 176–77; "Berichte. Berlin. Jüdischer Frauenbund für Turnen und Sport," JTZ no. 1 (1914), pp. 19–20.

56. Unna, "Unsere Palästinafahrt," p. 140. See also Miriam Rürup, "Auf der Suche nach den Ahnen?—Zu den Palästinafahrten deutscher jüdischer Studentenverbindungen 1913 und 1914," *Leipziger Beiträge zur Geschichte und Kultur der Juden in Deutschland* no. 2 (2004), pp. 167–89.

57. For example, Siegfried Rosenbaum, "Unsere Palästinaturnfahrt," JTZ no. 4 (1913), pp. 119–21; Fritz Blankenfeld, "Unsere zweite Wanderfahrt durch Palästina," JTZ no. 4 (1914), pp. 106–10.

58. Zlocisti, "Zum Geleit," p. 4. A physician, Zionist, and publicist, Zlocisti (1874–1943) was a founding member of Bar Kochba Berlin. During the First World War, he served as chief doctor of the Red Cross in Constantinople. He emigrated to Palestine in 1921.

59. See, for example, Rosenbaum, "Unsere Palästinaturnfahrt."

60. Zlocisti, "Zum Geleit," p. 4.

61. It was passed in an organizational convention held in Posen between April 26 and 28, 1912; the group of sponsoring delegates included Theodor Zlocisti. Cf. Yehuda Eloni, *Zionismus in Deutschland. Von den Anfängen bis 1914* (Gerlingen, 1987), pp. 273–79; König, "Herr Jud' sollen Sie sagen!".

62. Unna, "Unsere Palästinafahrt," p. 139.

63. König, "Herr Jud' sollen Sie sagen!", pp. 186–87; Eric Friedler, *Maccabi Chai—Makkabi lebt. Die jüdische Sportbewegung in Deutschland 1898–1998* (Vienna, 1998), pp. 29–32.

3. Sports and the Militarization of Jewish Society

Gideon Reuveni

THE RESEARCH ON modern Jewish militarism has concentrated primarily on questions relating to the extent of the militarization of Israeli society. Although there is no prevailing consensus as to either the form or the extent of that militarization, most older and more recent so-called post-Zionist studies trace Israel's militarism back to the armed conflict between Jews and the Arabs.[1] This approach is based on the view that Jews were and supposedly still are the victims of military action. Groundbreaking research on Jewish physical culture in the nineteenth century has shown, however, that the roots of Jewish militarism cannot be reduced to the Jewish-Arab conflict.

These studies draw our attention to the beginnings of a reform of the body, the aim of which was to regenerate the conception of the (above all male) Jewish body and liberate the Jews once and for all from their own clichéd physical self-image.[2] The bodily ideal of the warrior plays a central role in this context. As George L. Mosse noted in his seminal work *The Image of Man*, "The association of militarism and masculinity had always been present. . . . The military . . . had co-opted the neoclassical ideal of the male as formed, for example, through gymnastic exercise. Indeed, in its quiet strength and self-control this idea of masculinity was ready-made for the kind of discipline the military needed."[3] For many Jews, physical control, strength, courage, and daring made up this militaristic canon of masculine features, which it was thought the so-called "total Jew" would achieve above all with the help of sports.[4]

Some scholars regard these militarizing tendencies in the Jewish discourse of the nineteenth century as the internalization of foreign values, or as an essential reaction to the non-Jewish environment.[5] Viewed from this perspective, "unheroic conduct" is the only "authentic" Jewish way of life, as Daniel Boyarin postulates.[6]

In my opinion, the existence of such a distinctly unheroic physical ideal for Jews is altogether questionable.[7] It is also misleading to regard the Jews solely as a colonized group within Europe bludgeoned to absorb foreign notions of the body.[8] The European Jews made up an integral part of European society, thus the forces that influenced the society in general likewise influenced the Jewish part of society. Jewish sports serves as an excellent example for this process, for just as an ever-increasing importance was attached to sports in general, so too did sports gain importance as a medium for furthering and fostering a Jewish masculine identity.

Sports and Militarization

The special relationship between sports and militarism in Central Europe can be traced back to the beginnings of the German gymnastics movement at the turn from the eighteenth to the nineteenth century. From the very beginning there was consensus as to how so-called "German gymnastics" was to be applied as a means of premilitary education.[9] Nor did this tendency change much after the introduction of English sports during the second half of the nineteenth century. In the army and navy, sports became an integral part of training and leisure activities. It was in the military that thousands of young men had their first experiences as both active sportsmen and spectators.[10] While one consequence of this development was the entry of the sporting spirit in the military, another was that military spirit began to penetrate sports.

As a result of the First World War in particular, sports underwent a transformation from being a kind of recreational or social activity to being a platform to demonstrate the superior strength and skill both of single individuals and of the whole nation.[11] As Christiane Eisenberg has shown, the sports boom of the 1920s was primarily the result of the militarization of society, rather than of a mere desire for entertainment and distraction.[12] Hundreds and thousands of demobilized soldiers, who joined sports clubs in mass numbers after the war and also flocked to the stadiums as spectators, took sports as being a kind of "continuation of war by other means."[13] In postwar Germany this development was further accelerated by the call of leading politicians and military officers to institutionalize sports in the apparatus of state as a substitute for military service, which had been abolished by the victorious powers.[14] This seems not only to confirm Johan Huizinga's point that "the absence of compulsory general military training favored the opportunity and fueled the need for physical exercise,"[15] but also to corroborate Klaus Theweleit's analysis of the masculine identity in that period as a flight from femininity and "a struggle to contain the soldier male's fear of the desiring production of his own unconscious."[16]

A similar process—militarization of a demilitarized society through sports—took place in Jewish society as well. By making the body a site of Jewish regeneration, Jewish sports not only celebrated a warrior-oriented image of masculinity, but also became a vehicle of a process of militarization by which "society organizes itself for the production of violence."[17]

Displaying the "Tough Jew"

As early as in 1886, a group of students from Breslau announced that they were founding a Jewish student fraternity, the initial intention of which was to cultivate physical exercise. In their appeal, "Ein Wort an unsere Glaubens-genossen" ("A word to our fellow Jews"), they declared: "Alongside real physical strength and skill, self-confidence and self-esteem will grow too, and no longer will anybody be ashamed to be a Jew."[18] However, it was not until a decade later that an organized Jewish gymnastics and sports movement was founded, which started to put this aim into practice. According to Jewish sportswriting chronicles throughout the twentieth century, the systematic participation of Jews in sporting life, however, came hand in hand with the beginnings of the sports movement in general.[19] To be sure, many of these chronicles are not only celebrating Jewish achievements in sports, but also put much effort in displaying the so-called "tough Jews."[20] Thus we learn that perhaps the most important sport in which Jews made a name for themselves as outstanding sportsmen was boxing. The first reports about Jewish boxers appeared in England at the end of the eighteenth century; in this period, when boxing had still not become an exclusively male domain, there were even references to female Jewish boxers.[21]

The most famous boxer at the time was certainly Daniel Mendoza (1764–1846), who was English boxing champion from 1792 to 1795 and went down in Jewish sports history as "the first man to make boxing with proper rules and with gloves popular."[22] According to the Jüdisches Sportbuch (1937), from around 1817 until 1934 eighteen Jewish boxers won world championship titles.[23] In no other sport did Jews win so many world championships. Another discipline in which Jews excelled was wrestling. In the history of Jewish sports, as far back as the fifteenth century we find references to the two German Jews Ott and Thalhoffer, who apparently were known not only as talented wrestlers but as the authors of important manuals on wrestling.[24]

As active sportsmen and writers of teaching manuals Jews were also well-represented in another competitive contact sport: fencing.[25] According to George Eisen, bourgeois Jews were attracted to fencing in order to gain the ability to control the violence that was ascribed to it.[26] It thus appears that for the European Jews of the nineteenth century, who had to fight for their emancipation, the sword should not only be interpreted as a kind of phallic symbol, but it also has a close connection with the initiation of a myth, according to which there are "pure" weapons—a myth that is still of great importance in Israeli society today.

This tradition of the "tough Jews" was nurtured in Jewish gymnastics and sports clubs, which were established in many European cities from the end of the nineteenth century. The very names of many of these clubs testify to their aims. Such names as Maccabi, Bar Kochba, Hasmonea, Samson, Hagibor (the hero), or Hakoah (strength) demonstrate how sports was supposed to revive a past Jewish military heroism.[27] In his much-quoted appeal for "muscular Judaism," Max Nordau explains the choice of the name Bar Kochba for the Jewish gymnastics club in Berlin: "Bar Kochba was a hero who would not hear of defeat. . . . He was the last historical embodiment of a bellicose, militant Jewry. To evoke the name of Bar Kochba is an unmistakable sign of ambition. But ambition is well-suited to gymnasts."[28] This symbiosis of sports and militarism did not remain restricted to the symbolic level of the choice of names. Already in the second issue of the *Jüdische Turn-Zeitung* (JTZ) Richard Blum, one of the founding fathers of Jewish gymnastics, wrote a programmatic article entitled "Discipline." According to Blum, the subordination to one united will is an absolute prerequisite for the successful development of a gymnastics club.[29] In his view, discipline is the most important precondition for a gymnastics club to work properly, not only because of the practical necessity or its educational value, but primarily because of its function as a bridge to the military.

As the following shows, the connection between the military and gymnastics does not have its sole origins in the German gymnastics tradition. In the JTZ there are reports praising paramilitary organizations, such as the Jewish Lads Brigade, for instance, which was founded in London in 1897. The Lads Brigade was regarded as an alternative to the German gymnastics club. In contrast to the German gymnastics tradition, the English model comprised a mixture of strict discipline and real military drilling on the one hand, combined with a greater degree of freedom and independence in sporting activities on the other hand. According to the JTZ, the success of the Jewish Lads Brigade, which in April 1902 already had thirty-five hundred members, could be ascribed above all to the multiethnic character of the metropolis of London, where many eastern European Jews lived in wretched conditions.[30]

Paramilitary training was felt to be especially appropriate for regions in which ethnic and social tensions prevailed, such as in the Balkans, but as a more unfitting model for the German Jews, who lived in an extremely homogenous environment and under better conditions, as the JTZ pointed out. Despite this stance, the question of the relationship between the gymnastics club and the military remained a topic in the discourse of Jewish sports in Germany. In an article in the JTZ from May 1903, for example, Theobald Scholem, an avid supporter of German gymnastics, drew a clear dividing line between the gymnastics club, which aimed toward a harmonious balance between discipline and freedom, and purely (para)military organizations such as the German Jugendwehr, which in his opinion turned its members into "slavishly obedient creatures."[31] In the next issue, Julius Heilbrunn wrote a critical reaction to Scholem's misgivings. After a long and sophisticated discussion of the problematic relationship between the military and gymnastics in general, Heilbrunn makes the point that for the Jews, a close connection between military spirit and gymnastics club is indispensable. He attributes the special position of the Jews to the weak, or at least only nascent, sense of Jewish national identity. The Jews are "not accustomed to working in an organized way when it comes to Jewish affairs."[32] Ultimately, Heilbrunn continues, military spirit should play a key role in forming a self-confident Jewish life. In contrast to organizations such as German Social Democracy, which could ascribe their success to "the spirit of discipline that resides within a people which for generations has been through the school of the Prussian army,"[33] Jews had no such tradition to fall back on. Heilbrunn therefore draws the conclusion that "Jewish gymnastics clubs need to maintain even tighter discipline than is necessary in other clubs."[34] Above all, the feeling of political powerlessness, which according to David Biale was the precondition for a new Jewish politics of mass mobilization, gave rise to a militarized conception of gymnastics, which was seen to be central to the nationalist education.[35]

This militarism, which regarded the army as the "school of the nation," might also explain why the so-called transition from gymnastics to sports went so smoothly for the most part, above all within the Jewish-nationalist gymnastics movement.[36] The contribution of sports to the development of a strong will especially, as well as its combative nature, were positively stressed in this process.[37] Sports provided Jews in particular with a platform on which they could appear as equals to non-Jews and could show "what they can and would be able to do, if only they want to," in the words of the famous sports journalist Willi Meisel.[38] In addition, especially for the Zionists, this reorientation signaled a turning away from what was broadly speaking the product of a German-oriented assimilation—gymnastics—and toward sports, which after all was more in keeping with the transnational orientation of the Jewish-nationalist way of thinking than gymnastics was.[39] In this regard, the move of Jewish gymnastics toward sports—that is, the overcoming of the principles of order and bearing, and the adoption of the principles of competition and achievement—thus by no means involved a playing down of the role of militarism. In many respects sports increasingly became a medium that was to stimulate the fighting spirit of the Jews. It can therefore not be regarded, in this context, as an activity designed to reduce aggression.[40]

As I mentioned at the beginning of this essay, the First World War served to intensify the affinity between sports and militarism, and this is true of Jewish sports as well. The Jewish sports movement was zealously committed to the war and even took on "the training of our boys for their later military activities."[41] By focusing on Jewish sports we will further see that the attempt made during the war, above all on the part of the Zionists, to construct a vision of a new, strong, bellicose and de-individualized Jewish man, was far more widespread than has hitherto been presumed.[42] As we shall see now, the spirit that arose from the trenches made a great mark on Jewish sports.

Self-Defense and Military Sports

After the Great War, the Jewish-nationalist gymnastics movement was more strongly oriented toward Zionism than before. "The gymnastics movement," according to the first postwar issue of the *Jüdische Turn- und Sportzeitung*, "is a child of Zionism, and only as such does it have a sense and viability."[43] In concrete terms, this declaration represents the attempt to free Jewish gymnastics from its gymnastics club nature, and to build up a community of gymnasts in its place. From that point on, all gymnastics commands were to be given in Hebrew.[44] Far more significant, however, were Julius Hirsch's guidelines for the new construction of Jewish *Turnerschaft* (gymnastics) as a *Turnergemeinschaft* (gymnastics community). He proposes that the clubs should be broken down into small groups, in order that the interaction between their members would not be restricted only to the level of sporting activities, as was the case in the gymnastics clubs. He attached particular importance to the people who were to lead these groups. They were to be called *Mazbi* (army commanders).[45] In fact the "leadership principle" or "*Mazbi* principle" was indeed introduced in the various local groups, though with differing degrees of success. In Frankfurt am Main,

49

for example, the new method appears to have functioned excellently, while Leipzig and Munich complained about the lack of discipline and the passivity of their members and were not able to report similar successes.[46]

In view of the political instability and the rising number of attacks against Jews in the postwar period, the role of the sports clubs became increasingly important.[47] The Viennese attempt to use demobilized soldiers to form a kind of Jewish militia was regarded as a model example. However, as the authorities had prohibited Jewish organizations from being formed on a purely military basis, the Jewish National Council decided to integrate the Jewish soldiers in the Jewish-nationalist gymnastics and sports clubs. In the guise of a civilian sports club, the "Jewish Battalion" continued to exist, whereby at the same time the sports clubs almost in their entirety transformed themselves into a *Selbstwehr-Reserve* (self-defense reserve corps). In adopting semi-military training exercises in their sports program, they declared their readiness to "make their new members capable of defending themselves forcefully."[48]

In Germany the Reichsbund jüdischer Frontsoldaten (RJF, or Reich Association of Jewish War Veterans), founded in 1919, saw as its main task the fight against the rising antisemitism and the disparagement of Jews who had fought in the war.[49] Along with the usual written and verbal protests in public and with the authorities, the self-defense measures of the RJF included offensive actions such as ripping down antisemitic posters and disrupting antisemitic meetings, even to the point of forcing them to break off, if possible. In various places the RJF formed defense units and was prepared "to fight in the political struggle . . . with our own weapons."[50] The so-called "physical fitness training" played an important role in the self-defense concept of the RJF. In 1925, the RJF sports association Schild (Shield) was established—a name that symbolized "a soldierly bearing and readiness to defend ourselves against those who hold us in contempt and antisemites."[51] The main focus of the sporting activities of Schild was on martial arts such as boxing, judo, and wrestling, as well as gliding and small-bore rifle shooting, which were practiced with a view to their practical application.[52] The RJF placed particular emphasis on training with the "invisible weapon," jujitsu, and produced several German champions in this sport.[53] In spite of the ideological discrepancy between the German-nationalist oriented RJF and the Zionists, even before 1933 the two rival factions were already cooperating in matters concerning self-defense and sports.[54] Owing to the fears of the Jewish population, which felt more and more threatened by the nationalists and National Socialists, especially in Berlin, the Jüdische Abwehr Dienst (JAD, or Jewish Defense Service) was established.[55] Apart from the RJF, the Jewish boxing club Maccabi and the Zionist sports club Bar Kochba were the sponsors of this organization, whose members were given premilitary training.[56] The Jewish youths were therefore encouraged to pursue sports in order to be able to defend themselves against potential physical attack.

If it is the case, as Paul Yogi Mayer noted in 1934, that the frontline soldier was no longer a "military man" in 1918 but nevertheless often remained a soldier and frontline fighter, then we can definitely say that Jewish sports represented a key sphere in which the so-called "soldierly bearing" was propagated.[57]

The importance of military sports for Jewish sports organizations can furthermore be comprehended in their conception of competition. Competition in sports was not viewed as a neutral zone. There was far more at stake here than just victory or the number of points scored. For Jewish-nationalist sports, as Edgar Marx proclaimed for Bar Kochba Hamburg in 1927, "every fight that our team wearing the Mogen Dovid wins against our opponent is a fight for the Jewish club, and every time it is then somehow a Jewish matter."[58]

The Bund: Socialism and Militarism

The critical debate about sports and militarism chiefly took place against the background of the conflict between socialist and bourgeois sports. The discourse of Jewish sports was no exception in this respect. So-called Jewish-bourgeois sports were taken by Jewish socialists as being exclusively a part of the capitalist power structure. Those critics that held this view were generally Marxist anti-Zionist socialists, such as the Algemeyner yidisher arbeter bund in poyln un rusland (Jewish Labor Bund in Poland and Russia), which had been founded in Vilna in 1897.[59] The principles underpinning the sporting activities of the Bund are outlined in the book *Sport und Politik* (Sport and politics) by Julius Deutsch.[60] According to Deutsch, bourgeois sports, with their striving for individual top performance and above all setting records, epitomizes the capitalist social order, whereby "the stronger party triumphs over the weaker and rises to achieve honor, fame and fortune."[61] As an alternative to the competitive principle and "record-fanaticism" of bourgeois sports, Deutsch points to the collective achievement of mass sports. The sports organization of the Bund, Morgnshtern, estab-

lished in 1926, planned to put this model of proletarian sport into practice.[62]

The attempt to create an alternative to bourgeois sports quickly came
to a dead end.[63] Owing to the difficulties they met in finding recruits for
their socialist sports concept, Morgnshtern, like other socialist sports organizations, had to alter their conception of sports and concentrate more
on competitive sports, such as soccer, boxing, and table tennis.[64] It was not
only political pragmatism that lay behind this step; the reasons were also to
be found in socialism itself. The workers' movement did have peace as an
aim, yet from the socialist perspective, at least that of its Marxist core, there
was a class struggle in society, in which the workers had to defend themselves against exploitation, alienation, and the power of the capitalist ruling
classes.[65] This warlike tendency of the workers' movement ultimately determined the way it treated sports. The aim of proletarian sport was thus not
only to take the work-damaged body and create a "body beautiful," but first
and foremost "physical training for the fight for great social goals."[66] In this
context ideals of courage, sacrifice, and camaraderie—indeed the image of
the warrior himself—played a crucial role. It is no wonder, then—especially
against the background of the rapid spread of fascism in Central Europe—
that military sports became a fundamental element in the socialist sports
discourse between the wars.[67] At the 1927 congress of the Socialist Workers'
Sport International, in which Morgnshtern also participated, there was an
appeal for workers' sports associations to take up military sports in their
activity programs.[68] The Bund was already familiar with such defense activities from before the war, through its fight against antisemitism.[69] According
to historian Leonard Rowes, the Bund was the only Jewish party that managed to organize a militia that was successful in acting against antisemitic
hooligans.[70] It is doubtless no coincidence that the leader of the Bundist
Defense Corps, Bernard Goldstein, was also president of Morgnshtern in
Warsaw.[71]

Between the sports of Bundist workers and those of their adversaries,
above all Zionist sports, there thus appears to have been some common
ground—at least on a structural level. Both movements totally instrumen-
talized sports, thereby turning the body into a political variable.[72] Similarities can also be found in their respective conceptions of the body. While the
Zionists spoke of a "muscular Jew" with his broad chest, powerful limbs,
and valiant gaze, the physical ideal that Bundist workers had in mind in

their sports was that of a supple-limbed and steeled, powerfully built worker, who, just like the bourgeois Jew, should become more self-confident and free of any sense of subservience with the help of sports.[73] Thus, sports was much more than just an instrument for attracting new recruits or promoting solidarity. Even the importance of military sports, as a means of strengthening the Jews' capacity to defend themselves, cannot be put down to antisemitism alone. In the end, the target group of all the Jewish sports movements was the youth. As such, Jewish sports appears to take on the social role of the military as "existential threshold."[74] For in the same way that modern military service is supposed to transform the individual, taking him from boyhood into manhood, in order to confirm his entry into adult life, so was sports seen as the confirmation to strengthen the supposedly subservient Jews, and workers too, and turn them into proud, upstanding men and Jews.

"Neutral" Jewish Sports Organizations

Besides the Zionist, socialist and German-nationalist oriented sports clubs, the fourth pillar of organized Jewish sports consisted of those clubs that defined themselves as being neutral. These clubs were established as a result of the apparent refusal of many Jews to join either a Jewish sports association such as Maccabi or Schild or any non-Jewish clubs because of their personal philosophy. "We are not a new fighting club," declared the Hamburger jüdischer Sport- und Turnverein, founded in 1927, for example.[75] The message was thus that sport should not be seen as a political tool, but instead solely as a recreational activity.

Yet the attempt to depoliticize Jewish sports does not appear to be the only reason why "neutral" Jewish sports clubs were established. In 1925 the Verband jüdisch-neutraler Turn- und Sportvereine Westdeutschlands (VINTUS, or Association of West German Neutral Jewish Gymnastics and Sports Clubs) was founded in Essen as an umbrella organization for the neutral clubs. VINTUS was established as a result of the refusal of the Westdeutschenr Spielverband (WSV, Western German Sports Association) to accept Jewish clubs as members, their justification being that as "confessional" clubs they would contravene the association's rules on religious neutrality.[76] VINTUS was designed to offer Jewish sports clubs more chances for competition and so to prevent the exodus of club members to the more egalitarian, noncompetitive clubs, because of their competitive isolation. The allegedly neutral Jewish sports thus provided new opportunities for Jews who wanted or were obliged to participate in sports as Jews. When it came to the formation and preservation of Jewish identity in the interwar period, the endeavor to neutralize Jewish sports played an important role. Even the sports programs of the so-called neutral sports were not significantly different from those of the political clubs. They too promoted certain competitive disciplines, with the aim to bring forth strong, proud Jews. The name chosen for the neutral Jewish sports club in Essen is characteristic: the Hebrew name Hakoah (strength)—a name that symbolizes not only the Jewish convictions of the club, but also its ideal of a strong-willed, powerful Jewishness. It is therefore questionable as to what extent these sports clubs, which wished to stay clear of both intra-Jewish and general politics yet simultaneously defined themselves as Jewish, can really be described as neutral in such highly politicized times as the 1920s.

Whether there was a similar relationship between sports and militarism on the level of the individual athlete can hardly be ascertained without further research. We can assume that those to whom being Jewish was of existential importance would not have forgotten that they were Jews while they were engaged in sports, although it is almost certain that also those Jews to whom being Jewish meant very little would sooner or later have been descended upon by "name-hunters," whether Jewish or antisemitic, and "outed" as Jews. It comes as no surprise that the Jewishness of top-class athletes was a key feature of Jewish sports historiography, wherein the Jewish athlete was seen as the embodiment of a modern Jewish heroism.[77] One of the most highly celebrated Jewish sportsmen in the period between the wars, who made no secret of his Jewishness but did not belong to a Jewish sports club, was Daniel Prenn, German tennis champion between 1928 and 1932. In an interview given in 1929 he told the *C. V. Zeitung* that the outstanding achievement of Jewish sportsmen has to be seen as a direct consequence of a thousand years of oppression. He said that this had made the Jews particularly combative. To the question whether this observation did not actually conflict with the pacifism of many Jews, Prenn answered: "That is only an apparent contradiction, for having pacifist convictions can certainly go hand in hand with the enjoyment of competitive contact sport."[78]

Conclusion

In his treatise "Gymnastics and Sport in Fin-de-Siècle France," Eugen Weber points out that the fundamental question for every historical examination of physical exercise is that of why people pursue sports.[79] In the case of Jewish sports this is certainly a valid question, and, I believe, one that can

Zionist Gustav Krojanker as a student in Munich, circa 1910, wearing the uniform of the Jewish student fraternity KJV. Courtesy of the Beth Hatefutsoth Photo Archive, Tel Aviv.

be answered. For Jews, sports was not a value-free activity but a programmatic one. Even rival ideological tendencies promoted sports in a similar way and, above all, treated it as a Jewish affair, whereby a close connection between sports and Jewish identity was emphasized. It was claimed that by being strengthened physically, Jews could gain in self-confidence and assertiveness, and this not only made the ability to put up a fight a central element of the concept of masculinity, but at the same time it legitimated the organization and application of physical strength as a political instrument. In this deeper sense, sports was a medium that militarized Jewish society.

As we have seen, in Jewish sports discourse this militarizing tendency was made a central theme and even promoted. In many respects, sports groups were regarded as a surrogate army, which was not only supposed to defend Jewish dignity, but was also perceived as a kind of "school of the nation." It is probably no coincidence, then, that of all places Israel's National Center for Physical Education and Sport is not named for a great Jewish sports hero, such as Alfred or Felix Flatow, who were the first Jewish athletes to win gold medals in the modern Olympic Games, but instead bears the name Wingate, in honor of Major General Orde Charles Wingate, who trained Jewish special forces from 1936 to 1939 to fight in the great Arab uprising. After the state of Israel was founded, however, this naming act had only a symbolic value and virtually no practical application any longer, for by that time the Israeli army had already long since taken over the militarizing role of sports. Whether this development can be considered to be one reason underlying the relatively weak performance of Israeli athletes is an interesting thought that, however, I cannot pursue within the scope of this paper.

Translated from the German by Nicholas Jacob-Flynn

Notes

1. For an overview of this research, see Uta Klein, *Militär und Gesellschaft in Israel* (Frankfurt a.M., 2001), pp. 32–38; Moshe Zimmermann, "Militär, Militarismus und Zivilgesellschaft in Israel—eine europäische Erbschaft?" in Ute Frevert, ed., *Militär und Gesellschaft im 19. und 20. Jahrhundert* (Stuttgart, 1997), pp. 342–58.
2. On this see especially the articles by Daniel Wildmann and Moshe Zimmermann in this volume.
3. George L. Mosse, *The Image of Man: The creation of Modern Masculinity* (New York, 1996), p. 109.
4. Joachim Doron, " 'Der Geist ist es, der sich den Körper schafft!': Soziale Probleme in der jüdischen Turnbewegung," *Tel Aviver Jahrbuch für deutsche Geschichte* 20 (1991), pp. 237–58.

5. Sander Gilman, *The Jew's Body* (New York, 1991); Howard Eilberg-Schwartz, ed., *People of the Body: Jews and Judaism from an Embodied Perspective* (New York, 1992); Patricia Vertinsky, "The 'Racial' Body and the Anatomy of Difference: Antisemitism, Physical Culture, and the Jew's Foot," *Sport Science Review* 4 (1995), pp. 38–59.

6. Daniel Boyarin, *Unheroic Conduct: The Rise of Heterosexuality and the Invention of the Jewish Man* (Berkeley CA, 1997).

7. Desanka Schwara, *"Ojfn weg schtejt a bojm": Jüdische Kindheit und Jugend in Galizien, Kongresspolen, Litauen und Russland 1881–1939* (Cologne, 1999); Tamar Somogyi, *"Die Schejnen und die Prosten": Untersuchungen zum Schönheitsideal der Ostjuden in Bezug auf Körper und Kleidung unter besonderer Berücksichtigung des Chasidismus* (Berlin, 1982); Christopher D. Kenway, "Regeneration of the Volkskörper and the Jews' Body: The German Körperkultur Movement at the Turn of the Century," in Linda E. Feldman and Diana Orendi, eds., *Evolving Jewish Identities in German Culture: Borders and Crossings* (Westport CT, 2000), pp. 3–21.

8. On this view see for example Susannah Heschel, "Revolt of the Colonized: Abraham Geiger's Wissenschaft des Judentums as a Challenge to Christian Hegemony in the Academy," *New German Critique* 77 (1999), pp. 61–85.

9. Karl Heinz Schodrock, *Militärische Jugend-Erziehung in Preußen 1806–1820* (Olsberg, 1989), p. 189.

10. Hans Donalies, *Sport und Militär. Ein Handbuch für militärischen Sportbetrieb* (Berlin, 1911); Edmund Neuendorff, *Geschichte der neueren deutschen Leibesübung vom Beginn des 18. Jahrhunderts bis zur Gegenwart*, vol. 4 (Dresden, 1936), pp. 633–39; Guy Lewis, "World War I and the Emergence of Sport for the Masses," *The Maryland Historian* 2 (1973), p. 110.

11. Gertrud Pfister, "Sportler für den Krieg. Die Militarisierung der Turn- und Spiel-und Sportbewegung im wilhelminischen Reich," in Sven Güldenpfennig and Horst Meyer, eds., *Sportler für den Frieden* (Cologne, 1983), pp. 96–119; E. A. Wright, "Education," in "Sport and Militarism: Fascist Italy and Nazi Germany," Ph.D. Dissertation, University of Leicester, 1980.

12. Christiane Eisenberg, *"English Sports" und deutsche Bürger. Eine Gesellschaftgeschichte 1800–1939* (Paderborn, 1996), p. 232.

13. Eisenberg, *"English Sports" und deutsche Bürger*, p. 232; cf. also Michael Geyer, *Aufrüstung und Sicherheit: Die Reichswehr in der Krise der Machtpolitik 1924–1936* (Wiesbaden, 1980), p. 5.

14. On this, Hans Mommsen, "Militär und zivile Militarisierung in Deutschland 1914 bis 1938," in Ute Frevert, ed., *Militär und Gesellschaft im 19. und 20. Jahrhundert* (Stuttgart, 1997), pp. 265–76.

15. Johan Huizinga, *Homo Ludens* (Amsterdam, 1939), p. 317.

16. Kalus Theweleit, *Male Fantasies* (Minneapolis, 1987), p. 6.

17. Michael Geyer, "Militarization of Europe, 1914–1945," in John R. Gillis, ed., *The Militarization of the Western World* (New Brunswick, 1989), p. 79.

18. Quoted in Adolph Asch, *Geschichte des K. C. im Lichte der deutschen kulturellen und politischen Entwicklung* (London, 1965), pp. 44–51; cf. also Keith H. Pickus, *Constructing Modern Identities. Jewish University Students in Germany 1814–1915* (Detroit, 1999).

19. For a comprehensive blibliograpy on Jewish sports: Toni Niewert and Lorenz Peiffer, "Jüdischer Sport in Deutschland—eine kommentierte Bibliographie," *SportZeit* 1 (2001), pp. 81–106.

20. For a most provocative critique of the positive image of the tough Jews in post–World

War II American Jewish society see: Paul Breines, *Tough Jews: Political Fantasies and Moral Dilemma of American Jewry* (New York 1990).

21. Alien Bodner, *When Boxing Was a Jewish Sport* (Westport CT, 1997); Bernard Postal, Jesse Silver, and Roy Silver, eds., *Encyclopedia of Jews in Sports* (New York, 1965), p. 137.

22. Peter F. Radford, "Daniel Mendoza and his Circle: A Study of Social Integration in 18th Century Britain," *Sozial- und Zeitgeschichte des Sports*, 13 (1999), pp. 7–19.

23. Martha Wertheimer, Siddy Goldschmid, and Paul Yogi Mayer, eds., *Das Jüdische Sportbuch* (Berlin, 1937).

24. Postal et al., *Encyclopedia of Jews in Sports*, p. 513.

25. On the development of the competitive sports, cf. Henning Eichberg, *Leistung, Spannung, Geschwindigkeit. Sport und Tanz im gesellschaftlichen Wandel des 18. und 19. Jahrhunderts* (Stuttgart, 1978), pp. 61–80.

26. George Eisen, "Jewish History and the Ideology of Modern Sport: Approaches and Interpretations," *Journal of Sport History* 25 (1998), pp. 495, 507.

27. Ruben Ainsztein, *Jewish Resistance in Nazi-Occupied Eastern Europe: With a Historical Survey of the Jew as Fighter and Soldier in the Diaspora* (London, 1974).

28. Max Nordau, "Muskeljudentum," *Jüdische Turn-Zeitung* (hereafter *JTZ*) no. 2 (1900), p. 3; on this see also Ingrid Spörk, "Das Bild von 'Juden' in Texten Max Nordaus," *Transversal* 1 (2001), p. 12–18.

29. Richard Blum, "Disziplin," *JTZ* no. 2 (1900), p. 14. On Blum's rigid discipline as leader of the Bar Kochba gymnastics section, cf. the autobiography of Elias Auerbach, *Pionier der Verwirklichung* (Stuttgart, 1969), p. 131.

30. Ernst Tuch, "Einiges über 'Jewish Lads Brigade,' " *JTZ* no. 10 (1902), pp. 161ff; no. 11, pp. 178–82; no. 12 (1903), p. 215.

31. Theobald Scholem, "Turnen und Jugendwehr," *JTZ* no. 5 (1903), p. 85.

32. Julius Heilbrunn, "Militärische und turnerische Erziehung," *JTZ* no. 6 (1903), p. 102.

33. Heilbrunn, "Militärische und turnerische Erziehung," p. 102.

34. Heilbrunn, "Militärische und turnerische Erziehung," p. 102.

35. David Biale, *Power and Powerlessness in Jewish History* (New York, 1986), p. 130; on this aspect see also Fritz Simon, *Leibesübung und Nationalerziehung im Wandel der Geschichte* (Berlin, 1928); and Claire E. Nolte, *The Sokol in the Czech Lands to 1914: Training for the Nation* (New York, 2002).

36. In 1913 the association's publication had already changed its name from *Jüdische Turnzeitung: Monatsschrift für die körperliche Hebung der Juden* to *Jüdische Monatshefte für Turnen und Sport*. On the sports/gymnastics relation, cf. Hans-Jürgen König, "Die Anfänge der jüdischen Turn- und Sportbewegung," *Stadion* 15 (1989), p. 20.

37. Hermann Jalowicz, "Die Erziehung des Willens durch Leibesübungen," *Jüdische Turnzeitung* no. 3 (1901), pp. 29–34; Heinz Risse, *Soziologie des Sports* (1920; rpr. Münster, 1981), pp. 72–82.

38. Willi Meisel, "Dem Sport sein 'Schild,' " *Der Schild*, November 1926.

39. Hans-Jürgen König, *Die Anfänge der jüdischen Turn- und Sportbewegung*, p. 21; cf. George Eisen, "Zionism, Nationalism and the Emergence of the Jüdische Turnerschaft," *Leo Baeck Institute Yearbook* 28 (1983), pp. 247–62.

40. Allen Guttman, *From Ritual to Record* (New York, 1978), pp. 130–36.

41. "Bericht aus der Generalversammlung des Bar Kochba Hamburg," in Ina Lorenz, ed.,

Die Juden in Hamburg zur Zeit der Weimarer Republik (Hamburg, 1987), p. 984; cf. also John Bunzl, ed., *Hoppauf Hakoah* (Vienna, 1987), pp. 48.

42. Michael Berkowitz, *Western Jewry and the Zionist Project, 1914–1933* (Cambridge UK, 1998), p. 11; Greg Caplan, "Militärische Männlichkeit in der deutsch-jüdischen Geschichte," *Die Philosophin* 22 (2000), pp. 85–100.

43. Julius Hirsch, "Neuaufbau der Turnerschaft," *Jüdische Turn- und Sportzeitung* no. 1 (1919), p. 2.

44. Johanna Thomaschewsky, "Hebräische Turnkommandos," *Jüdische Turn- und Sportzeitung*, Organ der Deutschen Kreise der jüdische Turnerschaft, no. 9/10 (1919), pp. 24–26. It is indeed quite possible that some of the drill commands in the Israeli army, for instance קדימה צעד (Forward march!), הקשב (Attention!), שורה ערוך (Fall in!), ימינה שור (Eyes right!) can be traced back to this process of Hebrewization.

45. Hirsch, "Neuaufbau der Turnerschaft," p. 5.

46. "Protokoll der Sitzung des erweiterten Kreisvorstands in München am 8. September 1919," *Jüdische Turn- und Sportzeitung* no. 9/10, (1919) p. 12. See also pp. 43ff.

47. On this see also the article of Michael John in this volume.

48. "Selbstwehr und Turnvereine. Vorbildliche Organisation in Wien," *Jüdische Turn- und Sportzeitung* no. 1 (1919), p. 11.

49. Ulrich Dunker, *Der Reichsbund jüdischer Frontsoldaten 1919–1938* (Düsseldorf, 1977); Ruth Pierson, " 'Embattled Veterans': The Reichsbund jüdischer Frontsoldaten," *Leo Baeck Institute Yearbook* 18 (1973), pp. 139–55.

50. Dunker, *Der Reichsbund jüdischer Frontsoldaten*, p. 60; Caplan, *Militärische Männlichkeit*, p. 96.

51. Hajo Bernett, *Der jüdische Sport im nationalsozialistischen Deutschland 1933–1938* (Cologne, 1978), p. 50; on the history of Schild, see also Paul Yogi Mayer, "Equality—Egality: Jews and Sport in Germany," *Leo Baeck Institute Yearbook* 25 (1980), pp. 221–41; Paul Yogi Mayer, "Deutsche Juden und Sport. Ihre Leistungen—Ihr Schicksal," *Menora* (1994), pp. 287–311.

52. Dunker, *Der Reichsbund jüdischer Frontsoldaten*, pp. 96–104, 164–72. On military sport, see Michael Barrett, "Soldiers, Sportsmen and Politicians: Military Sport in Germany, 1924–1935," Ph.D. Dissertation, University of Massachusetts, 1977; Hermann Bach, "Volks- und Wehrsport in der Weimarer Republik," *Sportwissenschaften* 3 (1981), pp. 273–94; Hajo Bernett, "Wehrsport—ein Pseudosport. Stellungnahme zu Hermann Bach," *Sportwissenschaften* 3 (1981), pp. 295–308; Arnd Krüger and Frank von Lojewski, "Ausgewählte Aspekte des Wehrsportes in Niedersachsen in der Weimarer Zeit," in Hans Langenfeld and Stefan Nielsen, eds., *Beiträge zur Sportgeschichte Niedersachsens*, vol. 2, Weimarer Republik (Göttingen, 1998), pp. 124–48.

53. Dunker, *Der Reichsbund jüdischer Frontsoldaten*, p. 103; *Das jüdische Sportbuch*, p. 40; Rudolf Krotki, "Jiu Jitsu," in Carl Diem et al., eds., *Stadion. Das Buch von Sport und Turnen Gymnastik und Spiel* (Berlin, 1928), pp. 228–33.

54. On this cooperation, cf. also Jacob Borut, " 'Verjudung des Judentums.' Was there a Zionist Subculture in Weimar Germany?" in Michael Brenner and Derek J. Penslar, eds., *In Search of Jewish Community* (Bloomington IN, 1998), pp. 100–103.

55. On Jewish defense in the Weimar Republic, see Arnold Paucker, *Der jüdische Abwehrkampf gegen Antisemitismus und Nationalsozialismus in der letzen Jahren der Weimarer Republik* (Hamburg, 1968).

56. Dunker, *Der Reichsbund jüdischer Frontsoldaten*, pp. 63–69; Paul Yogi Mayer, "Deutsche

Juden und Sport," in Joachim H. Teichler, ed., *Körper, Kultur und Ideologie. Sport und Zeitgeist im 19. und 20. Jahrhundert* (Mainz, 1997), p. 129.

57. Paul Yogi Mayer, "Schwarzes Fähnlein," in Klaus J. Herrmann, *Das Dritte Reich und die Deutsch-Jüdischen Organisationen 1933–1934* (Cologne, 1969), p. 42; cf. also Hans Ries, "Sportsoldaten," *Die Kraft, Blatt für Sport und Jugendertüchtigung, Organ des Sportbundes im* RJF, December 1934.

58. Edgar Marx, "Das neue Jahr des jüdischen Turn- und Sportverein Bar Kochba e.V.," in Ina Lorenz, ed., *Die Juden in Hamburg zur Zeit der Weimarer Republik* (Hamburg, 1987), p. 988; cf. Felix Simmenauer, *Die Gold-Medaille. Erinnerungen an die Bar Kochba-Makkabi Turn- und Sportbewegung* (Berlin, 1989), p. 66.

59. Gertrud Pickhan, *Gegen den Strom. Der Allgemeine Jüdische Arbeiterbund "Bund" in Polen 1918–1939* (Stuttgart, 2001). On Jewish workers' sports, see Uriel Simiri, "Die Geschichte des Arbeitersports in Israel," in Arnd Krüger and James Riordan, eds., *Der internationale Arbeitersport* (Cologne, 1985), pp. 164–73; Elke Stiller, "Jüdische Sportvereine und ihre Beziehungen zu der deutschen und internationalen Arbeitersportbewegung 1923–1933," *Sozial- und Zeitgeschichte des Sports* 13 (1999), pp. 28–37.

60. Julius Deutsch, *Sport und Politik* (Berlin, 1928).

61. Julius Deutsch, *Sport und Politik* (Berlin, 1928), p. 23.

62. Bernard Goldstein, *20 Years with the Jewish Labor Bund in Warsaw 1919–1939* (New York, 1960), pp. 127–31; cf. also, Roni Gechtman, "Socialist Mass Politics through Sport: The Bund's Morgnshtern in Poland, 1926–1939," *Journal of Sport History* 26 (1999), pp. 326–52; on other Jewish sports organizations in Eastern Europe, see Moshe Kligsberg, "The Jewish Youth Movement in Interwar Polen" (Yiddish), in Joshua Fishman, ed., *Studies on Polish Jewry 1919–1939* (New York, 1974), pp. 137–228; Diethelm Blecking, "Jüdischer Sport in Polen," *Sozial- und Zeitgeschichte des Sports* 13 (1999), pp. 20–27.

63. Diethelm Belcking, "Marxismus versus Muskeljudentum. Die jüdische Sportbewegung in Polen von den Anfängen bis nach dem Zweiten Weltkrieg," *SportZeit* 2 (2001), pp. 31–52.

64. Gechtman, "Socialist Mass Politics," pp. 343.

65. Claus Tiedemann, "Die Stellung der Arbeitersportbewegung zu Frieden und Krieg," in Sven Güldenpfennig and Horst Meyer, eds., *Sportler für den Frieden* (Cologne, 1983), pp. 120–36.

66. Deutsch, *Sport und Politik*, p. 33; cf. also the brochure by Arthur Arzt, *Sport und Politik. Eine notwendige Klarstellung für Nursportler und Nurpolitiker* (Leipzig, ca. 1927), p. 6f.

67. On this, cf. also Borukh Yismakh, "Sport Clubs and Self-Defense," in Jack Kugelmass and Jonathan Boyarin, eds., *From a Ruined Garden: The Memorial Books of Polish Jewry* (New York, 1983), pp. 60–63.

68. Deutsch, *Sport und Politik*, p. 45f.; also Helmut Wagner, *Sport und Arbeiter Sport* (Berlin, 1931), pp. 175–80; Fritz Wildung, *Arbeiter-sport* (Berlin, 1929), pp. 151–54.

69. Henry Tobias, *The Jewish Bund in Russia. From its Origins to 1905*, (Stanford CA, 1972), pp. 221–35.

70. Leonard Rowe, "Jewish Self-Defense: A Response to Power," in Joshua Fishman, ed., *Studies on Polish Jewry 1919–1939* (New York, 1974), pp. 105–241. For history of Jewish self-defense in Eastern Europe and the different attempts to organize it see Jonathan Frankel, *Prophecy and Politics: Socialism, Nationalism, and the Russian Jews, 1862–1917* (Cambridge UK, 1981).

71. Goldstein, *20 Years with the Jewish Labor*, p. 130. According to Goldstein, he was only

honorary president, and not involved in the day-to-day business and organization of the Morgnshtern.

72. John M. Hoberman, *Sport and Political Ideology* (Austin TX, 1984).

73. Nordau, "Muskeljudentum," p. 10; Deutsch, *Sport und Politik*, p. 41.

74. Sabina Loriga, "Die Militärerfahrung," in Giovanni Levi and Jean-Claude Schmitt, eds., *Geschichte der Jugend* (Frankfurt a.M., 1997), pp. 20–55; cf. also Ute Frevert, *Die kasernierte Nation. Militärdienst und Zivilgesellschaft in Deutschland* (Munich, 2001), pp. 228–45.

75. "Der Hamburger jüdische Sport-und Turnverein," in Ina Lorenz, *Die Juden in Hamburg*, p. 988.

76. Fritz A. Lewinson, "Turn- und Sport-Klub Hakoah-Essen—einer der größten jüdischen Sportvereine, 1923–1938," in Hermann Schröter, ed., *Geschichte und Schicksal der Essener Juden* (Essen, 1980), pp. 283–89; Heiko Zielke, " 'Unsere Kraft unserem Volk.' Makkabi und den jüdische Sport in Düsseldorf 1924 bis 1938," in *In Düsseldorf und am Niederrhein. Aspekte jüdischen Lebens* (Düsseldorf, 1997), pp. 130–41; Pasqual Boeti, " 'Muskeljudentum.' Der Turn- und Sportklub "Hakoah Essen"—ein jüdischer Sportverein im Ruhrgebiet," in Jan-Pieter Barbian et al., eds., *Juden im Ruhrgebiet* (Essen, 1999), p. 609.

77. To give just a few examples from the interwar period: *Das Jüdische Sportbuch*, trans. Süssmann Muntner, "Leibesübung bei der Juden," *Menorah* (1926), pp. 381–93; Süssmann Muntner and Felix Theilhaber, "Sport und Körperkultur bei den Juden," in *Jüdisches Lexikon*, vol. 4 (Berlin, 1930), pp. 560–67; Leo Schindel, "Leibesübung bei den Juden," *Bayerische Israelitische Gemeindezeitung* (September 14, 1928), pp. 300–304; Siegfried Einstein, "Körperkultur und Sport bei den Juden," *Bayerische Israelitische Gemeindezeitung* (August 1, 1933), pp. 231–32; Willy Meisel and Felix Pinczower, "Sport," in Sigmund Kaznelson, ed., *Juden im deutschen Kulturbereich* (Berlin, 1935), pp. 926–36.

78. "Gespräch mit dem deutschen Tennismeister Prenn," *C. V. Zeitung* (July 26, 1929), p. 391.

79. Eugen Weber, "Gymnastics and Sports in Fin-de-Siècle France: Podium of the Classes?" *American Historical Review* 76 (1971), pp. 70–98.

4. Strongman Siegmund Breitbart
and Interpretations of the Jewish Body

Sharon Gillerman

I N ANTICIPATION OF the arrival in Berlin of the Iron King (Der Eisenkö-
nig), Siegmund Breitbart, in 1923, a journalist for Berlin's *Tägliche Rundschau* announced, "Samson is here, you Philistines of Berlin. The man described as the strongest man in the world since ancient times. Breitbart has
arrived."[1] Earlier that year, the city of Vienna had been overcome by a three-
month-long Breitbart mania that reached an intensity of adulation normally
reserved only for Vienna's greatest athletes. In Warsaw, where the Iron King
was known in Yiddish as "Samson our hero" (*unzer Shimshon hagibor*), the
Radziminer Rebbe summoned Breitbart to perform his feats of strength in
a private showing and bestowed a blessing upon him. During that same
visit, musicians performing in a Warsaw Jewish restaurant frequented by
the strongman greeted him with the playing of "Hatikvah."[2]

Siegmund Breibart, or Zishe, as he was known to his Yiddish-speaking
fans, was a Polish Jewish performer who astonished audiences with his
remarkable feats of strength. Blending spectacular showmanship with genuine muscular power, he earned his reputation as the "strongest man in the
world" by pounding nails into boards with his fist, bending iron bars, and
biting through chains. Breitbart's body-centered spectacles occupied a performance space that bridged sports and entertainment by offering up athletic feats in an artistic format. Having begun his career as a circus strongman in Germany after the First World War, Breitbart became a well-known
vaudeville star in the early 1920s and attracted a mass following in Europe
and America. For a few years following the end of World War I, Europe's
Iron King had become an icon of popular culture, indeed, even something
of a cult hero.

If Breitbart achieved a degree of superhero status while he was still alive,
he became positively larger than life in his death. Although his life and career came to a premature end in 1925 as the result of a stage accident involving a rusty nail that gave him a fatal dose of blood poisoning, his brother and
son carried on his act through the end of the twenties. Ironically enough,
his physical culture correspondence course, which was based in London
and New York, outlived its founder and continued to operate years after his

death, with correspondence still being signed "personally" by Breitbart. His eastern European Jewish fan base, which had been receptive to his message of Jewish empowerment, passed on stories about the Jewish strongman to their children that are still in circulation to this day. And in Central Europe, Breitbart joined the ranks of its illustrious musclemen, taking his place alongside the likes of Sandow, Beck, and Cronos. His achievements set a standard against which new strongmen and women were measured for well over a decade. Although he never concealed his Jewishness, and sometimes even capitalized on it, Breitbart's body became an object of admiration both for women and men, Jews and non-Jews. Indeed, the story of Breitbart's reception is all the more compelling for its emergence at a time of hardening racial attitudes. In this context, the Jewish strongman's public persona simultaneously challenged racial categories and undercut popular stereotypes of the Jew. Praising his body for its beauty as well as for its strength, many observers in Central Europe saw in Breitbart the embodiment of the contemporary ideals of strength and beauty. Breitbart's blue eyes, light hair, and perfectly sculpted musculature led Germans and Jews alike to claim him as a representative specimen of their race. While Germans commented frequently on his blonde hair as a sign of his natural beauty, for example, east European Jews pointed to his blonde curls as typical Semitic racial features.[3]

Breitbart's diverse audiences thus read his body in significantly different ways, rewriting the aesthetic qualities associated with his body into narratives that inhered with competing and sometimes contradictory cultural meanings. Accordingly, I am interested in tracing the multivalent images of race, masculinity, and strength that Breitbart projected in his performances, together with the construction of often quite opposing readings of these images by his audiences. Such an approach permits us to explore how Breitbart made his body into a surface upon which various meanings were inscribed; it became the site of simultaneous, competing discourses concerning, among other things, nation, gender, and race.[4] No less significant, this kind of analysis affirms the importance of distinguishing performance from spectatorship by probing the interplay between images as cultural products and the consumption of those images by diverse audiences.[5]

In order to consider the narrative uses to which Breitbart's male Jewish body has been put, I will discuss three texts—a novella, a screenplay, and a film—each of which integrated his body and his life story into a distinct framework of meaning. After beginning with a novella written by Paula Busch in post–World War I Berlin, I then discuss a Yiddish screenplay that appeared in Warsaw in 1928, three years after Breitbart's death. Moving into the twenty-first century, I close with a discussion of the 2002 Werner Herzog film *Invincible*, which was based on the life of the Jewish strongman. Each of these narratives was a product of a specific cultural and national context, and each presented Breitbart's masculinity as formative for the fashioning of very different notions of racial and national identity. In these competing constructions of Breitbart's masculinity and Jewishness, we see his Jewish body appear as at once concealed and exposed, triumphant and defeated, universalized and made to embody the tragic uniqueness of Jewish history.

Breitbart's performances are perhaps equally notable for their diversity and range as for the particular intensity of showmanship and spectacle Breitbart brought to each show. Sliding easily between diverse personae and identities, Breitbart effectively targeted individual performances to meet the desires of particular audiences. In addition to contributing significantly to the breadth of Breitbart's appeal, his fluidity as a performer effectively recast the "strongman" act as a form of performance drawing equally from the energies of the circus, the music hall, and the burgeoning physical culture movement. Whether dressed in the manner of a poor Teuton or barely dressed at all in his revealing Tarzan costume, Breitbart always strongly emphasized the display of the male body. Indeed, the elaborate regalia Breitbart would employ in his more exotic costumes was but another aspect of male display that served to accentuate and ironically underscore the spectacle he made of his physique when he would subsequently bare his body to the audience's gaze. The choice of personae further enhanced this effect with Breitbart's depiction of archetypal masculine figures such as the bullfighter, gladiator, and cowboy. These adopted roles directly echoed the tales of fantastic offstage exploits attributed to Breitbart such as fighting lion cubs and killing a bull with a blow from his fist. [6] Both onstage and off, Breitbart's image was carefully managed to reinforce an ongoing association with the masculine ideals of virility, strength, and courage. What was particularly notable about this effort was the ways in which it moved beyond simple questions of gender and an assertion of masculinity to encompass broader notions of racial and national identity. Thus, Breitbart's portrayal of the classical Greek hero not only provides a variation on the familiar theme of virility and strength but specifically reiterates the aesthetic paradigm of Aryan masculinity advanced by racialist thinkers of the period. These parallels become even more significant when one considers Breitbart's promotion of the accessibility of such strength and virility. With the physical culture correspondence course he developed in New York in 1924, Breitbart promised men that personal perfection could be achieved through cultivation of the body. Undercutting the racialists' logic, physical perfection could no longer be seen as a simple matter of genetics; it could be acquired.

The implications of Breitbart's performance emerge even more strikingly as one considers his signature role as a Roman centurion. Though Breitbart's personal fascination with ancient Rome is much in evidence from the more than two thousand volumes on ancient Rome he was said to have in his personal library, this personal interest cannot easily be separated from the wider German admiration for Rome as the most perfect embodiment of military and imperial greatness.[7] Breitbart clearly draws on such enthusiasms as he crafts a role for himself as a noble Germanic warrior. The strongest example of this may be his performance of his centurion act in Berlin to the accompaniment of Wagner's *Siegfried*. Rehearsing the narrative of a regenerate German nation, Breitbart prominently inserts himself into the narrative. In this way, Breitbart grafts the notion of the "muscle Jew" onto the idea of a virtuous masculinity that underwrites the belief in a regenerate German national identity. As a cultural outsider, he interprets and translates German national values to both Germans and non-Germans alike, incorporating his own physicality as an unabashedly public Jew into the narrative of German nationalism.

The boldness of this move becomes even more evident when we consider the ways in which Breitbart connected these very same images with the idea of a Jewish national revival. Just as his performance of the Germanic warrior's nobility draws on the legacy of Roman militarism, Breitbart's performance as the Jewish military leader Bar Kochba emphasizes a similar provenance. Indeed, the most astonishing example of Breitbart's linkage of militant Jewish nationalism with Rome involves an audacious invocation and *inversion* of religious identity. In a full-page advertisement in the leading trade journal, *Das Programm*, in 1925, Breitbart couples an oversized Star of David with the arresting German text: "Take note of two words—Siegmund Breitbart."[8] Underneath this, Breitbart inserts (in both German and Latin) the quotation, "In hoc Signio veritas vincet" or "In diesem Zeichen wird die Wahrheit siegen" ("In this sign the truth will prevail"). These are the words pronounced by the angel to the Emperor Constantine as he goes into battle under the emblem of the cross in 312 CE. The phrase makes for a deliberatively disruptive motto for the Jewish strongman with his name emblazoned under the Star of David.[9] Rather than the herald of a new era of

Christianity, Breitbart transposes Constantine's battle cry into a rallying cry for Jewish military conquest enunciated from the very center of European Christendom. In this way Breitbart enacts, through his performance and his adept self-promotion, the narrative of not one nation, but two. That this assertion of Jewish militancy would insert itself at the very root of European Christian hegemony underscores the notion of Jewish strength as at once an assertion of autonomy and an insistence on belonging within the form of the nation.

Of the three narratives I will consider here, only one was composed during Breitbart's lifetime. Paula Busch, the director of the preeminent German Circus Busch, discovered and hired Breitbart in 1919 and maintained a warm relationship with him until the end of his life. [10] Indeed, it was she who made the decision to market Breitbart as a Jew, and, as a result, it was she who also reaped considerable benefit from his overwhelming box-office success. [11] Breitbart was probably the most important strongman engaged by Circus Busch since the heyday of strongmen had ended earlier in the century. [12] In her novella entitled *Samson*, Busch relates the story of a circus strongman who was born with superhuman strength. Serialized in the Ullstein paper *Berliner Morgenpost*, it ran in July and August 1923, at the very time Breitbart was performing in Berlin. [13] The narrative includes a number of anecdotes that mirror events from Breitbart's career, in particular, stories that had themselves become a standard part of his own self-narrative. Busch's strongman character also bears a striking resemblance to descriptions of Siegmund Breitbart as a sweet, naïve, and extraordinarily generous person, characteristics that one might not necessarily assume were typical of strongmen in general. The novella, part bildungsroman part soap opera, follows the growth and maturation of a boy who is endowed with an equal measure of strength and beauty. It begins with a description of his childhood that substitutes the throbbing urban density of the historical Breitbart's impoverished neighborhood in Lodz with an idealized state of nature that has echoes in Hobbes and Rousseau. Busch's Kurt Bach grows up in a kind of primeval natural setting, evocative of a pedagogically cultivated state of nature in which children would be left to develop without the imposition of arbitrary social norms. Existing beyond the confines of time and place, Kurt and his seven brothers go about barefoot, wrapped only in togas, and remain until adulthood unencumbered by the usual demands of civil society. [14] As the older brothers leave their primordial paradise, Kurt's mother takes him to the city, whereupon he immediately joins the circus. It is in the circus that Kurt first has to contend with a social world driven by self-interest and vanity. Just as an ideal "natural man" would never be fully at home in society, neither could Kurt feel comfortable in the world of circus and professional sports that was governed, to a great extent, by appearances alone.[15]

In contrast to this compromised world of appearances, Kurt's strength and beauty throughout the novella serve as external signifiers that point to his wealth of inner resources. Thus, the frequent references to Kurt as "*der Blonde,*" rather than referring strictly to his physical beauty, have the effect of binding his internal moral qualities to his pleasing physical attributes. Along the way Samson meets his Delilah, and though temporarily waylaid by her, succeeds in having his biblical fate rewritten in a manner that allows him to find mature love with a kindred artistic soul. As Kurt matures into a full man he comes to embody the masculine ideal through his successful establishment of a harmonious balance between body and spirit.[16] And, by the very end of the story, he comes to understand that love, too, entails the perfect melding of body and mind.

In Busch's novella, the Kurt/Breitbart/Samson figure is integrated into and, indeed, made a representative of, the classic western narrative of the individual search for perfection that is to be achieved through the harmonious integration of body and mind. Fashioning a figure that literally embodies many of the cultural ideals that can be found in European literature, Busch draws on the Enlightenment, classical culture, the bildungsroman, and the physical culture movement. It is particularly striking, therefore, that Busch would take as her model for this universal man a Jew from Lodz. Yet Busch paints a portrait of a complex strongman whose values and qualities speak to the concerns and sensibilities of many post–World War I Germans. Elsewhere, Busch draws explicit connections between the form and content of circus performance with the political zeitgeist. In her view, for example, the era of the strongman in late-nineteenth-century German popular entertainment accompanied a period of military buildup and international competition for colonies when Germany had become the strongest of European nations.[17] Her post–World War I strongman appears to be temperamentally suited to much different times, for his exercise of strength is always accompanied by a sense of moral responsibility. Indeed, Kurt/Breitbart/Samson seems to stand as a warning against the destructive effects of the violence and aggression unleashed by war. Busch's beautiful strongman contests both the hedonistic cult of beauty in Weimar and the destructiveness of unchecked power rendered visible in the deformed male bodies inscribed with the wounds of war.[18] Her story concludes with the transformation of the very notion of Bildung, from an act of intellectual self-cultivation into one that combines the pursuit of the physical together with the spiritual. Tying together the values of physical culture and life reform movements, our hero achieves a state of perfection, with an inner spiritual life and the body in equal balance.

Casting Breitbart more as the tragic hero of the Hebrew Bible than as a model of the Greek heroic ideal, Y. M. Neuman presents the life and death of Zishe Breitbart in the form of a short Yiddish screenplay. Published in the first issue of the Yiddish-language journal Film Velt in 1928, the screenplay reflects the unique political significance that Breitbart held for east European Jews living in Central and Eastern Europe, as well as America.[19] Equally important, it represents perhaps the first attempt to give shape to an emerging oral tradition that had already begun producing collective memories of Breitbart. Whereas the German and Austrian Jewish middle classes were uneasy with Breitbart's sensational theatrical displays, paying them little attention and downplaying his position as an icon of popular culture and Jewish popular culture, the poorer, nationally oriented Yiddish-speaking east European Jews constituted Breitbart's specifically Jewish fan base.

Opening with the question, "Children, do you know who Zishe Breitbart was?" the screenplay has more the feel of a morality tale than a cutting edge modernist film project. What is clear is that the transmission of Zishe's legacy is central to this narrative. The story of Zishe's life is represented in a manner entirely consistent with his own account of his origins in his autobiography, which had been serialized in the popular Warsaw Yiddish daily Haynt just three years before. After we see young Zishe working beside his father in the family iron workshop, we move to one of the most dramatic moments of the screenplay. Scene 3 shows Zishe entering the circus arena in the garb of Bar Kochba, the second-century military and messianic figure who had come to symbolize, for Zionists in particular, an assertive Jewish nationalism and the ideals of the ancient national past.[20] Following Breitbart's stage entrance, antisemites begin heckling him and calling out that his act is a bluff. Zishe's feats of strength thus take on particular meaning as a means of refuting the antisemites and their charges. In vanquishing antisemitism and restoring the good name of the strongman, Breitbart's bodily strength represents a triumph not only for him personally but for the Jewish people as a whole. The "goyim," who throughout the screenplay appear interchangeable with the antisemites and speak always in one voice, realize that this fighting Jew is for real. When Zishe is crowned the defender of the Jews and Jewish honor, the goyim respond to his accomplishments with evident concern—and in Yiddish, of course. "Oy, a starker Yid," they remark to one another. "Who knows how many more there may be like him?"

Upon Breitbart's death in scene 5, however, there are still four scenes remaining. The setting of the screenplay now moves from this world to the next. We see Zishe ascend to heaven, where he is greeted by none other than Samson himself. "Welcome, my comrade of the twentieth century," says Samson. Understandably disoriented, Zishe asks Samson where he is. "In heaven my friend, in seventh heaven." "Samson, I've been thinking about you my whole life," Zishe tells him. He then asks Samson the question presumably on the mind of many potential Jewish film viewers: "Why are the times so difficult and bitter for the Jews? Why hasn't the Messiah already come to break our chains and make us free?" We never hear Samson's response. But the next scene opens with Neuman, the author, awakening from his sleep. He announces that Zishe came to him in a dream and passed on the secret of his strength. Without revealing Zishe's secret, Neuman nonetheless attempts to tear apart a chain. As Neuman breaks it apart, the chain of transmission, as it were, is now fully forged. Neuman himself is crowned the new Shimshon hagibor, accompanied by shouts of "Long live the new Samson!"

In Neuman's screenplay, Zishe is featured as a genuine Jewish folk hero whose overwhelming physical strength offered a means to meet a growing antisemitic threat. But Neuman's message transcends the achievements of Zishe the individual to illustrate how he inspired a people who felt itself in need of protection. In the screenplay, as well as in reality, Zishe offered his east European Jewish fans the example of self-defense and political mobilization as a meaningful response to Jewish political powerlessness. Indeed, for east European Jews, Breitbart's hero status fit easily into their own distinctive historical narrative of persecution and redemption. Gary Bart, the producer of Invincible and a descendant of the Jewish strongman, recounts a popular Yiddish saying that "were a thousand Breitbarts to arise among the Jews, the Jewish people would cease being persecuted." But like all tragic heroes, Breitbart too had a fatal flaw—and at the end of the screenplay we are told that his was a lack of religious observance. The screenplay concludes by admonishing "the children" to heed the lesson of Breitbart's death, for while Zishe possessed more earthly gifts than any man, there is nothing that can replace the fear of heaven.

In contrast to the two competing interpretations of Breitbart produced during his lifetime and immediately thereafter, Werner Herzog renders Zishe Breitbart as the latest instantiation in a long line of Herzog's visionary but ill-fated prophets. His film *Invincible* takes the Breitbart story as the basis for fashioning a grand Herzogian fable that pits a simple and innocent Jew against the dark forces of the occult, and, ultimately, against the Nazis themselves. [21] Breitbart is cast as the tongue-tied Moses, a prophet of few words but immeasurable vision. The plot line revolves around the contest between Zishe the strongman, played by a real strongman, Jouko Ahola, who earned the title "strongest man in the world" in 1998, and the infamous clairvoyant and con man Erik Jan Hanussen, played by Tim Roth. Throughout the film Hanussen enlists the dark powers of the occult in his ultimately futile drive to enhance his own wealth and power. In adapting the story to film, Herzog has changed both the time and place of the setting: he transported Breitbart's large family from a poor quarter of Lodz to a pious shtetl somewhere in the East. Even more significantly, he exchanged the early twenties for the early thirties, thus allowing the story to unfold on the eve of the Nazis' rise to power.

Herzog takes up his story at an historical moment far removed both from the Germany that gave rise to the universalizing impulses of Paula Busch, and from an Eastern Europe that had once been home to millions of Jews. In his first film to deal directly with the Nazi past, Werner Herzog creates a Breitbart figure that comes to symbolize the irrevocable break that took place between Germans and Jews, Germanness and Jewishness, as a result of National Socialism.

Set against Herzog's stunning cinematography, the film narrates the following story: Zishe Breitbart's display of unusual strength lands him an offer from a Berlin talent scout for a job on the Berlin stage. Though Breitbart initially resists leaving either his family or the shtetl, he eventually goes to Berlin and ends up working under Hanussen at his "House of the Occult." Hanussen, who fancies himself the logical choice for a cabinet position as minister of the occult in a future Nazi regime, cultivates the company of Berlin's Nazi top brass, despite having concealed his identity as a Jew. Under Hanussen, Breitbart becomes an overnight sensation. But he also witnesses the Nazi threat firsthand, and, by exposing Hanussen as a Jew, unwittingly contributes to the clairvoyant's murder by the SA. [22] Zishe soon realizes there is no place for him in Berlin and that he must return home to Poland. But before he leaves, he contacts the rabbi whom he had met when he first came to Berlin and who had warned him never to forget who he was. Having now become the true seer in the film, Zishe foreshadows the Holocaust, telling the rabbi that he foresees something terrible happening to the Jewish people. Zishe comes to understand that his strength, like Samson's before him, has been given to him by God for the purpose of saving his people. The rabbi is pleased that Zishe has found his way back to God and his roots, and cites a well-known Jewish legend, albeit with a telling Christian twist. The original legend has it that in every generation there are thirty-six righteous individuals whose merit sustains the world. In suggesting that Zishe may be one of the thirty-six, the rabbi turns a traditional teaching about the redemptive power of individual acts of righteousness into a tale of martyrdom and self-sacrifice, for Herzog's rabbi tells Zishe that he may be one of those thirty-six who will martyr themselves for the sake of the world. Upon Breitbart's return to Poland, he warns his brethren of impending disaster, attempting to rouse them to organize themselves and fight. But, blind to their danger, they spurn their prophet. Breitbart's vision remains unheeded, and he dies in Poland, two days before the Nazis assume power.

The turning point of the film is marked by Breitbart's public disclosure of his Jewishness. For unlike the historical Breitbart, Herzog's Zishe concealed his Jewish identity at the behest of Hanussen, as Hanussen believed "it wouldn't please the Nazis to see such a strong Jew." Passively assenting to his Aryanization, Breitbart dons a blond wig while performing his feats of strength alternately in the costume of the Roman centurion and the glorious Teuton. This masquerade finally comes to an end when, facing a hall full of drunken Nazis, Zishe unmasks the reality behind the image, casts off the blonde wig, and reveals his true self. It is this moment of self-disclosure that leads Zishe back to his people and readies him to heed the divine call. Breitbart had tried to conceal himself for a time, albeit unwillingly, but he is ultimately integrated back with his kinfolk in the shtetl—and in death.

Seen through Herzog's eyes, Breitbart has become yet another quixotic figure, a Jewish Kaspar Hauser, perhaps, one in Herzog's growing inventory of "holy innocents and prophets doomed to heroic failure," as one film critic put it. [23] But for Breitbart to retain this original, precivilized purity, Herzog found it necessary to alter one more highly relevant historical fact: that of the historical Breitbart's Zionism. Given the sometimes negative attitudes in Germany toward Israel during the second intifada, it may have been

Breitbart's fisticuff (Faustschlag). Courtesy of Pastor Martin Schaaff.
(Editors' efforts to track other rightsholders were unsuccessful.)

a good deal tidier for Herzog to keep Zionism out of the story altogether. Yet so long as purity and victimization remain bound together, there would also appear to be little room for Jewish agency in Herzog's vision. In a final twist of irony, Herzog transforms the very figure that had once been a symbol of Jewish power in the eyes of many east European Jews into the embodiment of Jewish powerlessness. This retroactive victimization of Zishe Breitbart certainly reflects a common trope in the representation of Jews in contemporary Germany. Indeed, already before 1933, the Jews in *Invincible* have become almost passive martyrs, while the mass death that awaits them at the end of the film still celebrates their fundamental purity in the face of unspeakable evil. Reading Breitbart through the lens of the Holocaust leads Herzog to reimagine the Jewish past as a history that is characterized primarily by Jewish victimhood, but that is simultaneously accompanied by idealizations of that pre-Nazi past. Whereas Busch sought to reaffirm the universalist legacy of the new Samson, and Neumann the national/political and God-given one, Werner Herzog's Siegmund/Zishe mocks any notion of either God or legacy in the face of the evil to come. In Herzog's *Invincible*, Breitbart thus becomes a Jewish prophet who martyrs himself to redeem an irredeemable world, the victim of a fate he could foresee but could not change.

As a site for the continuous production of conflicting meanings, Breitbart's body was viewed and ultimately "rewritten" by the audiences that watched him perform. In place of the familiar dichotomous racial representations of German and Jew, Breitbart's performances and reception appear to have undercut the potency of such images. Adopting the ideals of German masculinity while rejecting the notion of the Jew as emasculated other, the historical Breitbart produced a wide variety of images on stage that his audiences assembled and reassembled at will. Representing both universal man and Jewish national hero, Breitbart's body provided a model for Germans to reshape their own physicality and for Jews to become, as he told a journalist for *Haynt* in a 1925 interview, *kampffähig*—"battle-ready." Indeed, the legacy of Siegmund Breitbart compels us to consider how divergent narratives of nation and ethnicity, founded as they were in contemporary ideals of manliness, were able to coexist, uneasily perhaps—at least for a time.

Notes

1. Rumpelstilzchen (Adolf Stein,) *Tägliche Rundschau*, July 12, 1923.
2. *Haynt*, (Warsaw) April 1, 1925, p. 10; *Haynt*, October 21, 1925, p. 5.
3. *Haynt*, October 21, 1925, p. 5.
4. John J. MacAloon as cited in Marvin Carlson, *Performance, a Critical Introduction* (London and New York, 1996), p. 24–25.
5. Michel de Certeau, "The Practice of Everyday Life," as reproduced in *Cultural Theory and Popular Culture*, John Storey, ed. (Athens GA, 1998), pp. 484–85.
6. "Breitbart—zerquetscht! Leben und Sterben eines modernen Herkules," *Kleine Volkszeitung*, February 11, 1923 , p. 7; *Przygody nadzwyczajne, (Ausserordentliche Abenteuer. Siegmund Breitbart. Athlet des 20. Jahrhunderts)* (Warsaw, 1925) (n.a.), p. 1. I am indebted to Dietmar Winkler for providing me with the Polish biography along with his unpublished German translation, pp. 11–13.
7. "Breitbart, Modern Samson: First American Appearance of Jewish Superman," *The American Hebrew*, September 28, 1923, p. 497.
8. *Das Programm. Artistisches Fachblatt* (Hamburg), February 3, 1925, n.p.
9. Don Gifford, *Ulysses Annotated: Notes for James Joyce's Ulysses* (Berkeley CA, 1988), p. 94.
10. Gisela Winkler, *Circus Busch: Geschichte einer Manege in Berlin* (Berlin, 1998), p. 41.
11. A close friend of the Busch family, Rev. Martin Schaaf, said that Paula Busch was particularly interested in Breitbart because he was a Jew, and she was the one who decided to promote him as a Jew. Interview with Rev. Martin Schaaf, July 23, 2001, Berlin.
12. Paula Busch, *Das Spiel Meines Lebens: Ein halbes Jahrhundert Zirkus* (Stuttgart, 1957), pp. 124–25.
13. Paula Busch, "Samson. Roman von Paula Busch." *Berliner Morgenpost*, July 24–September 2, 1923.
14. Busch, "Samson," *Berliner Morgenpost*, July 24, 1923.
15. Busch, "Samson," *Berliner Morgenpost*, July 28, 1923.

16. George L. Mosse, *The Image of Man: The Creation of Modern Masculinity* (New York, 1996), p. 6.

17. Busch, *Das Spiel meines Lebens*, p. 125.

18. Sabine Kienitz writes about the war-wounded in "Der Krieg der Invaliden: Helden-Bilder und Männlichkeitskonstruktionen nach dem Ersten Weltkrieg," *Militärgeschichtliche Zeitschrift* 60.2 (2001), pp. 367–402.

19. *Film Velt*, September 1928, pp. 9–12.

20. Yael Zerubavel, *Recovered Roots: Collective Memory and the Making of Israeli National Tradition* (Chicago, 1995), p. 52.

21. *Invincible*, Fine Line Features and New Line Productions, Inc., 2002. In the spirit of full disclosure, I worked briefly for Gary Bart, the producer of the film, helping him to think about the historical significance of the Breitbart phenomenon.

22. Hanussen was in fact murdered by the SA two days after the Reichstag fire, and Breitbart did compete with Hanussen, though he never worked directly under him. On Hanussen see Wilfried Kugel, *Hanussen: Die wahre Geschichte des Hermann Steinschneider* (Düsseldorf, 1998); and Mel Gordon, *Erik Jan Hanussen: Hitler's Jewish Clairvoyant* (Los Angeles, 2001).

23. Timothy Corrigan as cited in Richard Falcon, "I Am What I Yam," *Sight and Sound*, April 2002, p. 2. Kaspar Hauser, a figure in Herzog's well-known film *The Enigma of Caspar Hauser*, was a boy found in the streets of Nuremberg in 1828. There exist many legends and literary accounts about his origins.

The Making of
Jewish Sports
in Interwar Europe

5. Jews in German Sports during the Weimar Republic

Jacob Borut

I N HIS ACCOUNT of Jewish youth in Germany, the historian Walter Laqueur made a clear distinction between the different generations during the Weimar years regarding their fields of interest. Whereas the older
generation was greatly involved in the rich cultural life of the day, in theater, music, and the arts, at a time when Germany was, in his words, the
"cultural center of the world," the younger generation had a different field
of interest: "For them the magic names were not Max Reinhardt, Piscator
and Furtwaengler; they followed with bated breath the results of the soccer
games each Sunday between Hertha BSC [of Berlin] and Schalke 04, the
leading club in the Ruhr. Their heroes were not Elisabeth Bergner or Emil
Jannings or Albert Bassermann, but Hanne Sobeck and Richard Hofmann,
the leading goal scorer of the day."[1]

Indeed, the younger Jewish generation of the Weimar Republic had a
great interest in sports, and many of its members participated in the sporting activities of their day. Sports were an important means of integrating
into society.[2] An outstanding example of successful integration through
sports was Daniel Prenn, the German tennis champion who in 1929, as a
member of the German Davis Cup team won his games against two members of the English team, thus leading Germany to their much acclaimed
victory over England. At that time, Russian-born Prenn was still a Russian
citizen,[3] but his sporting achievements brought him the kind of respect
rarely accorded to Russian Jews in Germany at the time. Such stories repeated themselves—on a much smaller scale—throughout Germany. Thus,
Abraham Dumb (Dotan) of Lübeck attested that he suffered from his antisemitic classmates in his *Mittelschule*, but the fact that he was an excellent
sportsman and won prizes for his class (especially in swimming) greatly
helped his social position.[4]

These examples indicate that success in sports was a powerful tool for
Jews to achieve integration into German society. As that integration came
under a growing threat, such successes became more and more important for the Jews. One sign of this rising importance might be seen in the
pages of the Jewish press. The most popular Jewish newspaper, the *Israelitisches Familienblatt* (henceforth IF), reported on sporting events in a section entitled—appropriately—"Sportecke" (sports corner), which appeared

on the last page of the second section of the paper (occasionally it was placed at the end of the first section). But in mid-1932, when the social and political position of German Jews was clearly deteriorating, athletic achievements received a prominent place in the news section, under large headlines. One such achievement was Daniel Prenn's within the German tennis team against Ireland in the Davis Cup, as were the two German jujitsu championships won by two members of the Berlin Schild jujitsu group.[5] The photographs of the athletes appeared next to the report about their achievements—an unprecedented honor in the pages of the IF.[6] Sports, then, gained among Jews an increasing importance as an avenue for achieving recognition by the surrounding society as equal and contributing members of that society.

An example for the potential acceptance of Jews was reported by the *Vossische Zeitung* during another Davis Cup tennis match in which Daniel Prenn excelled—this time against England. The reporter witnessed a change of attitude among some radical right-wing spectators, who referred to Prenn at the beginning as "Danny," but later as "Prenn," and finally "*Unser* [our] Prenn.*" The reporter concluded: "Can this people be united only in games?"[7] This was precisely the hope of German Jews, namely, that they would be considered members of a united German nation, first in the world of sports, and eventually in society as a whole.

Jewish achievements in sports also served to undermine existing antisemitic stereotypes about the social inferiority of Jews. This need also became more important in the last years of the republic. Thus, the *Gemeindezeitung für die israelitischen Gemeinden Württembergs*, a paper that hardly mentioned sports, chose in 1931 to publish in a leading place an article (taken from a Viennese journal) about Jewish achievements in the sport of boxing. It was followed by a report of Jewish sporting achievements in Ulm, which began as follows: "The old prejudice that we Jews achieve less in the realm of sports than our non-Jewish compatriots is again contradicted by the athletic achievements in Ulm."[8]

Jews could participate in sports either on an individual basis or as members of sports teams, where they were free to participate in Jewish or non-Jewish general sports clubs. This latter option was the one chosen by the majority of Jewish sportsmen and sportswomen during the Weimar Republic. Until the last years of the republic, Jews participating in German sports clubs did not encounter many obstacles; openly antisemitic clubs were the exception, not the rule.[9] Such obstacles did exist, however, and personal testimonies give reason to believe that antisemitism was more widespread than written sources reveal. For example, a Jew who grew up in the small town of Bensheim, in Hessen, told me that local Jews formed their own unofficial tennis club because Jews were not accepted as members of the Casino Verein, which was the local place for playing tennis.[10] That fact is not mentioned in a recently published study of the Jews of Bensheim.[11]

There were, however, two sports in which Jewish integration was noticeably hampered. The more famous case is that of the alpine clubs (*Alpenvereine*). The German *Alpenvereine* were part of a federation, the Deutsch-Österreichischer Alpenverein, which included the alpine clubs of Austria, the Sudetenland, and other German diaspora areas. At the initiative of the Austrians, the federation adopted an "Aryan clause" (*Arierparagraph*). The larger German local clubs, including those in Berlin and Munich, followed suit, adopting similar resolutions. In Vienna and Berlin the decisions led to the foundation in 1924 and 1925 of rival associations, called respectively Donauland and Deutscher Alpenverein Berlin, which were open to everyone.[12] The hopes of the founders to attract a large non-Jewish membership failed. Jews clearly constituted the majority in the dissident clubs, while most members of the now racially pure clubs remained where they were. German Jews did not, however, give up their open hostility toward the antisemitic clubs. For example, Jewish members of town councils opposed proposals for providing these clubs with financial support.[13]

Another type of a sports club with very little evidence of Jewish participation was the riding club (*Reitverein*) or the horse-breeding club (*Pferdezuchtverein*). In the places I have examined, these were elitist societies that developed in the small towns during the second half of the Weimar period, when motorization reduced the use of horses for agriculture and transport, and riding took on the character of a leisure activity. Horse-breeding in particular gradually became the domain of a wealthy elite to which Jews had very limited access. Some affluent Jews could have entered such *Vereine* had these societies developed earlier, at the beginning of the twentieth century. An example of such an individual is Hermann Gundelfinger in Württemberg, who cofounded such a club in Michelbach a. d. Lücke.[14] In the late Weimar years, however, Jews' social possibilities were no longer the same.

Antisemitism also existed in the field of gymnastics (*Turnen*)—a traditional haven for German nationalists since the days of Turnvater Jahn—and especially among the Deutsche Turnerschaft.[15] But despite its existence many Jews did participate in *Turnvereine* and reached high positions. In the villages and small towns, there was hardly any hint of opposition toward their participation. [16]

Apart from these fields, Jews participated widely in German sports life, won many awards, and—as the sources testify—truly enjoyed themselves and the companionship of other sportsmen and women, be they Jewish or not. Apart from active membership, they filled other important roles as officials, referees, and coaches. According to Paul Yogi Mayer, it was especially in soccer societies where Jews played such significant official roles. [17]

In fact, in some of the more remote rural areas, Jews—who had better contacts with the cities and the modern trends in urban life—played a major role in introducing soccer and other sports into the area, just as they played major roles in introducing other forms of culture and fashion. For example, Alfred Silberberg from Springe was a central figure in soccer in the Deister area of the province of Hannover. "He was not only a founding member and mentor of the Springer Fußball-Clubs von 1911, but was also one of the founders of the soccer clubs in the surrounding villages." [18] He was helped in those activities by his business contacts in the village. In 1927 he was elected as honorary chairman (Ehrenvorsitzende) of the soccer Kreisverband of Gau Deister, of which he was one of the founders.

Jews were members and officials in non-Jewish sports clubs. They felt integrated, but could Jews really reach the highest positions? Elsewhere I have examined the positions Jews could reach within local associations, [19] and I noted that Jews played a prominent role in founding and organizing them, as well as providing vital financial support. [20] Jews did, indeed, reach some high positions in local clubs—as treasurers, secretaries, and board members. They were especially prominent in merchant and trade societies. But there existed an invisible barrier limiting the access and the standing of Jews in German Vereine, and one of this barrier's manifestations appears when we look for Jews as chairpersons of local clubs—we hardly find any Jews that occupied such positions, even in clubs they had helped to found. Siegfried Hony, for example, an industrialist in Wissen near Betzdorf in the Rhineland, established a sports club in 1925 called Siegfried (his own name). This club was considered Jewish by the Nazis, who disbanded it when they came to power. But Hony himself held only the role of sports chairman (Sportobmann) in it and not of general chairman. [21] We find similar cases in other places. For a Jew to become chairman, such as Julius Zion in the Bonfeld Turnverein in Baden, or Hans Blum in the FC Eldagsen in the province of Hannover, was rare indeed. [22]

It should be emphasized that village Jews accepted these barriers and nurtured no resentment against them. They felt themselves "at home"—"zu Hause"—in their communities, wanted to belong to the local social system, and bore no grudge against it, even when its codes discriminated against them.

Jewish Sports Clubs

We now turn to those Jews whose sports involvement was limited to Jewish sports clubs. George Eisen, in his important study of Jewish gymnastics associations before World War I, noted that the "necessity for separate gymnastic societies" that "arose in the latter years of the nineteenth century" had two major causes: "outbreaks of antisemitic sentiments and the emergence of Jewish nationalism."[23] He noted that the majority of the groups in the early stages were Jewish nationalist, but they did not declare their ideology openly, and indeed did not engage heavily in ideology, in order to draw members who did not believe in the Zionist idea.[24]

When examining the Weimar period, we can observe a dramatic rise in the number and activity of societies that were not part of the Jewish nationalist movement. These were societies whose cohesive factor was—using Eisen's terminology—"the reaction to ostracism produced by a hostile environment."[25]

It is important to realize that during the Weimar period, the German-Jewish organizational system had attained its largest size and range since the decline of the traditional Jewish subculture in premodern times. The Zionists openly advocated the creation of a separate Jewish sphere, whereas the organizations of the majority of German Jews, such as the Central Verein deutscher Staatsbürger jüdischen Glaubens (CV) or the Reichsbund jüdischer Frontsoldaten (RjF), were opposed to the creation of what they saw as a "spiritual ghetto." These profound differences in aims and targets were expressed by the leaders of the various organizations and are accepted as the conventional historiographical wisdom.[26] In reality, however, the CV and the RjF did take an active part in the formation and expansion of the Jewish organizational system, as did the Liberal leadership of the larger Jewish communities, in contradiction to their written and spoken ideological premises.[27]

One realm that was especially developed by the Zionists at the local level was sports. In every community with a considerable Zionist group, a sporting society named Bar Kochba or Maccabi was formed.[28] The most popular branches were gymnastics—which had a long German tradition—soccer,

81

track and field, and in some places also boxing. The local Zionist societies competed against German sports associations in their locality or region. By the late 1920s, the number of Zionist organizations had grown sufficiently that they could also compete against one another without traveling too far. In western Germany, a *Westdeutscher Bezirk* was formed, and from 1930 onward it had its own soccer mini league.

In that regard, the Zionists were an exception among the ideological currents within German Jewry. For them, sporting activities had a significance beyond recreation or physical fitness. They served as a vehicle for creating a new youth, far different from the traditional diaspora Jew. Zionist sporting societies had an educational and ideological mission, and a large share of their activity was pedagogical in nature. In those activities lay, for the Zionist movement, the importance of the sports movement. Besides, in the late 1920s those societies proved to be an excellent means of drawing young members to the Zionist movement. Indeed, the 1929 convention of German Zionists in Jena accepted a resolution calling on local groups to give "powerful support" to sports societies, and for their representatives in community leadership organs to ensure financial assistance for such societies, stating explicitly that this was due to their "pedagogical and propagandistic significance."[29]

But the Zionists were not alone in the field of Jewish sports; in large Jewish communities and many of the medium-sized ones there were many other Jewish sports societies. Most of these considered themselves neutral, or not connected with any ideological current, while others were affiliated with the Liberals. In several places such as Frankfurt, Leipzig, Kassel, and the Rhine/Ruhr area there were Jewish workers' sports clubs, who competed with other societies associated with the workers' movement. The Liberals, unlike the Zionists, did not support sporting activities in uniquely Jewish sports organizations. Der Schild, the great sports organizational network of the RjF, was largely created during the Nazi period.[30] In the Weimar Republic there was no organized network, although some local sports societies of the RjF did exist, the most famous of which was the Berlin jujitsu group that—as mentioned earlier—held the German national championship for several years and was a source of great pride to all Jewish athletes (including the Zionists). But in principle, during the Weimar period the RjF did not support the activities of Jewish sports groups, and there were several cases in which activists who tried to form sports societies under its auspices had to turn them into neutral societies. Only in the early 1930s were some beginnings made for the creation of Der Schild as a national network, as many Jewish sportsmen were driven out of German associations due to the growth of antisemitism, and the leaders of the Reichsbund came to realize the value of training Jewish youths in defensive sports such as boxing and jujitsu.[31]

In fact, the indifference, or uncertainty, displayed by the leadership of Liberal organizations toward Jewish sports left the field open to local initiatives that made possible a rare cooperation between Jewish sportsmen of different ideological currents. On April 26, 1925, representatives of eleven Jewish sports associations in western Germany gathered in Essen and agreed to create a large regional organization called Vintus, which was declared neutral. The meeting was initiated by the local sports group Hakoach Essen, which was officially a neutral sports group, and among the eleven local associations three were Zionist while three were affiliated with the RjF.[32] Thus, we have a field in which Jews from various groups—Zionist, Liberal, and neutral—cooperated under one umbrella organization.

But there was even more cooperation. In Dortmund, the founder of the local Zionist boxing club was the teacher Siegmund Nussbaum, a very active Liberal leader, cofounder and vice-chairman of the local group of the Association for Liberal Judaism (Vereinigung für das liberale Judentum). He founded the Zionist club in his function as "chairman for gymnastics and sports of the RjF" (Obmann für Turnen und Sport des RjF). According to a report in the Jüdisch-Liberale Zeitung (JLZ), Nussbaum founded the boxing club "within the sporting movement of our community."[33] It is also noteworthy that the JLZ published the reports about cooperation with the Zionists without any comment, even though such cooperation clearly contradicted its standpoint, and in spite of the warning, it published otherwise about Zionist attempts to draw the support of Jewish youth through sporting activities.[34] There are other examples of Liberals and assimilationist Jews who played important roles in Zionist sports clubs.

To understand the circumstances that made possible such cooperation, we should try to understand the ambivalent relations of the Liberal leadership with such sports groups. The Liberals found it hard to encourage them, because it was the field of sports that had led to controversy between Zionists and Liberals when the first Jewish sports clubs were founded in the early twentieth century. On the other hand, it was not easy to discourage them, because the leadership could not ignore the need of the youth for sporting activities in an increasingly antisemitic society. Thus, it is in this field in which we can see a cooperation between local activists of various ideological shades, without outside hostile interference or even criticism, leading to the creation in western Germany of a neutral umbrella organization encompassing Zionists and Liberals alike. I believe that the existence of non-Zionist frameworks such as the Vintus and the many neutral sports societies all over Germany had enabled the Liberals to remain—in the realm of sports—loyal to their philosophy, which opposed the creation of specific Jewish organizations, without having to create an organizational system of their own. Otherwise, they might well have chosen to enter that field so that the Zionist challenge would not go unheeded.

Why was it the field of sports in which such cooperation could be achieved? Because sports is one area in which the activities are strictly neutral. In youth movements, talks and discussions were part of the routine. In cultural societies, such as Musikvereine, Sängervereine (singing societies), or Theatervereine, the content is open for debate—what songs should be sung? What play should be staged? The world view of the participants naturally played a role in such decisions. But world view hardly plays any role in the conduct of sports—there is no such thing as Zionist soccer tactics or a Liberal high-jump technique. Therefore Liberals, Zionists, and neutrals could compete without any fear of an ideological crisis, as long as they engaged only in sports.

During the second half of the 1920s in Germany one can observe a growing social exclusion of Jews. One manifestation of that tendency was a continuing decrease in the number of press reports about various public honors accorded to Jews by Vereine or by the Christian public. It was common, especially in villages and small towns, that at celebrations of important birthdays, golden anniversaries, or funerals of Jewish notables, the Vereine in which they were members would send a delegation, sometimes a small music band, or even hold a Fackelzug (torch procession). But as the decade was drawing to its close, such occasions, which had formerly evoked some form of public recognition, were now increasingly confined to Jewish circles. Reports with notes such as "the great popularity of the deceased was demonstrated by the large attendance of local inhabitants from all classes and religions" became far less common in the Jewish press, and reports about the presence of Vereine on Jewish social occasions were even more rare. [35] The percentage of reports in the IF indicating participation by non-Jews in Jewish personal social events in small towns dropped from 32 percent in 1926 to 22 percent in 1931, whereas the percentage of reports in which non-Jews did not participate rose dramatically from 2 percent in 1926 to 20 percent in 1931.

This could partly be attributed to the economic crisis and its severe effects on the Vereine, many of which were partly or completely paralyzed.[36] But the main reason is to be sought elsewhere, as is demonstrated by the reports themselves, including the few that did mention Christian participation in Jewish events. Some explicitly mentioned that this was in spite of the local public mood. A report about a torch procession held in Moers, for example, on the eighty-fifth birthday of a local Jew, noted that this happened "in spite of the anti-Jewish current, which unfortunately is strong also here."[37]

As this trend was getting clearer, local reporters and the editors of the IF were making efforts to blur the impressions that such reports could make. For example, more and more reports were formulated in a way that gave no indication whether non-Jews had participated or not. Birthdays were celebrated with the "many friends" of the guest of honor. At funerals, there was "great participation." The percentage of such vagaries in all reports of personal social events in small towns in the IF rose from 1 percent in 1928 to 11 percent in 1931. This change appears to have been editorial policy, as it became manifest in reports from all over Germany. What such a policy reveals about the social position, even of prominent Jews (only prominent Jews would be covered in a nationwide paper like the IF), hardly needs elaboration.

An indication of the dwindling social position of Jews is the sudden flourishing of Jewish Vereine in the small towns, and especially the creation of many local youth groups (Jugendbünde). Jewish youth, feeling rejected by the surrounding society, turned inwards. Jews who were already members of existing Vereine, however, stayed there until they were thrown out by the Nazis.

Following this, one might have expected a big growth in Jewish sports activities in those years. Indeed, the reports about such activities do show a clear trend of growth and development, but not a dramatic rise. In November 1931, a Jewish sports club was founded in Mainz—one of the more assimilated Jewish communities. In his opening speech, the chairman of the new group, named Tobias, stated that the club was established due to the great interest of Jewish youth. The new club, he told his audience, wanted to affiliate with an existing sports club—non-Jewish, of course— but no club would cooperate, claiming that their supporters and members came mainly from radical right-wing circles.[38] One would have expected more news pieces of this kind during those years, but the information from Mainz remains unique.

One major reason for that is the great hardship caused by the economic crisis of the time. In his Mainz speech, Tobias noted that the new club was opened despite the economic crisis. Other clubs suffered badly. In the annual meeting of Bar Kochba Breslau, for example, it was announced that the group was in deep financial trouble, as the local community drastically decreased its support for the club, while a part of the membership failed to pay its taxes. [39] It was hard to form new clubs, and existing clubs had to reduce their activities.

Another reason was, as mentioned earlier, that Jewish members of sports societies were not expelled from their clubs (except for the Jewish members of the *Alpenvereine*). They would have preferred to stay with their old clubs, train in the facilities that were well known to them, and work with coaches who knew them.

Despite these circumstances, the field of Jewish sports continued to grow. Two fields display a marked growth trend. One was swimming, and water sports in general. The membership of the swim club in Breslau jumped from two hundred to three hundred between 1930 and 1931—a gain of 50 percent. This is not hard to explain: as more and more athletes in Germany became Nazis, the sight of a Jew in a swimming pool was certainly not to their liking. We know of many cases in the Nazi period in which local Nazis tried to drive the Jews out of swimming pools and public bath institutions, even when there were no official instructions to do so. One can imagine that already before the Nazi rise to power Jews felt increasingly unwelcome in public swimming institutions, so they turned to Jewish societies.

The other field that enjoyed a steady growth was table tennis. The reports on the growth in this field come from central and southwestern Germany, a geographical area whose northern tip was Wiesbaden, and southern tip was Saarlouis in the Saar region. Only toward the end of 1932 do there appear reports of growing Jewish participation in table tennis in Leipzig, and then in Liegnitz in the northeast. [40] I have no definitive explanation for the growing popularity of this particular sport, but the Jewish trend may have reflected a general trend in the wider German society, perhaps because table tennis, which requires neither field nor stadium nor complicated equipment, suited the circumstances of the economic crisis. Jews entering this new sport in the social atmosphere of the early 1930s chose to do so in a Jewish framework; they felt unwelcome in German sports.

As mentioned at the beginning, success in sports was initially an effective means for Jews to integrate into German society. But as the Weimar Republic was nearing its end, even this avenue was gradually closed. *Sportvereine* in increasing numbers adopted the *Arierparagraph*—including groups connected with the universities, who were influenced by the right-wing radicalism prevalent among the students. In Hamburg, for example, the Institut für Leibesübungen at the local university conducted its practical work through such racist *Sportvereine*, which meant in practice that Jewish students were barred from using the university's sports facilities (some of which had been built with the help of Jewish contributions). [41]

Conclusion

In 1932 reports of discrimination against Jewish sports personalities made their way into the columns of the Jewish press. The Jewish coach of the soccer club 1. FC Nürnberg was fired, it was reported, after a local Nazi paper attacked him. [42] The Verein für Bewegungsfreiheit in Leipzig, upon looking for a new coach, sent a letter to the birthplace of a leading candidate to inquire about his origins. [43] Sports was no longer neutral; results alone were no longer the only decisive factor.

At least in one case the success of a Jew in reaching a leading position in a sporting club led, in fact, to his family being driven out of town. In Dolgesheim in Rheinhessen the local Nazis especially hated the Jew Nathan Frank, because he was the vice-president of the local gymnastics association. They claimed: "We National-Socialists hold the view that members of the Jewish people (*Volk*) are not allowed to act as referees for Germans, and, as strangers in Germany, should not exert any influence." [44] The local Nazi leader, Seemann, wanted to play a more important role in the association. The local chapter decided in a meeting in 1930 to drive Frank out of town by harassing his family members. From a nearby Nazi home they threw stones and lumps of coal onto his property, sang antisemitic songs in front of his home, and shouted slogans at him in the street. The flower boxes in front of his home were broken or stolen. A brick was thrown through a window of his house. Wild rumors were spread about him and repeated in a Nazi paper. The Franks did not leave their house when there were Nazis in the street, and their daughter only went out in the company of older people.

Finally, Frank decided to move elsewhere. During his last days in Dolgesheim a group of friends came to his house so as not to leave him alone. One night, a group of his friends leaving his home met a group of Nazis, and a brawl ensued in which two Nazis were wounded. The Nazis reacted immediately. Von Seggern, the local SA leader, and Seemann led a group of their followers to Frank's house, where the family had already gone to sleep. Someone from the mob broke a window, and the Nazis surrounded the house and shouted threats and abuse all night. The police were called and protected the house while the family spent the remainder of the night hidden in the attic. In the morning, they took their furniture and belongings and escaped to Worms.[45]

Even the most renowned Jewish sports hero, the tennis player Daniel Prenn, came under a dark cloud. In 1931 Prenn negotiated with the Hammer tennis racquet factory, hoping to become a representative for the company after the end of his tennis career. When the negotiations failed, the factory filed a complaint against Prenn with the German Tennis Association, accusing him of having violated the principle of amateurism. After the association dismissed the complaint, the company took Prenn to court, accusing him of libel. Prenn won the case, but the tennis association nevertheless decided to suspend his career for six months, until the matter could be clarified. This last step was a hard blow not only for Prenn but also for his many admirers. The IF openly accused the tennis association of maintaining a double standard, claiming that had Prenn not been a Jew and native of Russia he would have been treated much more fairly.[46] Prenn resumed his career after the suspension and was able to score some major tennis wins for Germany in the Davis Cup.[47] But the bitter experience of the disgrace inflicted upon a Jewish idol and symbol of integration must have remained with many Jewish athletes and sport enthusiasts. Prenn himself left the German sports association, becoming a member of the Berlin Bar Kochba, where apart from tennis, he also played on the handball team.[48] The following story is the best indication that Jewish success was a provocation to Nazis: In 1932 members of the Bar Kochba Berlin participated in a large athletics competition in Rostock. As Jews won several events, the crowd responded by whistles and shouts of "Hep Hep." This behavior dismayed the leaders of the German clubs, who threatened to pack up and go home.[49]

All these stories show that already before 1933 Jewish success in sports represented a provocation to large parts of the German public, and, accordingly Jews were blocked even from this road to acceptance within German society. It was only a matter of time—and a short time—until this exclusion became official policy.

Athletes at the anniversary sport festival of the VBAV (Verband Berliner Athletik-Vereine) at the German stadium. Berlin, June 1924. Courtesy of the Felix Simmenauer Collection of the Jewish Museum of Berlin.

Notes

The research on which this article is based was partly funded by the Vidal Sassoon International Center for the Study of Antisemitism at the Hebrew University of Jerusalem and by the Leo Baeck Institute Jerusalem.

1. Walter Laqueur, *Generation Exodus: The Fate of Young Jewish Refugees from Nazi Germany* (Hanover NH, 2001), p. 8.
2. Hajo Bernett, *Der jüdische Sport im nationalsozialistischen Deutschland 1933–1938* (Schondorf, 1978), p. 17; Paul Yogi Mayer, "Equality—Egality: Jews and Sport in Germany," *Leo Baeck Institute Year Book* (henceforth LBIYB) 25 (1980), pp. 221–41, here p. 227.
3. *Central-Verein Zeitung* (henceforth CVZ) 8, no. 30 (July 26, 1929), p. 391. On Prenn see also Mayer, "Equality—Egality," p. 225.
4. *Yad Vashem Archive*, 03/10887, p. 3.
5. Israelitisches Familien blatt, IF, 34, no. 24 (June 16, 1932), p. 3, on Prenn, who won his two singles games against Irish rivals and played a major part in the German win at the doubles match; IF 34, no. 27 (July 7, 1932), p. 3 (jujitsu).
6. The IF did print photographs of prominent Jewish personalities mentioned in its news section, but those were printed together at the bottom of the page. Photographs printed next to the news article were extremely rare.
7. *Vossische Zeitung*, November 7, 1932, quoted in IF 34, no. 29 (July 21, 1932), p. 10.
8. *Gemeindezeitung für die israelitischen Gemeinden Württembergs* 8, no. 6 (16 June, 1931), p. 62.
9. Bernett, *Der jüdische Sport*, p. 16.
10. Interview with Professor Eliyahu Lehmann, March 13, 2002.

11. Geschichtswerkstatt Geschwister Scholl, *Geschichte der Bensheimer Juden im 20. Jahrhundert, mit Erinnerungen und Betrachtungen von Hans Sternheim* (Bensheim, n.d.).

12. On the reactions within the Jewish membership of the Alpenvereine to these developments, see the file in the archive of the Central Verein deutscher Staatsbürger jüdischen Glaubens (CV): Central Archives for the History of the Jewish People (CAHJP), Jerusalem, Fond 721, Delo 2256. On the relations between the CV and the Alpenverein, see CAHJP, Fond 721, Delo 3433. On antisemitism in the D. Ö. Alpenverein see Frank Bajohr, *"Unser Hotel ist Judenfrei": Bäder-Antisemitismus im 19. und 20. Jahrhundert* (Frankfurt am Main, 2003), pp. 68–69.

13. For example, see the effort of Mr. Laaser, a member of the *Stadtparlament* of Tilsit and a member of the CV, to block a request by the *Verein* for a 500 RM donation toward the funding an *"Ostpreußenhütte"* it wanted to build near Salzburg: CV Archive, CAHJP, Film HM2/8828, file 3433, frames 48, 50.

14. Joseph Walk, ed., *Pinkas Hakehillot Württemberg-Hohenzollern-Baden* (Jerusalem, 1986), p. 113 [Hebrew]; Utz Jeggle, *Judendörfer in Württemberg* (Tübingen, 1969), p. 248 (the year of foundation was not given). Richard Strauss, a leading businessman in Ulm and later the founder of the Strauss dairy products company in Israel, was a member of the riding club in his town (Walter Strauss [ed.], *Signs of Life: Jews from Wuerttemberg* [New York, 1982], p. 326.) This club in Ulm was certainly a leisure club.

15. On antisemitism in the *Turnbewegung* before 1914, see Hartmut Becker, "Antisemitismus in der deutschen Turnbewegung vor dem ersten Weltkrieg," in Manfred Lämmer, ed., *Die jüdische Turn- und Sportsbewegung in Deutschland 1898–1938* (Sankt Augustin, 1989), pp. 1–8 (I would like to thank Professor Lämmer for providing me with a copy of this important book). On later cases of antisemitism, see Hans-Jürgen König, "Die Anfänge der jüdischen Turn- und Sportsbewegung," in *Die jüdische Turn- und Sportsbewegung*, pp. 9–28; Hajo Bernett, "Opfer des Arierparagraphen—Der Fall der Berliner Turnerschaft," in *Die jüdische Turn- und Sportsbewegung*, pp. 29–43.

16. See Jakob Borut, " 'Bin Ich doch ein Israelit, ehre Ich auch den Bischof mit': Village and Small Town Jews within the Social Spheres of Western German Communities during the Weimar Period," in Peter Pulzer, ed., *Jews in Weimar Germany* (Tübingen, 1998), pp. 120–21; Jakob Borut "Juden im gesellschaftlichen Leben süd- und westdeutscher Dörfer und Kleinstädte zur Zeit der Weimarer Republik," in *Nebeneinander—miteinander—gegeneinander? Zur Koexistenz von Juden und Katholiken in Süddeutschland im 19. und 20. Jahrhundert*, Haus der Geschichte Baden Württemberg, ed. (Gerlingen, 2002), p. 168.

17. Mayer, "Equality—Egality," p. 225.

18. Hans-Christian Rohde, *"Wir sind Deutsche mit jüdischer Religion." Geschichte der Juden in Eldagsen und Springe, Benningsen, Gestorf, Völksen* (Springe, 1999), p. 56.

19. Borut, "Bin Ich doch ein Israelit," pp. 124–25; Borut, "Juden im gesellschaftlichen Leben," p. 174.

20. See Bernhard Deneke, "Fragen zur Rezeption bürgerlicher Sachkultur bei der ländlichen Bevölkerung," in Günter Wiegelmann, ed., *Kultureller Wandel im 19. Jahrhundert* (Göttingen, 1973), pp. 50–71; Ernst M. Wallner, "Die Rezeption stadtbürgerlichen Vereinswesens durch die Bevölkerung auf dem Lande," in *Kultureller Wandel*, pp. 160–73; Jeggle, *Judendörfer in Württemberg*, p. 248.

21. Günter Heuzeroth, "Jüdisch-deutsche Bürger unserer Heimat," pt. 3, *Heimat-Jahrbuch des Kreises Altenkirchen* 19 (1977), p. 124. Of course, "Siegfried" is a very old German

name, but the fact is that the local inhabitants thought that Hony had named the society after himself, as shown in Jeggle, *Judendörfer*. Hony could not have been so secluded from local life as not to realize the implications of giving the society his own personal name, yet that is precisely what he did.

22. Jeggle, *Judendörfer*, p. 248; Rohde, *"Wir sind Deutsche mit jüdischer Religion,"* p. 57.
23. George Eisen, "Zionism, Nationalism and the Emergence of the Jüdische Turner-schaft," LBIYB 28 (1983), pp. 247–62, here p. 247. For a debate about the reasons for choosing a Jewish or a non-Jewish sports association see Frith Themal, "Wo sollen wir Juden Sport treiben?" *Gemeindezeitung für die israelitischen Gemeinden Württembergs* 5, no. 11 (18 September, 1928), p. 140, and the reply by Fritz Glück, Themal, "Wo sollen wir Juden Sport treiben," no. 14 (16 October, 1928), pp. 170–71.
24. On that subject see also König, "Die Anfänge." On Jewish women see Gertrud Pfister, "Die Rolle der jüdischen Frauen in der Turn- und Sportsbewegung (1900–1933)," in *Die jüdische Turn- und Sportsbewegung*, pp. 77–81.
25. Eisen, "Zionism," p. 253.
26. See, for example, Yehoyakim Cochavi, *Jewish Spiritual Survival in Nazi Germany* (Hebrew) (Tel Aviv, 1988), pp. 11–12.
27. For further details on this subject, see Jacob Borut, " 'Verjudung des Judentums': Was There a Zionist Subculture in Weimar Germany?" in *In Search of Jewish Community: Collective Jewish Identities in Germany and Austria 1918–1932*, Michael Brenner and Derek Penslar, eds. (Bloomington IN, 1998), pp. 92–114.
28. See Robert Atlasz, *Barkochba: Makkabi—Deutschland 1898–1938* (Tel Aviv, 1977), esp. pp. 86–109; on local groups in Germany, see Mayer, "Eqality—Egality," pp. 227–30.
29. *Jüdische Rundschau* 35, no. 3 (January 10, 1930), p. 21.
30. Ulrich Dunker, *Der Reichsbund jüdischer Frontsoldaten 1919–1938. Geschichte eines jüdischen Abwehrvereins* (Düsseldorf, 1977), pp. 96, 102–4, 164; Mayer, "Equality—Egality," pp. 230–31. For a local study proving this point, see the detailed description in Guenter Erckens, *Juden in Mönchengladbach* (Mönchengladbach, 1988), vol. 1, pp. 559–68. See also Pfister, "Die Rolle der jüdischen Frauen," p. 83.
31. On the new perception of Jewish defensive sports in view of rising antisemitism see "Von jüdischen Boxern," in the CVZ 7, no. 34 (August 24, 1928), p. 473.
32. JLZ 5, no. 20 (May 15, 1925), 1st Beilage, p. 3; JLZ 5, no. 34 (August 21, 1925), 1st Beilage, p. 3. On Hakoach Essen see Fritz Levison, "Turn- und Sport-Klub Hakoach Essen," *Münster am Hallweg* 32, Heft 1/4 (January 1979), pp. 42–48; "Hakoach—Die Kraft: Ein jüdischer Turn- und Sportverein in Essen," in *Zwischen Alternative und Protest: Zu Sport und Judenbewegungen in Essen 1900–1933* (Essen, 1983), pp. 8–25.
33. JLZ 6, no. 52 (December 24, 1926), Beilage, p. 1.
34. JLZ 6, no. 29 (July 16, 1926), p. 2.
35. I am currently engaged in a numerical analysis of such reports, which I hope to publish in a different framework.
36. Oded Heilbronner demonstrated this point about the *Vereine* in the Schwarzwald region. See Oded Heilbronner, "Der verlassene Stammtisch. Vom Verfall der bürgerlichen Infrastruktur und der Aufstieg der NSDAP am Beispiel der Region Schwarzwald," *Geschichte und Gesellschaft* 19 (1993), pp. 178–201.
37. IF 33, no. 6 (February 5, 1931), p. 5.
38. IF 33, no. 46 (November 17, 1931), p. 6.
39. IF 33, no. 44 (October 29, 1931), p. 6.

40. IF 34, no. 44 (November 1, 1932), p. 5 (Leipzig); IF 34, no. 50 (December 15, 1932), p. 6 (Liegnitz).

41. IF 33, no. 32 (August 6, 1931), p. 1.

42. IF 34, no. 34 (August 25, 1932), p. 4.

43. IF 34, no. 31 (August 4, 1932), p. 3.

44. CVZ 10, no. 13 (March 27, 1931), pp. 151–52 (the quotation was taken from a declaration by the Nazi lawyer, Jung, during the ensuing trial).

45. CVZ 10, no. 13 (March 27, 1931), pp. 151–52.

46. IF 33, no. 30, (July 23, 1931), p. 4, and no. 32 (August 6, 1931), p. 4; Pfister, "Die Rolle der jüdischen Frauen," p. 76.

47. See notes 5 and 7.

48. IF 34, no. 24 (June 16, 1932), p. 3.

49. Robert Atlasz, "Der jüdische Sport in Deutschland vor und nach dem Jahre 1933," Yad Vashem Archive O.1/233, pp. 5–6.

6. The Politics of Jewish Sports Movements in Interwar Poland

Jack Jacobs

I N OCTOBER 1998 Miryam Shomrat, an official of the Israeli government, gave an address at the opening of an exhibit on Jewish sports held in Berlin. She indicated that during the period before the Second World War, Jewish sports clubs had promoted the Zionist movement and the establishment of the State of Israel. [1] This claim is far too broadly stated, at least as applied to interwar Poland. Like Polish Jewry itself, the Jewish sports movements of interwar Poland were by no means united either in their approach to Zionism or on other issues of interest to Polish Jewry. Moreover, an analysis of membership trends suggests that the Jewish sports movement affiliated with the anti-Zionist Bund was ascending in the period immediately preceding the Second World War. It simply is not true that Jewish sports clubs of interwar Poland in general promoted the establishment of the Jewish state.

Large-scale Jewish sports movements tended to emerge marginally later in Congress Poland than in Jewish communities in German-speaking Europe. The propensity of orthodox Jewish authorities to frown upon activities perceived as distracting from the study of religious texts, and the restrictions on Jewish organizational life imposed by the Czarist regime, hindered the emergence of a large-scale Jewish sports movement in Congress Poland in the first years of the twentieth century. There may well have been local Jewish sports clubs in specific towns or cities. [2] There were not, however, unified Jewish sports movements per se.

The German occupation of Congress Poland during the course of the First World War, however, created a dramatically freer atmosphere for the Jewish population and allowed Jewish communal and cultural groups far greater leeway than they had previously experienced. One result was the emergence of Maccabi groups in Warsaw, Vilna, and Plock. The Jewish sports club Bar Kochba, which was based in Lodz and allegedly affiliated with the Maccabi world union at a later point in time, also dated from this period. In 1921, a network of Maccabi clubs in Poland was officially established.

Polish Jewry, however, was internally divided along any number of different—albeit somewhat overlapping—fault lines. There were strongly held differences of opinion not only between religiously observant and secularized Jews, but also between Yiddishists and Hebraists, Zionists and anti-Zionists, liberals, socialists, and communists. Maccabi was a sizeable and vibrant movement in Poland throughout the interwar period. By the 1920s if not earlier, however, it was widely thought of as particularly attractive to middle-class and wealthy elements of the Polish Jewish community, and to those sympathetic to the mainstream General Zionists. This perception helped to spark the creation of a number of new sports movements and clubs, each of which had ties with a specific, different, Jewish political party. The sports movement known as Gwiazda, for example, founded in 1923, was affiliated with the Poalei Zion-Left.[3] Morgnshtern, officially established at the end of 1926, was run by Bundists.[4] Hapoel, a sports movement linked to the Poalei Zion-Right, also operated in Poland in the years between the two world wars.[5] There were, moreover, individual sports clubs, though not full-fledged sports movements, sympathetic to the Revisionist-Zionists[6] and to the autonomist movement of the Folkistn.[7] At least one local sports club—Skała (Rock)—consisted primarily of members of the Jewish Section of the Communist Party.[8] To be sure, the range of opinion among the leaders of the Jewish sports movements was not quite as broad as was the range of perspectives within Polish Jewry as a whole. The orthodox political party Agudes Yisroel, for example, did not create sports organizations of its own. Nevertheless, there were significant differences among the Jewish sports movements of Poland rooted in the differing ideologies of their leaders or parent parties.

Dr. Pribulski, the long-term head of Bar Kochba, for example, insisted that Hebrew be the language of command of Jewish sports clubs. In an interview conducted in 1924, Pribulski explained that his club strove to help create a Jewish sports movement that would operate simultaneously in numerous countries, and suggested that only Hebrew was suitable to act as a lingua franca for such a movement.[9] He argued that Hebrew was the symbol of Jewish unity, and that, in any event, Yiddish was insufficiently standardized to serve as a command language. Though Pribulski also insisted that his club was apolitical and that it ought to be opposed on principle to affiliation with any political party, the stance taken by Pribulski on the language question as well as numerous other questions of the day was interpreted by others as indicating that Bar Kochba—and Maccabi—occupied a specific, reactionary niche in the political and social spectrum of Polish

Jewish life. Both Morgnshtern and Gwiazda were ideologically committed to the use of Yiddish, and critical of groups such as Bar Kochba or Maccabi in part because of the failure of these groups to commit themselves to the use of Yiddish. Moreover, both Morgnshtern and Gwiazda perceived Bar Kochba and Maccabi as bourgeois. A public statement issued by the Lodz branch of Morgnshtern in 1931, for example, condemned Bar Kochba and Maccabi in no uncertain terms. "Under the mask of physical education," the statement read, "there are produced in the Maccabis, Bar Kochbas . . . slaves for the . . . capitalist order; nationalists are raised there, supporters of militarism, of shiny epaulets and ringing little swords. The bourgeois sports clubs are the nest of hatred against the working class and its ideals of liberation."[10] Just as the working class had to create its own organizations in politics and in the economic arena, the Bundists reasoned, so too was it necessary to create separate socialist sports organizations to tear working-class youth away from the injurious influence of bourgeois sports.

The Left Labor Zionists' Gwiazda certainly would have agreed, for it insisted that "the worker-sportsman struggles for the liberation of the working class; sports is for him not a goal in itself, but a means by which to educate a physically developed and class-conscious member of the international family of workers. . . . [T]he chief goal of the worker-sportsman is socialism. An individual victory has value only if it brings something useful to humanity. Private interests must yield to second place; the collective is the essential thing."[11]

But, though members of the Bundist-oriented Morgnshtern and the Left Labor Zionist Gwiazda both thought of themselves as left-socialist in orientation, they differed significantly from one another—at least initially. To be sure, the spirit of Morgnshtern was closer to that of Gwiazda than to that of most other Jewish sports movements. Though the Bund was staunchly anti-Zionist, both the Bund and the Poalei Zion-Left were Marxist and secularist, as well as Yiddishist.[12] Bundists and Left Labor Zionists cooperated in the context of the TSYSHO (the Central Jewish School Organization), and at times even entered into electoral agreements.

The differences in emphasis between Morgnshtern and Gwiazda are quite revealing. Morgnshtern, for example, concentrated on activities in which large numbers of individuals could engage simultaneously (such as gymnastics, hiking, and cycling) and played down such widely popular sports as soccer and boxing.[13] Unlike the other Jewish sports movements,

Morgnshtern explicitly fought against the formation or promotion of individual stars at the expense of other members. [14]

Gwiazda, on the other hand, asserted that there was no such thing as a proletarian sport. "The bourgeois or proletarian character" of a sports movement, the *Arbeter-tsaytung*, a Left Labor Zionist organ, proclaimed in 1931, "depends only on who leads the sport organization and on its goals." Thus, though there were dissenting voices within the Poalei Zion-Left as to the appropriateness of this policy, Gwiazda promoted soccer from the time of its founding. [15] In 1928, when the Warsaw Gwiazda claimed to be the single strongest Jewish workers sports club in Poland, it proudly listed its soccer section first in a public description of its activities and accomplishments, emphasizing the fact that seventy of the three hundred members in the Warsaw Gwiazda were in its soccer section, and that its soccer team had played numerous matches outside of Warsaw. [16]

The leadership of Morgnshtern, on the other hand, feared that soccer (at least as played by Gwiazda and by bourgeois sports movements) placed too much emphasis on individual accomplishment and the glorification of "champions." "Sports-business, commerce in soccer and with . . . convictions," an organ of the Bundist youth movement sneered in 1929, "our sportsmen leave for the 'experts' in the field of political and societal commerce." [17] There were soccer teams affiliated with Morgnshtern even in the 1920s. Soccer, however, was not as important to Morgnshtern as it was to other sports associations.

The differences between Gwiazda's position on boxing and that of Morgnshtern were somewhat deeper and longer lasting. For a number of years, Bundists were among the sharpest opponents of boxing within the Socialist Workers' Sport International (SWSI). [18] The Warsaw local of the Left Labor Zionist sports movement, on the other hand, is known to have had twenty-five members in its boxing section in the late 1920s, and to have competed against Polish boxers from the Polish workers' clubs. [19] By 1933, Shepsl Rotholts, a member of the Warsaw Gwiazda, was the best boxer in his weight class in all of Poland. [20] The supporters of boxing within Gwiazda's ranks argued that it was not true that boxing per se fostered brutality, bloodthirstiness, chauvinism, and egoism (as their socialist opponents claimed). Labor Zionists who made such a claim, one supporter of the pugilists alleged, erred because of the way that bourgeois sports were conducted. Gwiazda, a part of the proletarian movement, had a Marxist perspective, this supporter insisted, and a "socialist proletarian ethic."

One simply did not find among Gwiazda's boxers, imbued with this ethic, he continued, the attitudes that boxing's opponents feared. Boxing made youths stronger, ready for struggle, and prepared them to undertake successfully the task they ought to perform, that of aiding in the victory of the international proletariat over the bourgeoisie. Thus, the misgivings of certain labor Zionists notwithstanding, if boxing could help to create healthy, conscious worker-fighters, it should be supported.[21]

Despite continuing objections to boxing within its own ranks, the Warsaw branch of Morgnshtern—by far the largest branch of Morgnshtern in all of Poland—created a boxing section in the second half of December, 1935.[22] In the late 1930s, this section was competing not only with Gwiazda and with Polish clubs, but even with Maccabi. The spokesmen for the boxers affiliated with Morgnshtern insisted that health concerns that had earlier been raised by opponents of boxing had proven to be unfounded. They also pointed out—in what may have been a political analogy—that boxing was first and foremost a defensive sport, but that it teaches an "important truth about life, that one can best defend oneself if one attacks."[23]

Did Morgnshtern cave in to bourgeois values in making a place for soccer and boxing within its organization? Possibly. One alternative explanation is that its leadership responded to the desires of its membership. Just as the national program of the Bund in Czarist Russia was allegedly influenced by pressure from below, so too, it would appear, was the program of Morgnshtern in interwar Poland. These changes, however, also made Morgnshtern far more similar to Gwiazda than had earlier been the case.

In certain respects, on the other hand, Morgnshtern continued to be notably different from its Left Labor Zionist equivalent. Unlike Gwiazda, which had a women's section (at least in its Warsaw local),[24] Morgnshtern deliberately chose not to create a special commission for women and stressed that such a commission was not necessary because women already played a prominent role in the organization. In Morgnshtern's Warsaw branch, approximately half of the members in the gymnastics, handball, and other sections were female. Moreover, according to a report on its activities in 1938 issued by the Warsaw branch, "women participate actively not only as 'sports consumers,' that is, as members, but also as 'producers,' or instructors . . . and activists of the society."[25]

Morgnshtern's choice of affiliations also deserves a closer examination, and hints at another continuing difference between it and Gwiazda. The Left Labor Zionist sports movement was instrumental in the formation of the

Polish Workers' Sport Federation (zrss), which was dominated by members of the Polish Socialist Party.[26] Though Gwiazda disapproved of the relatively positive relationships that the zrss maintained with bourgeois Polish sports movements and with the Polish governmental authorities concerned with physical education, and though it also disagreed with the decision of the zrss to expel certain left-oriented clubs from the federation, Gwiazda continued to be active within the zrss even after losing critical votes on these issues.[27] Gwiazda believed in principle in "unified class organizations," and thus believed that it ought to remain in the zrss so long as it continued to have the right to express its opinion within that organization, and the possibility existed that it could have an impact on that organization's policies.[28]

Unlike Gwiazda, Morgnstern was scarcely involved with the zrss.[29] The Bund had a complex and not altogether smooth relationship with the Polish Socialist Party—which was, from the Bundist perspective, too reformist in orientation, too nationalistic, and insufficiently decisive in combating antisemitism.[30] In the late 1920s, the possibility of Morgnshtern and certain other movements promoting physical education and athletics affiliated with the zrss were explored. In the course of these exploratory talks the zrss held discussions reminiscent of debates on the so-called "organization" and "national" questions that had rocked the Russian Social Democratic Workers' Party before the First World War, and agreed to reorganize itself as a federal organization that would presumably have contained Polish, Jewish, German, and Ukrainian sections.[31] Gwiazda, however, declared that it would only form a Jewish section with Morgnshtern within the zrss under certain very specific conditions (which it knew the Bund would not accept), and negotiations faltered.

But the differences between Morgnshtern and Gwiazda—and the extent to which these differences narrowed over time—only hint at the range of opinion and activities within the world of the Polish Jewish sports movements in Poland's largest cities. It is worth bearing in mind that sports clubs affiliated with a number of different movements often had a broad range of activities, including many activities that one would not automatically associate with movements created to foster sports and physical education. The Vilna branch of Morgnshtern, for example, had a mandolin orchestra operating under its auspices, as well as a dramatic group and a reading room.[32] Morgnshtern's Warsaw branch organized lectures, trips to the theater, and outings to movies.[33]

Sports movements affiliated with a variety of political parties also helped to provide physical defense for the Jewish population. Yekhiel Dobekirer, who was active in Hapoel in Vilna, described in an interview how, during a period in which antisemites would demonstrate in front of Jewish stores, breaking windows, and waving signs reading "Don't buy from Jews," Hapoel members in Vilna responded by attempting to force the antisemites to move on—and on one occasion even killed a demonstrator with a stone.[34]

It ought also to be borne in mind that the political distinctions I have described were easiest to maintain in Poland's largest cities, and that the situation in the smaller towns and cities of Poland could often be quite different than that in such places as Warsaw or Lodz. Borukh Yismakh, writing in the *Memorial Book Sefer Vishkov*, has described the formation of Maccabi, Gwiazda, and the Jewish Communist sports club Skała in his home town, and adds, "when one of the teams had a match in a different town, it borrowed players from the other teams. There were also instances of betrayal. When, for example, Gwiazda had a match against a bourgeois club from a different city and borrowed a player or two, the latter deliberately played poorly, in order that their political comrades might win. But things were different when a Polish club challenged one of ours to a match. Then Maccabi and Gwiazda were in complete solidarity, aiming to play their hearts out and win."[35]

It is, to be sure, difficult to document and to assess the relative strengths of the Jewish sports clubs of interwar Poland on a local level, though there was an ambitious attempt to do so in the years immediately preceding the Second World War. In 1935 the Yidisher visnshaftlekher institut (YIVO), a scholarly institution based in Vilna and dedicated to the study of the language, history, and culture of east European Jewry, created a branch specifically devoted to the Jewish sports movements. This branch publicly announced its intention to create a central archive of materials by Jewish sports movements both in Poland and elsewhere, to organize a sports library and reading room under YIVO auspices, to issue publications, to act as an advisor for athletes, and to aid Jewish sports organizations operating in outlying areas.[36] The YIVO group developed a questionnaire containing forty-three questions and distributed it to numerous Jewish sports clubs throughout Poland. The questionnaire asked for information on each club's affiliations, activities, and facilities, the date of its founding, the language in which work was conducted, the number of active and of passive members, the genders and professions of members, publications issued, and so forth.[37] A report

99

published early in 1936, however, indicates that no more than forty-eight clubs had submitted responses to the questionnaire.[38] Minutes of a meeting held in May of 1937 demonstrate that, though the YIVO had established contact with the central coordinating bodies of Maccabi, Morgnshtern, and Gwiazda, the total number of questionnaires that had been completed and returned to YIVO was still so small that academically valid conclusions could not be drawn on the basis of the data in hand. Only 13 of the 107 branches of Morgnshtern had submitted responses, for example, as had a mere 11 of the 44 branches of Gwiazda, and 31 of the 190 Maccabi clubs.[39] This disheartening result seems to have led the project to fizzle out. Moreover, most of the completed questionnaires received by the YIVO seem to have been lost; only five responses to the YIVO questionnaire have thus far come to light—all of which, it is worth noting, were among materials stored in Lithuania throughout the postwar years, and all of which are from clubs affiliated with Morgnshtern. Thus, conclusions as to the size, nature, and extent of the Jewish sports movement in interwar Poland can currently be made only on the basis of fragmentary documentation.

But there is at least one conclusion which can in fact be made: The Bundist movement Morgnshtern grew dramatically in the Polish capital city in the years immediately preceding the Second World War. In its formal report on activities for the year ending February 1, 1936, for example, the Warsaw branch of Morgnshtern indicated that it had 956 active members.[40] A year later this same branch had increased the number of its activists to 1,500 and claimed that it had thereby become the single largest local sports organization—Jewish or Polish, socialist or not—in all of Poland.[41] By February of 1938, the total membership of Morgnshtern's Warsaw branch had grown to 1,855.[42] It is almost certainly the case, moreover, that Morgnshtern increased its strength in Warsaw not only in absolute terms, but also relative to its Jewish rivals. The Warsaw branch of Gwiazda, for one, is known to have had 700 active members in February of 1937, but only 400 activists in January of 1939. The Bund itself, it is worth recalling, attained its most impressive electoral victories in the municipal elections of 1938 and 1939. The increasing membership of Morgnshtern in the period leading up to these elections—and the decline in the membership of Gwiazda—strongly suggest that the electoral successes of the Bund were indicators of more deeply rooted changes in political affiliation among Polish Jews.

Like Polish Jewry itself, I conclude, Polish-Jewish sports movements were sharply divided along ideological lines. Jewish sports movements were

"Into the ranks of the 'Shtern'!"
A poster produced in conjunction with a membership drive conducted by the movement
for sports and physical education affiliated with the Left Poalei Zion in Poland.
Courtesy of the archives of the YIVO Institute for Jewish Research.

by no means necessarily devoted to Zionism, nor, for that matter, to any other specific political program. The growth of Morgnshtern, led by explicitly anti-Zionist Jewish socialists, underscores the fact that any intimation that the Jewish sports movement as a whole advocated the creation of an independent Jewish state distorts the historical record.

Notes

1. Friedhard Teuffel, "Bar Kochba Berlin—Ursprung der internationalen Makkabi-Bewegung. Der erste jüdische Sportverein in Deutschland wurde 100 Jahre alt," *Frankfurter Allgemeine Zeitung*, October 29, 1998, p. 39. Cf. Diethelm Blecking, "Jüdischer Sport in Polen," *Sozial- und Zeitgeschichte des Sports* 13, no. 1 (March, 1999), p. 22.

2. Minutes of a meeting of the YIVO Branch for the Jewish Sports Movement suggest that the oldest Jewish sports club operating in Poland in the late 1930s had been founded in 1901. However, the minutes do not indicate the location in which this club had been created (and thus leave open the possibility that it had been in a location which was part of the Austro-Hungarian Empire rather than the Russian Empire at the time of the club's establishment); Minutes [of the YIVO Branch for the Jewish Sports Movement], May 5, 1937, YIVO Institute, New York (YIVO), RG 29, file 86.

3. Shtern (Giwiazda) traced its ancestry back to a group known as Spartakus, which was established in Warsaw by the Labor Zionist youth organization Yugnt in 1920; P. Frim, "Fun varshever arbeter sport-klub 'shtern,'" *Di fraye yugnt* 5, no. 2 (February 1928), p. 18. The name Spartakus was almost certainly meant to invoke the memory of the German Marxist group with which Rosa Luxemburg had been closely identified during the First World War, and which, in 1918, founded the Communist Party of Germany. In 1923 the Polish Jewish sports group Spartakus united with Gwiazda (the Polish word for star), a sports group made up of middle school students, and this union began to refer to itself as the Shtern (Star) Workers' Sport Club. The creation of the Shtern club in Warsaw gave an impetus to the establishment of similar groups in other areas of Poland. The Shtern group in Lodz—Poland's second largest city, with a particularly large number of Jewish workers—was organized around 1925, and began to operate around 1926. By 1928, it had a gymnastics section, a soccer section with fifty active members, and a ping-pong section. The bulk of the leadership of the Lodz group at that time was made up of members of either the Poalei Zion-Left or the youth movement of that party. On this, see B. R., "Fun lodzsher sport-klub 'shtern,'" *Di fraye yugnt* 5, no. 5 (May 1928), p. 17; cf. "Rirevdike tetikayt fun lodzsher sport-klub 'shtern,'" *Arbeter-tsaytung* 5, no. 8 (February 21, 1930), p. 10. In the mid-1930s, however, a political dispute within the ranks of the labor Zionist movement led to the dismantling of the Shtern branch in Lodz. A new sports club, Typhoon, acted as a de facto replacement for the earlier club. On this, see A. Lagerist, "Prekhtiker derfolg funm sport-lager funm lodzsher 'tyfun,'" *Arbeter-tsaytung* 10, no. 24 (June 14, 1935), p. 8; B. Sh. "Unzer sport-bavegung in lodzsher reyon," *Arbeter-tsaytung* 10, no. 35 (August 30, 1935), p. 6; M., "Opklangen fun der 'aktivistisher' provokatsie kegn lodzsher 'shtern,'" *Arbeter-tsaytung* 10, no. 40 (October 11, 1935) p. 7; and "Erev dem turn-yontef fun lodzsher 'tyfun,'" *Arbeter-tsaytung* 11, no. 6 (February 7, 1936), p. 6. Reports by local Shtern groups were regularly printed in the labor Zionist press.

4. I have adapted portions of an earlier essay I wrote about the history and ideology of Morgnshtern for use in this piece. See Jack Jacobs, "Creating a Bundist Counter-Culture: Morgnshtern and the Significance of Cultural Hegemony," in *Jewish Politics in Eastern Europe: The Bund at 100*, Jack Jacobs, ed. (New York, 2001), pp. 59–68.

5. N. Kantorowicz (Kantorovitsh), "Die tsienistishe arbeter-bavegung in poyln," in *Yorbukh "Alef*," (New York, 1964). The leaders of Hapoel were Meyer Peker, Dov and Mietek Zilberman, and Khayim Glavinski.

6. Dovid Rogoff, "Sport in vilne," *Forverts* (September 8, 2000), p. 20.

7. "An onfrage tsum varshever sport-klub 'samson,'" *Arbeter-sportler* 5 (November 1, 1929), p. 7.

8. Borukh Yismakh, "Sports Clubs and Self-Defense," in *From a Ruined Garden: The Memorial Books of Polish Jewry*, Jack Kugelmass and Jonathan Boyarin, eds. (New York, 1983), p. 61. Yismakh's piece was first published in 1964.

9. I. R-g., "Di yudishe sport-bavegung. A gesprekh mit'n dr' pribulski," *Sport-tsaytung* 2 (July 15, 1924), p. 4.

10. "Arb[eter] gezelshaft far fizisher dertsiung 'morgnshtern' in poyln, optaylung in lodz," *Vendung* (Lodz, February 1931), in Bund Archives, YIVO, MG 9-159.

11. Shtern membership book of Bolek Lemberger, YIVO, RG-28, folder 60. The membership book also contains a selection of edifying quotes from Karl Marx and Ber Borochov. For additional insight into the relevant views of Left Labor Zionists toward the goals and tasks of a worker sport movement, see I. A-tsh, "Arbeter-sport," *Arbeter kultur*, September 28, 1928, p. 4; "Di oyfgabn fun arbeter-sport," *Arbeter-tsaytung* 5, no. 23 (July 11, 1930), p. 6.

12. The single best study of the Bund in interwar Poland is that of Gertrud Pickhan, "*Gegen den Strom." Der Allgemeine Jüdische Arbeiterbund "Bund" in Polen 1918–1939*, Schriften des Simon-Dubnow Instituts Leipzig, vol. 1 (Stuttgart, 2001). On the Poalei Zion-Left see Bine Garntsarska-Kadari, *Di linke poyle-tsien in poyln biz der tsveyter velt-milkhome* (Tel Aviv, 1995), and the excellent article by Samuel Kassow, "The Left Poalei Tsiyon in Inter-war Poland," in *Yiddish and the Left*, Gennady Estraikh and Mikhail Krutikov, eds. (Oxford, 2001), pp. 109–28.

13. Mass activities were stressed because they could be easily engaged in by amateurs and beginners, because they promoted health, and because they did not require a great deal of practice. The individuals who were part of Morgnshtern, it was presumed, did not have a great deal of time at their disposal and could not afford sports requiring large amounts of expensive equipment. These were not, however, the only activities—or types of activities—conducted under Morgnshtern's auspices. Chess, for example, also attracted some support.

14. "Vi azoy darf oyszen a sotsialistishe sport organizatsie?" *Arbeter-sportler* 9–10 (November 15, 1930), p. 7.

15. Moshe Kligsberg, "Di yidishe yugnt-bavegung in poyln tsvishn beyde velt milkhomes (a sotsiologishe shtudie)," in *Shtudies vegn yidn in poyln 1919–1939. Di tsvishnshpil fun sotsiale, ekonomishe un politishe faktorn inem kamf fun a minoritet far ir kiem*, S. Fishman, ed. (New York, 1974), pp. 221–22. There were Poalei Zionists who argued that soccer and boxing were not proletarian sports. The leadership of Shtern, however, did not agree. See the *Arbeter-tsaytung* 6, no. 43 (November 6, 1931), p. 70.

16. Frim, "Fun varshever arbeter sport-klub 'shtern'."

17. Sh. Tshernetski, "Unzere sportler marshirn faroys (der ershter tsuzamenfor fun unzere sport-organizatsies)," *Yugnt-veker* 10 (May 15, 1929), p. 4.

18. Arbeter-gez. far fizisher dertsiung "morgnshtern" in poyln. varshever optaylung, *A yor arbet. tetikayts-berikht far der tsayt fun II.1 1937 bizn II.1 1938*, p. 21, (Bund Archives, YIVO, RG 29, file 86).

19. Frim, "Fun varshever arbeter sport-klub 'shtern'."

20. Natan, "Kh. sh. rotholts boks-mayster fun poyln," *Arbeter-tsaytung* 8, no. 17 (April 28, 1933), p. 5. Rotholts went on to win widely noticed victories over three German boxers, as a result of which the Nazis removed these boxers from the German national boxing team; see letter to the editor from Ben Tsheisin, *Forverts*, March 9, 2001, p. 21.

21. Nekhamia, "Boks un der arbeter-sport (diskusie artkil)," *Arbeter-tsaytung* 8, no. 17 (April 28, 1933), p. 5.

22. Arbeter-gezelshaft far fizisher dertsiung "morgnshtern" in poyln (yidishe sektsie fun arbeter-sport-internatsional). varshever optaylung, *Barikht tsu der alg. farzamlung dem 14tn fevruar 1936 far der tsayt—1. II. 1935–1. II. 1936*, p. 5, YIVO, RG 29, file 86.

23. Varshever optaylung, *Barikht tsu der alg. farzamlung*, p. 5. Cf. Mik, "Boks derobert birger-rekht," *Der nayer arbeter-sportler* (June 1937), p. 7.

24. Frim, "Fun varshever arbeter sport-klub 'shtern'." In 1933, the women's section of the Warsaw Shtern conducted a recruitment campaign: "Verbir-aktsie fun arb. froyen-sportlerins," *Arbeter vort* 11 (May 10, 1935), p. 5. Shtern urged women to enter the workers' sport movement because women suffer from "capitalist oppression and exploitation." It encouraged women to "become healthy free people" (in part) through "the collective creation of the workers' sport movement" ("Di arbeter-froy in di reyen fun der arb. sport-bavegung"), *Arbeter vort* 11 (May 10, 1935), p. 5.

25. Arbeter-gezelshaft far fizisher dertsiung "morgnshtern" in poyln. varshever optaylung, *1938. yor barikht*, p. 7, Bund Archives, YIVO, MG 9–158.

26. A. V. "Di proletarishe sport-bavegung," *Di fraye yugnt* 5, no. 1 (January, 1928), p. 17. Titlman and Yitskhok Gotlib (1902–1973) were elected as representatives of Shtern to the managing committee of ZRSS in October 1927. In 1929 Dr. Ber Opnhaym (born in 1892) of the Shtern was elected to the presidium of the third congress of the ZRSS, and he served as vice-chairman in the presidium. See "Arbeter-sport—kongres," *Arbeter-tsaytung* 4, no. 6 (February 8, 1929), p. 7; and "Driter kongres fun arbeter-sport-farband in poyln," *Arbeter-tsaytung* 4, no. 7 (February 15, 1929), p. 6. For biographical information on Gotlib, Opnhaym, and other Shtern activists (e.g., Dr. Hersh Liberman), see Shlomo Schweizer (Shloyme Svaytser), ed., *Shures poyle-tsien. portretn* (Tel Aviv, 1981).

27. The governmental agency responsible for physical education also had responsibility for military education and preparation. The leadership of Shtern worried that the influence of this agency, therefore, might lead to the militarization of the workers' sport movement, and to the "fascistification" of young workers. See "Der aroystrit fun 'shtern' forshteyer in z.r.s.s. kegn der militarizirung fun di sport-klubn," *Arbeter-tsaytung* 4, no. 35 (August 23, 1929), p. 7.

28. *Arbeter-tsaytung* 6, no. 43 (November 6, 1931), p. 7. Cf. A. V-s., "Finf yor arbeter-sport-farband," *Arbeter-tsaytung* 5, no. 10 (March 7, 1930), p. 6. Relations between the ZRSS and the Shtern deteriorated in the late 1930s. See "6ter kongres fun arbeter-sport-farband in poyln," *Arbeter-tsaytung* 12, no. 11 (March 12, 1937), pp. 6, 8.

29. A representative of the Morgnshtern, Lucian Blit, greeted the ZRSS at the Third Congress of the ZRSS in 1929, pointed to the continuing divisions within Poland among

workers sport movement, and proclaimed that he hoped that these movements would work together toward common goals in the near future. See "Driter kongres fun poylishn arbeter-sport-farband," *Naye folkstsaytung* 4, no. 42 (February 17, 1929), p. 4. Blit's greeting was described by a Labor Zionist reporter as having made a "pitiful impression;" N., "Driter kongres fun arbeter-sport-farband in poyln," *Arbeter-tsaytung* 4, no. 7 (February 15, 1929), p. 6. A small number of Bundist delegates attended the Sixth Congress of the ZRSS; see "6ter kongres fun arbeter-sport-farband in poyln." None bothered to attend the Seventh Congress (at which 24 of the 140 delegates represented Shtern, and 2 delegates represented Hapoel). See "Der 7ter kongres fun arbeter-sport-farband in poyln," *Arbeter-tsaytung* 14, no. 4 (February 19, 1939).

30. Abraham Brumberg, "The Bund and the Polish Socialist Party in the Late 1930s," in *The Jews of Poland between Two World Wars*, Yisrael Gutman et al., eds. (Hanover NH, 1989), pp. 75–82; Piotr Wróbel, "From Conflict to Cooperation: The Bund and the Polish Socialist Party, 1897–1939," in *Jewish Politics in Eastern Europe*, Jacobs, ed., pp. 161–65.

31. A. V., "Di proletarishe sport-bavegung."

32. Cf. the questionnaire prepared by the Yidisher visnshaftlekher institut optsvayg far der yidisher sport bavegung, completed by the Arbeter gezelshaft far fizisher dertsiung "morgnshern" in poyln, vilner optsvayg, and accessioned by YIVO on January 19, 1936; YIVO, RG I.1, file 600.

33. Arbeter-gezelshaft far fizisher dertsiung "Morgnshtern" in poyln. varshever optaylung, 1938. *Yor barikht*, Bund Archives, YIVO, MG 9-158.

34. Inteview with Yekhiel Dobekirer conducted by Jack Jacobs, February 5, 2000, New York. Dobekirer also indicated that the member of Hapoel responsible for the killing was smuggled out of Poland.

35. Yismakh, "Sports Clubs and Self-Defense," 61.

36. "Optsvayg far der yidisher sport-bavegung," *Yedies fun yivo*, December, 1935, 4 [54], p. 7.

37. "Optsvayg far der yidisher sport-bavegung," *Yedies fun yivo*, March, 1935, 2 [51], pp. 10–11.

38. "Fun optsvayg far der yidisher sport-bavegung," *Yedies fun yivo*, January–March, 1936, 1–2 [54–54a], p. 11. Twenty-five of the clubs from which answers had been received were affiliated with Maccabi, twelve with Morgnshtern, ten with Gwiazda, and one with Hapoel. The clubs were located in thirty-three different locations.

39. "Minutes [of the YIVO Branch for the Jewish Sports Movement]," May 5, 1937, YIVO, RG 29, file 86.

40. Arbeter-gezelshaft far fizisher dertsiung "morgnshtern" in poyln. yidishe sektsie fun arbeter sport internatsional. varshever optaylung, *Barikht tsu der alg. farzamlung dem 14-tn fevruar 1936 far der tsayt fun 1. II. 1935–1. II. 1936*, YIVO, RG 29, file 86.

41. Arbeter-gezelshaft far fizisher dertsiung "morgnshtern" in poyln. yidishe sektsie fun arbeter sport internatsional. varshever optaylung, *Barikht fun der tsayt 1.II.1936 -1.II.1937*, Bund Archives, YIVO, MG 9-158.

42. "Arbeter-gez. far fizisher dertsiung 'morgnshtern' in poyln. varshever optaylung, *A yor arbet. tetikayts-barikht far der tsayt fun II.1 1937 bizn II.1 1938*. During this period, the Morgnshtern branch in Lodz also increased in strength. Cf. *Tetikayts-barikht. "morgnshtern" optaylung in lodz. 31 mai 1937 bizn 1 marts 1938*.

7. Hakoah Vienna

Reflections on a Legend

John Bunzl

W HEN HAKOAH VIENNA was founded in 1909, sports were already on the verge of a social breakthrough. Sports events began to be great social affairs, soccer games frequently drew around ten thousand spectators. The number of active players and clubs was already considerable (there existed, for instance, in 1907 already seventy soccer clubs in Vienna, and the members of the mainly German Austrian clubs of the workers' gymnasts association numbered over fifteen thousand in 1911).

Although the sports boom occurred relatively quickly and, within a brief period of time, people from nearly all social layers and political movements participated in it, athletes had to fight hard for their social recognition. For decades, sports continued to have about it the air of the street, rabble, and vulgarity in the public's mind—apart from disciplines in which mainly academics participated (mainly fencing), and in equestrianism, which had its own development. In that sense, the Jewish sports movement, too, faced skepticism and rejection—both as a sports movement and as a Jewish movement—from the majority of Viennese Jews at least until the end of the First World War. [1]

Sports was then largely dependent on the initiative of individual athletes and on their willingness to put aside professional, material, and non-sports related private interests. The prospect of receiving at some point a reward other than the joy, self-confidence, and fulfilled life that the sports activity and the experience of community or victory themselves could provide was nonexistent.

Still, organized sports of the first decades of the twentieth century were as far away as today's sports from the realization of the amateur ideal, from the model of an athlete who was always self-disciplined and fair, who was not primarily motivated by success, and who practiced sports primarily as an end in itself. After all, from the beginnings until 1945, most sports clubs connected their activities to political and ideological goals, or, in any case, goals outside of sports. In that sense the foundation of a sports club with a national Jewish agenda was nothing exceptional. Even if sports was in the center for many, probably for most of the athletes of all persuasions, as soon as they organized themselves they were under an agenda, they were exposed to the educational endeavors of coaches and functionaries, and specific political movements were publicly attributed to them.

Sports is always political, but it is not always practiced as politics. The following remarks on the various political trends in sports should not create the impression that the athletes were mostly motivated by political goals, and that sports until 1938 was characterized by open political disputes. But to understand Hakoah, the political framework of sports is as important as the technical development of sports, the general social conditions, and the survival and developmental strategies of the Viennese Jews.[2]

At the time Hakoah was established, there already existed two strong politically oriented trends in the gymnasts and sports movement. The gymnastics clubs had initially been an open-minded pan-German movement, and until the 1880s and beyond, many Jews had belonged to them. But the majority of them had developed into the circle of the Deutsche Turnerschaft and were mostly German nationalist to *völkische*, antidemocratic, antisemitic oriented organizations.[3] Sports organizations within the labor movement— for many years under the suspicious observation of the Social Democratic Party—had developed since the 1890s. But many other clubs as well embraced, officially or unofficially, political trends, world views, and goals beyond sports. Viennese Czechs, for instance, had had since 1866 their own gymnastics clubs, the Sokol (founded in Prague in 1862 for all Czechs). These clubs saw their sports and educational activities as part of an "elevation of the Czech nation to complete independence and sovereignty." By 1910 they had around 1,800 members.[4]

The founding of the Austrian republic in 1918 and the growing political confrontations from the end of the 1920s onward increased the interest of political parties in sports and sports clubs. The open and deliberate functionalization of sports for extra political goals continued, while at the same time sports clubs were trying to distance themselves from any ideology. The German-nationalist gymnastics clubs formed the Deutscher Turnerbund (German Gymnastics Association) in 1919, an organization of more than 110,000 members (in 1933), which per statute excluded "non-Aryans" from admission, represented increasingly Nazistic positions, and partially acted as a cover organization after the prohibition of the Austrian Nazi party. The labor sports movement, united in the Arbeiterbund für Sport- und Körperkultur Österreich (ASKÖ) (Austrian Workers' Association for Sport and Physical Culture), as the organization was called from 1924, grew to an organization of almost 250,000 members by 1931; the worker-athletes rejected competitions and games with athletes from other associations, with "athletes only," as well as with athletes of different political persuasion and professionals. Together with the other associations of the Sozialistische Arbeitersport-Internationale (Socialist Workers' Sport International) they organized their own workers' Olympic games in Vienna in 1931. [5] With the establishment in 1914 of the Verband der christlich-deutschen Turn-erschaft Österreichs (Association of Christian-German Gymnastics Clubs in Austria)—the first Christian-German gymnasts club in Vienna had been founded in 1900—the Christian Socialists and political Catholicism, too, had their own gymnasts' movement (in 1928 a sports movement was added with the Reichsbund-Turn- und Sportgemeinschaft). The Christian-German gymnasts, who already had 30,000 members in 1925, also had an Aryan paragraph in its statutes. [6]

Besides the large movements, there were numerous independent clubs, which were in close contact with antisemitic movements (mostly rowing and fencing clubs, but also the Wiener Sportklub and the Erster Wiener Amateur-Schwimmklub (EWASK) were close to the movement represented by German gymnasts), and unmistakably antisemitic oriented associations (the ski association, for instance, introduced the Aryan paragraph in 1926, whereupon the opponents left). But there were numerous clubs that explicitly distanced themselves from any association and dispute. In the mid-1920s, professional soccer clubs were officially permitted, to which the Hakoah soccer players belonged as well. And there was also the Öster-reichische Hauptverband für Körpersport (Austrian Sports Federation), an alliance, organized according to sports branches, of all clubs and sections that wanted to carry out joint sports competitions and championships beyond the limits of clubs, political ideologies, and roof organizations. (The "Austrian champions" were not representative for all athletes.) Many Hakoah sections belonged to the association—and they also had their functionaries there.

The destruction of the republic by the Dollfuß government in 1934, and the attempts he and his successor Schuschnigg made to establish an authoritarian Ständestaat (corporate state), did not leave sports untouched. The clubs and associations of the workers' sports movement were prohibited after the armed conflict in which some Social Democrats unsuccessfully tried to resist the Dollfuß government in February 1934. The Deutscher Turner-bund was dissolved in July 1934, after the failure of the Nazi putsch. All legal sports clubs and associations had to join one organization, the Österreich-ische Turn- und Sportfront (Austrian Gymnastics and Sports Front) under the leadership of the Heimwehr leader Ernst Rüdiger [Fürst von] Starhem-berg, whose organizers were largely functionaries of the Christlich-Soziale Turnerschaft (Christian-Social Gymnastics Association). For Hakoah, much changed during those years.[7]

Later on, the Nazis were much more successful and radical than the rep-resentatives of the corporate state in the "systematic control of sports activ-ity" (Starhemberg) by the state. After the entry of German troops in March 1938, Austrian sports became state-organized and National Socialist. The Turn- und Sportfront was incorporated into the Deutscher Reichsbund für Leibesübungen (German Reich Association for Physical Exercises), the as-sociations were purged of inconvenient functionaries and athletes, clubs became state regulated and were reorganized, followers of the regime were installed as the associations' leaders, all Jewish clubs were prohibited, and Jews were excluded from clubs and expelled from swimming pools by de-cree. Indeed, the Nazi regime never managed to completely control what went on in clubs, on the sports fields, and among the spectators, but free-dom was very limited, and, after some time, did not exist at all for Jews.[8]

Goals and Significance of Hakoah

Hakoah was founded around the following goals and functions:

1. Gathering all Jewish athletes who were unable to join other clubs because of hidden or open antisemitism or the Aryan paragraph;
2. The training of physical strength and thus of defense abilities and of self-confidence of the Jews;
3. Deliberate proof to the public—to Jews as well as non-Jews and the antisemites among them—that Jews were not inferior to other parts of the population in physical strength and in the ability to be an all-round educated people;
4. Advancement of Jewish national awareness.[9]

On that basis, Hakoah developed within a few years into a club with over 1,500 members and many followers, an association that was active in a dozen sports disciplines and that produced champions and record holders in many of them. Hakoah was not the only Jewish sports organization: there were the Jewish gymnastics clubs, which added other sports disciplines as well. In addition, a number of smaller Jewish sports clubs were founded in Vienna (among others, Ahduth, Hapoel, Hasmonea, Jewish Athletics Club, Kadimah) and in other cities (such as Hakoah Innsbuck, Hakoah Graz, and Hakoah Linz). Hakoah and the other Jewish sports clubs—together they formed the Jüdischer Turn- und Sportverband (Jewish Gymnastics and Sports Association)—were by no means the only organizations where Jews were active in sports: after the First World War, many Jews belonged to non-Jewish clubs because they felt comfortable there and did not want to declare themselves as Jews, or because they rejected national-Jewish alliances (a high proportion of Jews were in the clubs of the workers' sports movement and also, among others, in the Wiener Amateur-Sportverein, called Austria from 1926 and the Vienna. Moreover, Jewish organizations that otherwise did not consider themselves sports clubs began to introduce sports into their range of activities. Such organizations included Zionist associations, the Jüdische Studentenschaft Judäa (Jewish Students Association Judea), and the youth from the Union österreichischer Juden (Union of Austrian Jews, the group that managed the Israelitische Kultusgemeinde [Jewish Community] in the 1920s).[10] But Hakoah had a unique position: it became the most important all-round sports club and the most publicly visible crystallization point of Jewish self-confidence in Austria. The rise was not only a result of the changes regarding the position of Jews and sports within society. It was also because Hakoah had a core of open-minded and active people who established new sections, did public relations, and organized club life outside the sports activities; it was also a result of the club's political and sports program and practice.

Hakoah was a club based on Jewish identity—non-Jews were permitted only as coaches—and structured according to liberal principles. Anybody who did not principally reject this Jewish framework could become a member and feel at home without having to compromise political and other convictions. Thus Hakoah was—to mention the extremes—a club for Jews who, without any programmatic intentions, wished nothing else but to practice sports quietly, that is, without the burden of open or latent antisemitism so rampant in many Austrian sports clubs; but also a club for Jews who saw their sports as part of the Zionist project and as preparation for the physical strains of life in Israel/Palestine. And even though the club embraced the Zionist movement—also publicly through its membership in the international Jewish sports federation Maccabi, founded in 1921—this orientation did not deter athletes of other persuasions insofar as they did not reject a Jewish sports club altogether.

But also within Austrian society, Hakoah held a position like no other Jewish organization. While all the political Jewish associations, the Jewish professional and cultural organizations, the religious, educational, and charitable associations were active to a large extent only within the Jewish public or specific segments of the Viennese Jewish population, Hakoah organized itself as an Austrian club highly visible to the general public. And it did so in an area that was politically the least tricky, because competition and regulated fight were part of its foundations. [11] Thus, on the one hand, Hakoah offered Jews who were, for whatever reasons, skeptical toward national-Jewish projects—because they counted on assimilation as solution to the "Jewish question," or feared that a collective political appearance as Jews would foster antisemitism, or because of something else—the opportunity to participate in a collective Jewish program. Of course, to many Jews even this was too much because as radical socialists, assimilated bourgeois, die-hard German nationalists, or monarchists they rejected any form of collective appearance of Jews as Jews; or because for them as consistent Zionists the establishment of an Austrian sports club within the Austrian sports scene hid the danger of an arrangement with Austrian society; or because as Orthodox religious persons they dealt with entirely different issues; or because they were principally against sports.

On the other hand, Hakoah offered Jews an area—and probably the only one—where they were able and allowed to celebrate success as Jews in Austria and where they were even officially recognized. In politics that was impossible: a Jewish National Party that stood equally beside other Austrian political parties did not get elected by the vast majority of Jews (in the parliamentary elections of 1923, it received 2.4 percent, in 1927, 0.9 percent, and 1931, 0.2 percent), and the fight against antisemitism and for the civil rights of Jews was fought rather as a battle of retreat during that period. In other areas it was difficult at the least: the pioneering achievements of a Jewish physician, the revolutionary innovation of a Jewish composer, and such were celebrated as success in consciously Jewish circles and may have contributed to the strengthening of Jewish self-confidence, but these were achievements of individual people who were also frequently assimilated or baptized Jews. However, the victories of a sports club, one that openly declared itself as a collective Jewish action and as such competed against general and partially explicitly "Aryan" clubs in open competition, were from the start inseparable from acknowledging Judaism. Only with Hakoah was it possible to win with the Star of David on the chest. Hakoah as such was not primarily a political club, but its activities were inseparable from politics, independent of the individual athlete's will, and that led to its success to a large degree. In the end, that blend could not be separated even in competition—also as far as the sports adversaries were concerned. With few exceptions (such as the water-polo matches between Hakoah and EWASK [First Viennese Amateur Swim Club]), sports meetings between Hakoah teams and non-Jewish clubs were not, a priori, fought as ideological or national battles. The fans of just a few clubs came to the field already with the intention of engaging in Jew-bashing. Systematic bias against Hakoah by juries and umpires occurred in only a few sports disciplines, especially in swimming. If, therefore, in such sports disciplines where the contestants faced each other, competing became rough at times, it was in most cases the result of athletic rivalry. Similarly, the fanaticism of the audience was the result of its watching each competitor from a club perspective. As far as toughness, unfairness, and fanaticism are concerned, most matches of the Hakoah soccer players were probably not very different from games between Rapid and Sportklub or Austria and Hertha. Nevertheless, there was a priori something about games and other competitions where Hakoah participated that did not exist in meetings among non-Jewish clubs. After all, it was one thing when Admira fans cursed Wacker players as "filthy swine," and an entirely different thing when they called a Hakoah player "Judensau" (Jew pig). And there was an enormous difference whether an angry fouled player called the wrongdoer "scum" or "Drecksjude" (dirty Jew). The tougher the going for reasons of sportive rivalry, the more antisemitism (and the Jewish response) rose to the surface. And the more the atmosphere was heated by antisemitism, the less the disputes were of a sportive nature. The nonsportive element was in general more important to the audience than to the athletes.

Hakoah's success, however, was also the result of the club's ideas regarding sports. Thanks to its goals, its history, and its carriers, Hakoah was able to express needs that originated in society and in the sports movement. Hakoah was free of the conservatism of the gymnastics clubs—in fact, from the start it left gymnastics to the gymnastics clubs—and of the limitations of clubs with just one sports discipline. It did not take up the positions of the workers' sports club (rejection of professionalism, aversion to catering to the audience and record-hunting, limitation of competition) and was more favorable toward women's sports than many other clubs and associations. The Jewish club fostered sports for the general public as well as for topnotch athletes; in addition to founding a professional soccer club as well as a tourist club, it organized a range of other disciplines that included swimming, track and field, wrestling, hockey, fencing, handball, ice hockey, table tennis, tennis, skiing, chess, and, partially, boxing. Hakoah was also active in advancing the youth and catered to cultural needs outside of sports, organizing an orchestra, lectures, balls, and so forth.

The sports achievements of Hakoah, its records, championships, and game results can be examined in the lists and charts of the Austrian sports associations. The most famous success among its many titles was undoubtedly the Austrian soccer championship in 1925. The place the club is entitled to in the development of a new collective Jewish identity may one day be identified in more detail by historians of the national-Jewish and Zionist movements in Austria. The significance the club had for the lives of many of its members and adherents clearly emerges from contemporary sports reports and from recollections of the participants. Hakoah was for numerous people a place where they were able to realize abilities and needs, sportive and others, that otherwise might have remained unfulfilled. It was a space where they found and created community, self-confidence, and joy in living, an activity that gave their lives more meaning. This is the true significance of Hakoah, even when viewing Hakoah's entire history of the 1920s and 1930s from the Auschwitz perspective. After all, twenty, ten, or even two years of a "little happiness" and a more or less fulfilled life cannot be erased by an ensuing catastrophe. Besides, the education and dynamism that Hakoah provided for its supporters greatly assisted in the timely escape, through emigration, of the larger part of the club members from Hitler's annihilation machine.

In one respect, however, the year 1938 sealed Hakoah's failure, which had been—or could have been—obvious long before the Nazis prevailed. At its establishment, one of the goals Hakoah had set for itself was to refute antisemitism. With their sports activities, Hakoah actives were to demonstrate to the public that Jews were the same people as non-Jews, that they could compete in will power, physical strength, and discipline, and that the antisemitic view of the Jew as weak, deceitful, word-twisting, whining, dishonorable, and idle parasites did not conform to reality. Individual athletes might certainly have changed their views through contact with Hakoah actives. Overall throughout society, and on the level of sports, however, antisemites were not shaken at all by the fact that Hakoah set Austrian records or prevailed in competitions over non-Jewish athletes who appeared as Aryans,

Medal from the sport club Hakoah Wien. Vienna,
undated. Courtesy of the Jewish Museum of Berlin.

Christians, or something else. All these achievements were for antisemites another proof of the danger, slyness, and guile of the "Jewish race." Hakoah failed in this respect just as the Jewish dueling fraternities, Jewish World War I veterans' associations, officers' associations, and all the other Jewish groups failed in their fight against antisemitism.[12]

Notes

This contribution is based on part of a book I edited on Jewish sports in Austria: John Bunzl, ed., *Hoppauf Hakoah: Jüdischer Sport in Österreich* (Vienna, 1987).

1. For a description of the emergence of a Jewish sports movement in the Austrian part of the monarchy, see Adolf Gaisbauer, *Davidstern und Doppeladler* (Vienna, 1988), esp. p. 424.
2. There is a huge literature on the sociopolitical environment of early-twentieth-century Austria. I refer here only to the classic: Albert Fuchs, *Geistige Strömungen in Österreich 1867–1918* (Vienna, 1949).

3. For background on *völkisch* movements in Austria, see Francis Ludwig Carsten, *Faschismus in Österreich: Von Schönerer bis Hitler* (Munich, 1977); and Bruce F. Pauley, *Hitler and the Forgotten Nazis: A History of Austrian National Socialism* (Chapel Hill NC, 1981).

4. On the Czech minority in Vienna see Monika Glettler, *Die Wiener Tschechen um 1900* (Munich, 1972); on Sokol, p. 85; for a general view of ethnic diversity in Vienna see Michael John and Albert Lichtblau, *Schmelztiegel Wien, einst und jetzt: Zur Geschichte und Gegenwart von Zuwanderung und Minderheiten* (Vienna, 1990).

5. There are many books on Austro-Marxism and the development of a social-democratic subculture in Vienna between the wars. As a general introduction consult Josef Weidenholzer, *Auf dem Weg zum "Neuen Menschen": Bildungs- und Kulturarbeit der österreichischen Sozialdemokratie in der 1. Republik* (Vienna, 1981). For a more specific view on youth culture see Wolfgang Neugebauer, *Bauvolk der kommenden Welt: Geschichte der sozialistischen Jugendbewegung in Österreich* (Vienna, 1975); on soccer, see Mathias Marschik, *Wir spielen nicht zum Vergnügen: Arbeiterfussball in der Ersten Republik* (Vienna, 1994), and idem, *Vom Herrenspiel zum Männersport: Die ersten Jahre des Wiener Fussballs* (Vienna, 1997).

6. As an introduction see Alfred Diamant, *Die österreichischen Katholiken und die Erste Republik, 1918–1934* (Vienna, 1960).

7. The Dollfuß-Schuschnigg era (1934–1938) is covered by Emmerich Talos and Wolfgang Neugebauer, eds., *Austrofaschismus: Beiträge über Politik, Ökonomie und Kultur 1934–1938* (Vienna, 1984).

8. Effects of the Anschluss of Austria are analyzed in Emmerich Talos, Ernst Hanisch, and Wolfgang Neugebauer, eds., *NS-Herrschaft in Österreich, 1938–1945* (Vienna, 1988); see also Evan Burr Bukey, *Hitler's Austria: Popular Sentiment in the Nazi Era, 1938–1945* (Chapel Hill NC, 2000).

9. Tha classic account of Hakoah history is Arthur Baar, *50 Jahre Hakoah 1909–1959* (Tel Aviv, 1959).

10. On the history of the Jewish community in interwar Vienna see Harriet Pass Freidenreich, *Jewish Politics in Vienna, 1918–1938* (Bloomington IN, 1991).

11. See Mathias Marschik, " 'Muskel-Juden': Mediale Repräsentation des jüdischen Sports in Wien," in *Davidstern und Lederball: Die Geschichte der Juden im deutschen und internationalen Fussball*, Dietrich Schulze-Marmeling, ed. (Göttingen, 2003), pp. 263.

12. The most comprehensive study of Austrian antisemitism can be found in Bruce F. Pauley, *From Prejudice to Persecution: A History of Austrian Antisemitism* (Chapel Hill NC, 1992).

Antisemitism
and Sports

8. Antisemitism in Austrian Sports between the Wars

Michael John

I N 1918–19 SEVERAL new states came into being in the area that had been ruled by the Habsburg monarchy. Above all, Austria, the former center, was marked by an ongoing economic and political crisis in the 1920s and 1930s. In this situation antisemitism developed into a mass phenomenon and took on a noticeably more aggressive form. The antisemitism of the German nationalists was augmented by that of hundreds of thousands of immigrants from the non-German-speaking regions of the monarchy: in postmonarchic Austria they strove to compensate for the "stigma" of their origins through chauvinism and antisemitism. In addition there was the antisemitism of the middle classes, but also of many workers, who viewed the class struggle from an antisemitic perspective. All of this manifested itself in the sporting life of the times. This article aims to examine the appearance of aggressive forms of antisemitism on the basis of some exemplary cases. The focus is on competitive team sports, whereby fencing has been included as well, because the whole field of "fencing and fighting" also brings in clashes involving students and student fraternities (Burschenschaften) in the university domain.

Antisemitism on the Soccer Pitch

The sporting conflicts between Jews and the rest of the population were repeatedly focused on the expressly Jewish teams, that is to say, Hakoah (Hebrew: Strength) and other Zionist or Jewish-nationalist oriented clubs. In Austria the registered soccer clubs at one time included Hakoah Graz, Hakoah Linz (Upper-Austria), Hakoah Innsbruck, Hasmonea, Unitas, Kadimah (Hebrew: Forward), and Hakoah Vienna. Hakoah Vienna, founded in 1909, had by the far the strongest team, and was thus at the center of attention of people who followed sports.

The first massive manifestations of antisemitism on the soccer field came just months after the collapse of the Habsburg monarchy. Being an election year, 1923 was particularly eventful—but it was also a year of frequent antisemitic rioting, as antisemitism was very prominent in the political discourse at the time. In August 1923 there were violent incidents at the match between Hakoah and Ostmark, whereby "the mob tried to start a riot, spitting and throwing stones at cars and their occupants. [*Evidently these were the cars of the Jewish spectators.*—MJ] The initiator was the barred Ostmark player Lackenbauer."[1] In November the *Wiener Morgenzeitung* reported about rioting on the soccer pitch:

> People who abide by the rules of common decency and manners in everyday life become brutal terrorists at Hakoah matches. . . . What went on at the game between Admira and Hakoah, for instance, is quite simply beyond belief. There was a veritable orgy of verbal abuse, including the repeated use of the words "Jewish pig," and wild threats could be heard from all sides. Scarcely a match takes place at which the Hakoah players are not insulted and threatened in the basest manner. At their own ground in Krieau a whole team of mounted watchmen is needed to keep the hordes of spectators at bay.[2]

Following these incidents, Hakoah announced that they would no longer participate in the championships. A few months earlier, the team president, Körner, had been physically attacked by a WAF (Viennese Soccer Association Club) player in the course of a championship match. WAF was a Viennese upper class club. Against the background of Hakoah's withdrawal from the championships in connection with the attacks during matches and the behavior of antisemitic spectators, the following comment appeared in the *Prager Presse*, a German-language Czech newspaper: "The Czech teams will understand the motives underlying the Jewish club's decision, which was surely not taken lightly, for every time they played in Vienna against one of the local teams, they had to struggle not only against eleven players, but also against the great mass of fanatical, raging, hate-filled supporters."[3]

Diverse groups and classes took part in the antisemitic riots of the 1920s, and the incidents on the soccer fields were generally not of an organized nature. Physical assaults were carried out by young men above all, although teenagers, too, were involved in the constant violence and fighting. In the sports press, reports about the young assailants appeared repeatedly: "With the words, 'That one looks like a Jew too,' this young horde set upon individual adults and beat them black and blue. This naturally triggered off a great tumult, in which thousands of people (some more actively and some more passively, of course) participated."[4] In the meantime, the antisemitic incidents were no longer restricted to Hakoah Vienna. At the second-league match between the Zionist club Hasmonea and Josefstädter SF, rioting among the players and the spectators led to the game being canceled, with the decision in Hasmonea's favor.[5] In the little Tyrolean town of Wörgl, at the match between Wörgl and Hakoah Innsbruck, the Tyrolean Hakoah players were also subjected to insults. According to the *Wiener Morgenzeitung*, "The Wörgl players, stirred up by the crowd with shouts like 'Jewish pig,' 'Give the Jewish trash a good thrashing,' 'Let's have a pogrom,' etc., gave the Hakoah players a real going over with all kinds of fouls."[6] When two of the Jewish players were injured and the insults of the spectators became more and more threatening, Hakoah Innsbruck gave up.[7] Some teams in Stryria refused to play matches against Jewish players; Leobner Deutscher Sportverein, Grazer AK, Leibnitzer SV and SV Knittelfeld had introduced the so-called *Arierparagraph* (the Aryan paragraph, comprising regulations prohibiting non-Aryans from participating), which was otherwise generally rare in the field of soccer.[8]

The Existence of an Alternative Scene

In the 1920s and '30s, the Jewish population in Vienna numbered between 180,000 and 200,000, so it is no surprise that there was an alternative scene as well. This included a range of key figures from that form of soccer culture that—as is often said—was infiltrated by elements from the Bohemian and coffeehouse culture and was associated with theater, journalism, and other cultural fields. Poetry, essays, and intelligent bon mots were produced by these circles of soccer-lovers in especially large quantities. For example, the author Friedrich Torberg wrote a well-known poem about the Austria player Matthias Sindelar ("Ballad of the Death of a Soccer Player"), the opera star Leo Slezak was also a great soccer enthusiast, and the essayist Alfred Polgar can be mentioned in this context.[9]

Hakoah Vienna made an essential contribution to this scene, too. The Jewish club was one of the first teams to promote soccer as a professional sport and to organize international tours. In 1925 Hakoah Vienna became the first Austrian champion in the professional league; in the same year Hakoah became national champion in another "tough" contact sport, too, namely hockey.[10] Thanks to two highly publicized and successful tours, the soccer team made a name for itself in the United States as well.[11] Wiener Austria (formerly Amateure) also won the Austrian soccer championships —indeed, several times.[12] Amateure/Austria had a reputation as being the team of the assimilated, liberal-minded Jewish bourgeoisie and intellectu- als—the team included several Jewish players, and the top officials were

Jews. Antisemitic incidents also occurred in connection with Austria, though less frequently than at Hakoah matches. Unlike Hakoah, the team was not a purely Jewish affair, but rather an integrated professional club. What is more, there was intense rivalry between the two clubs, which sometimes even led to physical fights between their supporters, as the Hakoah club magazine reported.[13] On the one hand, the social background of the respective club supporters played a part in this tension between the clubs; on the other hand, it was also partly due to their different origins: assimilated, old-established Viennese Jewry versus east European Jewish immigrants.

The frictions that arose in connection with teams whose fans came from the so-called *Vorstadt* (working-class suburbs) or from Vienna's lower classes were far greater, however.[14] When Amateure played against Wacker or the Simmering club Red Star, the motto of the day was "Here come the Jews." It was similar with matches against the record championship-winners Rapid. According to Karl Geyer, "Whenever Rapid played against Amateure, [Rapid coach Dionys] Schönecker used to say, 'Watch out boys, we're playing the Jews today. You know what to do—give them a good thrashing, then they'll end up where they belong.' He used to say that before every match against them. And we took his words to heart."[15] In the *Illustriertes Sportblatt* the difference between Rapid and Amateure (Austria) was formulated like this: "Rapid is a team of the people and never neglects its roots. The Green-Whites are a 'Vorstadt' club in the best sense of the word." In contrast, Amateure were referred to as "a team of soccer mercenaries, dazed by the stifling fog of the coffeehouse."[16] Amateure won the championships in the seasons of 1923/24 and 1925/26.

Hakoah won the championships in the 1924/25 season; after that, the Jewish nationalist club no longer played a role in the fight to win the title, having instead to struggle against relegation. After the 1927/28 season Hakoah was in fact transferred to a lower division, but later went up again to play in the top league. On the one hand, the relegation might well have to do with the fact that some players had left the club to play in the United States, having been recruited during Hakoah's big tour there; on the other hand, there is also some evidence pointing to the possibility that winning the championships in 1924/25 was related to the Hakoah players being "super-motivated." This phenomenon is familiar from more recent cases, such as Germany's surprise victory in the 1954 world championship, as well as their victory in 1990, after reunification; and Croatia's good performance in 1998 after their independence from Yugoslavia and the end of that phase of war in the Balkans. In such cases, the normal motivation is heightened by an additional motivating force of an ethnic, nationalist, or social nature or something similar. In the case of Hakoah, in the first professional championships they wanted to prove that in this sport Jews are not the underdogs, but can in fact be better than the other teams. Antisemitism might thus temporarily have acted as a spur that led to success.[17]

During the Economic Crisis—Water Sports
Scandals in Linz, Krems, and Vienna

In the course of the economic crisis there was a new increase in overt antisemitism. For instance, the newspaper of the Jewish community in Linz wrote of "heavy economic and political attacks that are being planned, declared, and implemented against us" and of "malicious machinations," and arranged a lecture called "Crisis and Decision in Jewry" in the hall of the merchants' association. There it emerged that the reaction of the local Jewish population was one of surprise.[18] Shortly after that, in the summer of 1931, the first campaigns by circles close to the National Socialists began. The Linz swimming champion and NS sympathizer Sepp Staudinger behaved in a grossly unsporting fashion toward the Jewish Hakoah swimmers, who were leading in some disciplines in the state championships in the Linz Parkbad, and stirred up the spectators into shouting antisemitic comments.[19] One report on the incidents went as follows:

> Antisemitic scandals in Linz. The athletic performance was weak. The interest of the Linz citizens in the competition, which was more of an advertising event than anything else, was very low. . . . The scheduled water polo match could not take place, as EWASK [Erster Wiener Amateur-Schwimmklub, an antisemitic club that was close to the National Socialists. —MJ] refused to play against a team of Jews. And so the "propaganda" event of the swimming club ended in a big scandal. During the competition, and even more so afterwards, the success of Hakoah led to ugly antisemitic scenes. . . . In the end the Hakoah swimmers were forced to fend off an attack that was made on them on their way to the station themselves, since the police did not arrive until just before the train was due to leave.[20]

The day after these events, the social-democratic *Tagblatt* reported a further incident at Linz station. This time it was not Hakoah, but socialist athletes who were involved: "At Linz station a group of worker athletes left the train to take a stroll during the stop at the station. The Linz railroad official Ziegler and a friend of his did the same. They were both wearing the swastika. Ziegler's friend insulted the workers, calling them Jewish riff-raff and telling them to go and get out of Linz." This led to a big fight.[21]

In 1932 the water polo team of EWASK beat Hakoah 3–2 in a key championship match after a hard fight, even though Hakoah had been in the lead and was by far the stronger team in the second half. Among the supporters there was violent fighting during this match, as a group of EWASK supporters had been heard shouting, "Death to the Jews."[22] In an outraged article the Jewish newspaper Die Stimme made the following plea:

> It is time to put an end to this! We all still remember the negotiations that took place with the Ewask bosses after the fighting in Linz and the (unsatisfactory) compromise that was agreed on, which was designed to put a stop to the offensive swastika insults. Now the same Ewask bosses, who swore blind at the time to keep politics and sport separate from each other, have revealed their true colors. The water polo match Ewask versus Hakoah was blown up as if the whole of Austria would be saved by virtue of this one victory against Hakoah. . . . There was unprecedented violence, far removed from the sports arena.[23]

The Jewish newspaper thus called on Hakoah to withdraw from the championships.

In the same year, 1932, the Deutsch-Österreichische Tages-Zeitung viewed "Zionists, repulsive, disgusting hook-noses" in the midst of a "Jewish mob, snorting with rage," which increased in intensity to reach an "Asiatic frenzy," first and foremost as the aggressors at sports events. In the view of the nationalist paper, there were "Jews as far as the eye can see" at the stadium swimming pool, with "the occasional Aryan sitting shyly in between them." The newspaper made it clear in no uncertain terms that in their opinion, Jews had no business taking part in sports: "The events of the day serve to show all Aryan athletes, and our gymnasts too, how important it is not to leave sport to the Jews, but rather to break into the international domain with a vigorous attack, to conquer it for the German people, and to utilize the values that undeniably exist in a sporting education for the good of our nation alone."[24]

The aggressive formulation "with a vigorous attack" was not an empty threat—not in Linz, as has already been shown, nor in Krems, in 1932 at the river swimming championships, or to be more precise, after the competition was over:

A group of people from Krems attacked the Hakoah swimmer Lichtenstein in his changing room at the Krems pool, beat him up, and threw him out. When he was fleeing in his car, a bucket of red paint was thrown at it, causing considerable damage. A group of Hakoah swimmers of both sexes, who were looking after Lichtenstein, had stones thrown at them, as did a second car, which took the Hakoah swimmers into the town and was also badly damaged. The one single police officer who was there proved to be powerless. The Hakoah swimmers gathered in a hotel in the town, where they were subjected to insults from the National Socialists who had congregated on the street outside. The police had to protect them while they "made their retreat" out of Krems. The police started an investigation and managed to apprehend some of the attackers. Legal proceedings were then set in motion.[25]

Fencing and Fighting

In 1910 Hakoah had established a fencing section; during World War I all activities came to a halt, but in 1919 fencing was reactivated. Unlike in Hungary, for instance, where Jewish fencers commanded a strong position, in Austria Jews did not play a particularly important role in this sport. One of Hakoah's greatest successes came in 1926 at the European foil-fencing championship in Budapest, and even then they only came eighth.[26] It was a long-standing complaint of Jewish sportswriters that there was not only a lack of training possibilities, but also a lack of motivation, and young men were called upon to show more interest in fencing as an organized sport.[27] The hidden message that was meant by "organized" was deliberate: the only area in which Jewish fencers were able to achieve noteworthy success was the university championships, which were not tied to any club membership. Jewish students and academics won quite a few such championships, in both the individual and the team competitions. It was no accident that successes were concentrated on the university domain. Fencing was very common at the universities, yet frequently it happened outside the sphere of sports organizations. In the so-called *Burschenschaften* (student fraternities), fencing was both a test of courage and also a matter of image. In Vienna these student organizations can be classified into three movements: The predominant all-German (German radical) fraternities; the liberal German-democratic ones, which accepted Jews and rejected racist antisemitism; and the Zionist fraternities.[28] "The aim of these Zionist fraternities," according to the writer and former fraternity student Arthur Köstler,

> was to prove to the world that Jews could hold their own in dueling, drinking, and singing just like other people. . . . The founders of the first Zionist fraternity, Kadimah, spent eight whole hours a day for six months training in the art of saber-fencing in the "German high style"; they then made their first entrance in full dress in the assembly hall of Vienna University. Once the Teutons, Saxons, Goths, and Vandals had recovered from their initial astonishment, a big violent brawl started. The consequence of this brawl was a series of duels, in the course of which the Kadimah students inflicted a considerable number of scars on their opponents. After Kadimah, my own fraternity, Unitas, was founded; there then followed Ivriah, Libanonia, Robur, Jordania and the rest. . . . "Lebanon" and "Jordan" came to be the most-feared "blades" of the university.[29]

The Waidhofener Resolution of the German nationalist fraternities was set down in 1896, according to which Jews were not only to be barred from joining fraternities, but were also to be regarded as not capable of giving satisfaction through dueling. Köstler describes the consequences of the "Waidhofener principle" during his student days in the first half of the '20s:

> It remains an open question whether the infamous resolution was passed as a result of the aversion to accepting a thrashing from Jews, as the Jewish side claimed, or whether there were other reasons; in any case, it put the Jews in a difficult position. As they could no longer fight their opponents using knightly means, they had to prove how tough they were with their fists and with clubs. Vienna University thus became the scene of constant and bloody fights. These generally happened on Saturday mornings during the traditional stroll in the colonnades of the assembly hall. . . . The brawl was started almost always following the same pattern. A Libanonia or Jordania student would feel "provoked" by a real or imagined action, such as a challenging look or being brushed against by a passing elbow; he would then walk up to the Saxon or Teuton, click his heels smartly and challenge him in a cutting tone of voice: "Sir, you have provoked me. I request that you follow me to the ramp (in front of the main entrance)." Thereupon the further proceedings would be negotiated by the opponents.

In general, according to Köstler, what ensued was the question put by the offending party: " 'Sir, are you an Aryan?' Under the rules of the Jewish fraternities, their members were obliged to respond to this question by punching the offender in the face or hitting him on the head with a stick."[30] This blow was usually followed by clashes between the fraternity students who were present.

The clashes between German nationalist and Zionist fraternity students, which had originally seemed to be of a ritual kind, were to undergo a lasting change in nature in the course of the 1920s; occasionally they even took the form of an organized chase. A German nationalist majority attempted to throw students whom they took to be Jews out of the university; in the end they hounded Jewish students, of both sexes, through the corridors and beat them up. The violence reached a peak in 1923 when, according to a police report, on November 19, "150 German nationalist students" occupied the entrance to the Anatomical Institute of Vienna University; it came to clashes with "liberal, Jewish nationalist and social-democratic students."[31] The next day there was a serious riot at the University of World Trade; anybody who "acted provocatively against Aryans," to use the formulation of the Christian Social *Reichspost*, was beaten with rubber truncheons and sticks, dragged up to the ramp in front of the main building and thrown off it.[32] The next peaks came in the rioting at the university in 1927 and 1929; in 1929 especially, police reports repeatedly told of clashes between German nationalist and Jewish students—for example on the ramp of Vienna University on June 8, 1929, where there was fighting involving between eighty and a hundred students; one of the German nationalists was arrested, and several Jewish students reported injuries.[33]

The riots escalated again in 1931. Several people were badly injured in attacks by nationalist students, in which steel bars, whips, knives, and brass knuckles were used. Frequently there were also students from the United States among the injured Jews. On one occasion, American students were forced to pull down their pants—to show whether they were circumcised. On June 27, 1931, Jewish students protested against these attacks, which were increasingly taking on the form of an organized persecution, at a large-scale and peaceful demonstration. There, the main complaint of the Zionists was the lack of "sporting spirit" on the part of their antisemitic opponents.[34] In the course of time, in fact, the activities of the German nationalist fraternities at the university had blended together increasingly with riots organized by the National Socialist party, and by the beginning of the '30s the party had taken over complete control in this respect. The "Radical Zionists" protested against the activities of the National Socialists at the university in a demonstration of their own.[35]

A U.S. pressure-group (Liga zum Schutze der ausländischen Studenten in Wien, i.e., League for the Protection of Foreign Students in Vienna) eventually wrote a strongly worded protest against the university riots:

> We the undersigned Americans hereby protest against the repeated attacks on foreign minorities, such as those against Hungarians, Poles, and Jews, at Vienna University. We came here full of admiration and respect for Austrian culture. However, we are outraged in the utmost as a result of the scandalous behavior we have had to experience, and we deeply regret that the rest of the civilized world, too, will come to know of these events and will be similarly horrified. As American citizens we protest against the cowardice, the inhumanity, and the lack of sporting spirit that allows groups of 50 to 100 people to attack single foreign students. We have witnessed foreign students being beaten mercilessly. Even women were injured.[36]

In the '20s and '30s, hundreds of American medical students, most of whom were Jews, studied in Vienna. In connection with the petition cited above, U.S. ambassador Gilchrist Baker Stockton began to intervene in the affair, meeting the Christian Social Chancellor Dollfuß several times in person. He made an official protest, as did the diplomatic representatives of Poland, Bulgaria, Yugoslavia and Romania.[37] As a result, from the autumn semester of 1932 onwards, the level of violence at the university began to diminish.

The Situation during the Authoritarian Regime, 1934–February 1938

During this period, reports about antisemitic riots at soccer and swimming events, which had been frequent in the 1920s and early '30s, were few and far between. On the one hand, it is possible that the nature of the reporting had changed; on the other hand, though, hardly any such cases can be found in the political records, either in those of the state police or the chancellery. What is clear is that from 1933/34, when democracy was eliminated in Austria, at least in the first years of the authoritarian regime—which stood as a competing dictatorship to that of National Socialism—overt manifestations of antisemitism on the sports fields were clamped down on, these being regarded as National Socialist activities and thus forbidden. The activities of the nationalist fraternities were monitored as well. The German nationalist Turnerschaft (gymnastics association), too, was under permanent observation in the Ständestaat years.

After the First World War, three clubs in Austria were merged to form the DTB (Deutscher Turner-Bund, or German Gymnastics Society), and the DTB implemented an *Arierparagraph*. In March 1934 the *Bundesturnzeitung* of the DTB was still writing such comments as: "The Jews . . . are a foreign body in our nation . . . and every foreign body is damaging."[38] A few months later the DTB was banned by the Austrian regime. What triggered the ban was evidently above all the involvement of the gymnasts in the July putsch of 1934, whereby the association's gymnasium was known to be the meeting place of the National Socialist Dollfuß assassins. Furthermore, there had clearly been collaboration between the gymnasts and the SS-Standarte 89, an organization that was banned in Austria at this time.[39]

What is clear is that the regime acted altogether ambivalently. On the one hand, some laws were passed containing measures that can only be interpreted as antisemitic, and the discrimination against Jews in everyday life continued to increase; on the other hand, Jewish institutions and businesses were regarded as allies against National Socialism. According to Bruce Pauley in his history of Austrian antisemitism, the authoritarian government was under pressure from various sides—especially from American intervention—to protect the Austrian Jews, but also from Austrian antisemites both within and outside the Vaterländische Front (Fatherland Front) to do precisely the opposite; in addition, from 1936 on there was increased economic and political pressure from Hitler's Germany. The Ständestaat dictatorship chose a compromise: on a lower level, antisemitism was condoned and partially promoted, and on a higher level it was rejected. The latter policy included the prohibition of large-scale antisemitic rioting—at the universities, on the Ringstraße, at important championship matches; in short, all those incidents that would have led to headlines in the foreign media were to be prevented.[40]

Karl Haber, president of Hakoah for many years, described the situation at the time of the authoritarian Ständestaat (1934–38) as follows:

> It would be wrong to believe that the Vienna sports scene only consisted of antisemites [at that time]. There were clubs with which we had good relations . . . and in most types of sport the players themselves certainly acted fairly. With the individual sports there were hardly any clashes. . . . There was violence with the team sports,

though. From the onset the playing was tougher, and whereas at a normal match someone might have shouted, "Watch it, I'll get you" following a foul, at one of our matches what they shouted was "Jewish pig," of course. But we didn't put up with any of it. When anyone shouted something antisemitic, we yelled back "Nazi bastard" or "filthy Nazi"—for us, an antisemite was a Nazi. And we had a kind of solidarity protection service for dangerous situations, in which the wrestlers were particularly active.[41]

Nevertheless, in the years 1934–38 as well, the aggressive antisemitism should not be underestimated; it was less spontaneous, and to an increasing extent carried out by National Socialist activists. "We were used to anti-semitic comments—they came at us all the time, and we hardly even registered them any more. But it was above all Nazis that carried out targeted attacks," according to Norbert Lopper, a Hakoah and Austria player and official born in 1919: "Sometimes masses of people got swept up in it all too, though, like at the Strassenbahn-Hakoah match; that was frightening—there I really did get scared somehow. They really got stuck in to us Jews there." Lopper continues: "To give an example, in 1936, I was a plumber's apprentice, and my boss tried to push me off the ladder I was standing on. He was an antisemite. I threw a hammer at him then, and handed in my notice. But all the same, I never really felt I was in danger, never thought that anything would happen to us."[42] The aggressive potential inherent in the National Socialists' activities at soccer matches was considerable at any rate. On March 25, 1935, they planned to totally disrupt the international match between Austria and Italy. The Austrian state police had reports from informers that the illegal Austrian SA had received ten thousand tickets from Berlin, in order to massively boo and heckle the Italian team and the government members who would be present in the stadium. The informers reported that the plan was to let down a huge swastika flag on balloons during the game. Beer glasses and other objects were to be thrown, and ten thousand people would chant "Heil Hitler," in order to force the match to be stopped, to bring discredit to the Austrian regime, and to damage relations with Italy.[43] Three radical party members were said to have the chance to get onto the VIP rostrum, where they were going to let off "specially con-structed firecrackers containing swastikas." Ultimately—according to the informer—"the National Socialists plan to cause a tumult at matches where Jewish teams are playing." The police used all the possible means at their disposal to prevent the international match from turning into a political demonstration. The state police records only contain a few mentions of a planned attack on a Jewish team, Makkabi Brünn (Brno), who were playing in Vienna in 1935, and their aim to prevent it from being carried out.[44]

Reactions from the Jewish Side

The Jewish self-help that has already been mentioned was certainly very widespread. Already in the 1919/1920 season, when the aim was to be promoted to the top league, the *Neues Sportblatt* reported about an "amassed crowd of Hakoah supporters who had turned out in full," around eight thousand people. After the decisive match, which got Hakoah promoted, there were riots among the spectators for the first time at a Hakoah game: "When the final whistle blew, the furious Germania players started to attack the Hakoah team. . . . On the way to the changing rooms the pugnacious players from Schwechat were then given their just deserts by the [Hakoah] supporters."[45] Throughout the 1920s there is a whole string of examples of crowd fighting in which the Jewish fans themselves played no small part. In 1925, after Hakoah Vienna won the championships in water polo, hockey, and soccer, undoubtedly the most popular sport of the day, the Maccabi-Verband (Maccabee Club) chose the following words, taking stock of the situation at the time: "The much-ridiculed Jewish youths have now become young Jews after all. The world organization of Jewish gymnasts and athletes is not an empty concept; it is a total reality. Jewish dignity and Jewish self-confidence are indeed in good hands now; the ludicrous caricature of the bandy-legged, timid, contemptible Jew is already an anachronism, since countless Jewish victories have borne witness to the superb condition of the powerful Jewish physique."[46]

The fact is that from the 1920s, Jewish youths, but also young Jewish men (and sometimes women as well) no longer reacted purely defensively or merely verbally to gross expressions of antisemitism; this applied to both the universities and the sports fields, and there are dozens of examples attesting to this. In *Die Stimme*, for instance, reporting on the match between Vienna and Hakoah: "Machu [Vienna] was sent off in the 60th minute for a whole string of provocative fouls. Some of the Hakoah fans then lost control and started bombarding the Vienna players with bottles. The consequence was that the police had to intervene and there were tussles in the crowd."[47] At a match between Hakoah and Floridsdorfer AC there was rioting, too: one Floridsdorfer player was seriously injured and the blue-white (Hakoah) fans launched an attack; in the end the police intervened here as well.[48]

The behavior of the Hakoah fans eventually became a topic of discussion for the sports press—discussed partly in an openly antisemitic fashion in certain papers, but there was also more objective commentary, too. The center-left newspaper *Der Tag* for example, in an article about the match between Hakoah and WAC (Wiener Athletiksport Club) in December 1926, made the following comment:

> We hope that we stand above suspicion of being spiteful or unobjective when we describe the quite inexplicable attitude of one group of spectators as anti-sport through and through. All credit to the enthusiasm of the Hakoah supporters, for it shows that there is a deep bond between them and their team. But fanaticism is dangerous. The Hakoah team surely needs the enthusiasm of its supporters to accompany it along its often thorny path; fanaticism, however, is only detrimental to their efforts. . . . Those Hakoah supporters that belong to the group of front-line fighters should bear this in mind.[49]

Reporting on the match between Slovan and Hakoah, the *Sport-Tagblatt* writes of the "terrorizing crowd"—and it is the Hakoah supporters who are being referred to here.[50] The articles led to ripostes in the Hakoah club magazine; one typical statement ran as follows:

> The Hakoah supporters have formed a deep bond with the team; they sense the healthy spirit and should not let themselves be shaken by the polemics in various newspapers, but should rather back the team in its hard struggles when it looks as if it needs a boost. This heroically fighting team needs to feel the support, not only at away matches, as has been the case up to now, but also at home. . . . Anyone who knows the Jewish mentality knows that our supporters can spur the players on without sinking to the level of the mob that has terrorized us, unhindered, in countless matches. . . . Woe betide us, however, when just once we stray beyond the bounds of sporting decency! Then virtually the whole of the sports press falls on us like a pack of wolves. . . . Hakoah fans, you do have the right to protest when the referee is obviously ruling against us. Our players are not fair game—you must protect them![51]

In the '20s and '30s there was a rising generation of young male Jews who did not shy away from physical confrontations and had a well-developed sense of "Jewish dignity." Thus Richard Kadmon, for example, a successful

Hakoah wrestler, recalls a group of Viennese Jews of both sexes going for a Sunday walk at the Franz Josefs-Kai in Vienna. This brought antisemites onto the scene, who arranged an "antisemites' stroll" in order to attack the Jewish walkers. But then wrestlers from the Hakoah team intervened, and "a few slaps and thumps were enough to send the Teutonic heroes scurrying away." [52] Walter Frankl, a successful track and field athlete, records something similar: "In Hakoah we were one big family. When the organized antisemitic demonstrations started in Vienna, we from Hakoah formed 'Haganah groups' [*defense units*], which were ready at all times to protect the Leopoldstadt Jewish quarter with all their might." [53]

In the face of such rampant antisemitism, the reactions of young athletic Jews were highly emotional at times, as has already been shown in Arthur Köstler's memoirs, for example, and can also be seen in the recollections of individuals who were involved. Erich Feuer, for instance, born in 1917, track and field athlete and member of the Tiberias student fraternity, reinforces this: "We wouldn't stand anything, my fraternity brothers and I. I was also with the Haganah, and whenever anyone was pestered or there was any trouble, we reacted straight away. We didn't put up with any nonsense whatsoever." [54] And Hans Selinko, born in 1919, recalls: "We were standing on the Schwedenbrücke after swimming training. All at once, two or three lads approached us. One of them said 'Jewish pig' and gave me a shove. Suddenly, the other started hitting me too; I was dumbfounded. Then we had a vicious fight—I didn't put up with it. Then he even started kicking me, and I just saw red. . . . And then, well, I just grabbed one of them and threw him off the bridge into the Danube Canal. Yes, I threw him in. The other antisemite, he was petrified with fright, and then he just ran away as fast as he could." [55]

The reaction of active athletes to the growing antisemitism stood in stark contrast to the official reaction of Jewish sports clubs, especially of the most important one, Hakoah. In the years before the National Socialist takeover, the clubs had taken an unequivocally defensive line. After Hitler seized power in Germany, all the workers' sports organizations were disbanded. No Jew was allowed to belong to a German sports club. For the sake of demonstrating a little tolerance in the eyes of the rest of the world, however, Jewish sports and gymnastics clubs were allowed to continue to exist. Abroad, including in Austria, the response was a kind of "policy of appeasement" in sports. Hakoah athletes took part in the 1936 Olympic Games in Berlin—a majority of club officials had voted in favor of participating; this led to an intra-Jewish controversy with the Austrian Maccabi-Verband, which had called for a boycott. Some young women swimmers did in fact decide not to participate and left Hakoah.[56] As late as in 1937 Austrian Jewish sportsmen took part in competitions in Germany. In August 1937 soccer and hockey players from the Viennese clubs Hakoah and Hasmonea traveled to Berlin, Frankfurt, and Leipzig. Shortly before March 1938, many Jewish officials were still of the opinion that things under Hitler would not be as terrible as had been prophesied. [57] On March 12, 1938, German troops crossed the Austrian border and the Anschluss of Austria to the German Reich was proclaimed—with all the well-known consequences. In the area of sports the National Socialists began their purge immediately: Jewish sportsmen were barred from the ongoing championships; the executive board of the club Austria Vienna was removed from office, club president Emanuel "Michl" Schwarz was arrested as a Jew, and the club was put under a temporary management. The Jewish club Hakoah Vienna was disbanded and its assets confiscated; the results of the Jewish teams that had been playing in the championships were annulled. [58]

Antisemitism as a "Cultural Code"—Farewell to a Thesis?

According to the currently prevailing thesis of Shulamit Volkov, in the pre–World War I German-speaking world the term "Jew" also functioned as a synonym for a negative figure and as an anti-emancipatory metaphor. Antisemitism was used as a catchword, first and foremost symbolically and not translated into concrete, thought-out actions. [59] This function of antisemitism was also important for communication within specific groups, such as the German national (völkische) patriots as well as parts of the Austrian "home-guards," and antisemites with Christian Social orientation. Cultural symbols, however, have a certain tenacity, and, according to Volkov, they therefore continue to circulate in a new social, political, and cultural context—in Volkov's discussion, that of the Weimar Republic. "For millions of Germans and for the majority of the German Jews, 'antisemitism' remained a cultural code. They felt secure in the assumption—though it was no longer completely unchallenged—that they were dealing with a familiar bundle of opinions and attitudes."[60] In his standard work The German Jews, Moshe Zimmermann also believes that the level of violence cannot be regarded as a reliable indicator for the intensity of antisemitism in the Weimar Republic. [61] Albert Lichtblau adapts this thesis for Austria: "Until then [1938], antisemitic attitudes were regarded as socially and politically acceptable, as a 'cultural code.' Antisemitic stances broadly met with a positive response, which in the First Republic only occasionally led to antisemitic actions, however."[62]

In view of the crass antisemitism in the '20s and early '30s—in view of all the physical violence, the fighting, the injuries, on the Austrian sports fields and at and around the universities (and indeed attacks, even murders, unconnected with sports), the question arises as to whether the thesis that interprets the antisemitism of the time as a "cultural code" should not be dispensed with. Punches in the face, bloody noses, kicking, dueling with sabers, brass knuckles, steel bars—all this does not make up some vague "cultural code"; rather, they are very concrete phenomena. In the words of then-ninety-one-year-old Marcel Prawy, for many years active in the Austrian cultural scene as an opera expert and probably one of the last witnesses who was directly involved: "As Jewish students we were beaten up at the university, and it was Austrians who did it. The police stood outside, under the command of the future chancellor, Schober, who had ordered them not to intervene. Thus they stood by and watched us being bloodily beaten." Prawy is regarded as a conciliatory Viennese Jew, who does not actually attach much importance to the perception of antisemitism. Yet for the period between the wars he speaks in no uncertain terms of the "everyday atrocities" at the university.[63]

The aggressive, physical nature of antisemitism in Austria definitely went beyond the purely mental forms of hatred toward Jews. From 1919 to 1932 Austria, and in particular Vienna, which must be seen as the focal point of the phenomenon, was the scene of very many violent acts between Jews and non-Jews. From 1933 until annexation in March 1938 these occurred less frequently, but on a more private or semipublic level they still occurred nevertheless. How, then, can one explain this aggressive, physical antisemitism, which has been described with numerous examples and whose nature and extent the author believes represents a clear break to what preceded it in the days of the Empire? First, as the consequence of an anomaly: In the period between the wars, Austria was basically in a permanent state of crisis. The consequences of disintegration after the fall of the Habsburg Empire, which Austria had yet to come to terms with, and the related difficulty of adapting to the new situation—a problematic economic policy and inhibiting sociopsychological factors triggered by the sudden transformation from a great empire to a small state—together with unfavorable global economic conditions, all led ultimately to the diminution of the national product for whole chunks of the period from 1919 to 1937. Political instability, corruption and a one-sided legal system further compounded the situation.

Second, this development in society led to a certain decivilizing in general, not only with regard to the treatment of Jews, and to an increase in the readiness to use political (and not only political) violence.[64] Both the spontaneous and the organized violence on the sports fields, in the swimming pools, or on the university ramps would seem to fit into this category. On the one hand, this was a general phenomenon. Violent clashes in general occurred frequently during soccer matches in Austria in the interwar period.[65] On the other hand, it was a process of specific importance, for in this period physical attacks on Jews had increased considerably in comparison to the empire days. In this context, Albert Lichtblau refers to the "brutalization" of antisemitism.[66]

Third, the new readiness to use violence against Jews went hand in hand with a likewise comparatively new phenomenon: the readiness of Jews to react and indeed to be proactive. With the ideological advance of Zionist attitudes and the socialization of young Jews in the Austrian crisis-society of the interwar period, the signs of Jewish resistance to antisemitic attacks increased; this, or at least its beginnings, could be seen on a massive scale on the soccer pitches and in the universities. In order to uphold the "cultural code" in its ideal form, we would have to presume that Jews' basic position was a defensive one, that is, Jews would not question or attack this specific antisemitic practice. Yet in addition to this came the socialization of the younger Jewish generation, growing up in the harder social climate of the 1920s, and even more so in the '30s. Even internal Jewish conflicts, whether related to sports or to politics, were sometimes dealt with physically.[67]

Finally, the young people growing up with Zionist attitudes, indeed the whole following of the Hakoah sports club with all its different sections, adhered to the ideal of the physically strong and self-confident Jew. In the society of the Austrian Jews, characterized by its Zionism, this was emphasized constantly. Aggressive antisemitism was not played down at all in any of the Zionist magazines and newspapers, at least until 1933, and was interpreted as a real, concrete danger. Indeed, aggressive, violent antisemitism was sometimes seen as an argument to bring young people and adults into the Zionist camp, and to justify the demand for a greater degree of resistance and Jewish self-confidence.

Hakoah spectators. Everybody wanted to see matches against Hakoah in the mid-1920s.
The Jewish club won the Austrian championship in 1925. Courtesy of Walter Beer.

A considerable proportion of the older generation of the time, however, held the view that the more aggressive climate toward Jews could be tempered by means of adaptation and by making concessions. These people did not go to such places as stadiums and pools, and therefore they usually did not experience physical attacks first-hand and thus were not really fully aware of this type of Austrian antisemitism in its concrete form. In this context, Leon Botstein has spoken of the "passive depoliticizing of the Jewish fellow-citizens in Austria"; the state-led suppression of the overt, confrontational type of antisemitism of the illegal National Socialists in Austria from 1933 was surely a major factor behind this attitude.[68] Thus the aggressive, physical antisemitism hardly registered with one part of the Jewish population; the other part, especially the younger generation, felt such aggressive antisemitism very acutely. Physical confrontations were often put down to a certain degree of "sporting spirit," however, wishful thinking though this was. At the same time, among the young Zionists the assumption took hold that this aggressive antisemitism could be countered both by the individual and by means of Jewish defense organizations.[69] This was not the case, as was to be proved in March 1938, when masses of old men were forced to do gymnastic exercises and old women to scrub the streets; the pogrom-like riots, which repeatedly centered on "the body" and "corporeality," were a feature that at the time were observed in the German Reich with amazement. In the first weeks of the new regime, more than eighteen thousand Jewish men were arrested and sent to concentration camps or held in police cells. The taboo of not physically attacking Jews, which in the main was upheld during the time of the empire, had, however, already started to crumble fast in the years following the end of the First World War.[70]

Translated from the German by Nicholas Jacob-Flynn

Notes

1. Ernst Vogel, *Fußballdämmerung* (Brünn, 1924), p. 90.
2. *Wiener Morgenzeitung*, 8 November 1923, p. 5.
3. *Prager Presse*, 12 November 1923, p. 7.
4. *Sport-Tagblatt*, 27 November 1923, p. 9.
5. *Wiener Morgenzeitung*, 23 November 1923, p. 10.
6. *Wiener Morgenzeitung*, 18 November 1923, p. 9.
7. *Wiener Morgenzeitung*, 18 November 1923, p. 9.
8. Cf. Vogel, *Fußballdämmerung*, pp. 92–93.
9. Cf. Roman Horak and Wolfgang Maderthaner, *Mehr als ein Spiel: Fußball und populäre Kulturen im Wien der Moderne* (Vienna, 1997), pp. 113–40.
10. Cf. *Jüdischer Sport* (Official Publication of the Makkabi-Weltverband and the Jüdische Turn- und Sportverband), 9 July 1925, p. 1.
11. John Bunzl, ed., *Hoppauf Hakoah: Jüdischer Sport in Österreich, Von den Anfängen bis zur Gegenwart* (Vienna, 1987), p. 69; cf. also Arthur Baar, *Fußballgeschichten—Ernstes und Heiteres: Hakoah, Wien* (Tel Aviv, 1974), pp. 80–87.
12. Cf. Roman Horak, "Fußballkultur in Wien," SWS-*Rundschau* 30 (1990), pp. 371–376, 372–373.
13. *Hakoah* (official publication of the Hakoah sports club), 5 August 1926, p. 5; *Hakoah*, 18 September 1925, p. 77.
14. On soccer clubs in interwar Austria, cf. Michael John, "Sports in Austrian Society 1890s-1930s: The Example of Viennese Football," in *Urban Space and Identity*, Central European University, Budapest, History Department, Working Paper Series 3 (Budapest, 1995), p. 140.
15. Karl Geyer, quoted in Michael John and Albert Lichtblau, eds., *Schmelztiegel Wien, einst und jetzt: Geschichte und Gegenwart der Zuwanderung nach Wien: Aufsätze, Quellen, Kommentare* (Vienna, 1993), p. 437.

16. *Illustriertes Sportblatt*, 8 October 1928, p. 3.

17. The hopes of anyone who expected that winning the championships would cause a lasting weakening of the antisemitism were disappointed, however. Not immediately, it is true, but the moment it became clear that Hakoah was struggling against relegation, the rioting and violent confrontations started again.

18. *Mitteilungen für die jüdische Bevölkerung der Alpenländer*, 13 February 1931, p. 2.

19. Cf. *Mitteilungen für die jüdische Bevölkerung der Alpenländer*, 14 August 1931, p. 2; 28 August 1931, p. 2.

20. Arthur Baar, *50 Jahre Hakoah 1909–1959* (Tel Aviv, 1959), pp. 111–12.

21. *Linzer Tagblatt*, 4 August 1938, p. 6.

22. *Die Neue Freie Presse*, 20 June 1932, p. 11.

23. *Die Stimme*, 23 June 1932, p. 8.

24. *Deutschösterreichische Tages-Zeitung*, 21 June 1932, p. 7.

25. *Neue Freie Presse*, 11 July 1932, p. 11.

26. *Hakoah*, 2 July 1926, p. 7.

27. *Jüdischer Sport*, 9 July 1925, p. 4; *Hakoah*, 2 July 1926, p. 7.

28. Cf. Harald Seewann, " 'Mit Wort und Wehr für Judas Ehr!' Die jüdischen Verbindungen in der Monarchie," in *Juden und Deutsche: Vergangenheit und Zukunft*, Walter Simon et al., eds. (Graz, 1994), pp. 150–57.

29. Arthur Köstler, *Pfeil ins Blaue: Bericht eines Lebens 1905–1931* (Vienna, 1953), pp. 100–101.

30. Köstler, *Pfeil ins Blaue*, p. 102.

31. Österreichisches Staatsarchiv (hereafter ÖStA), Bundeskanzleramt (hereafter BKA), Sgn. 22 in genere, 1923: Aktenzahl 60.146 bis 61.999–29.

32. *Reichspost*, 20 November 1923, p. 2.

33. ÖStA, BKA, Sgn. 22 in genere, 1929: Aktenzahl 132.645 bis 132.648–29.

34. *Die Stimme*, 3 July 1931, pp. 1–2, 5, 7.

35. *Der jüdische Arbeiter*, 4 December 1931, p. 1.

36. *Die Stimme*, 3 July 1931, pp. 7–8.

37. Cf. Bruce Pauley, *Eine Geschichte des österreichischen Antisemitismus: Von der Ausgrenzung zur Auslöschung* (Vienna, 1993), p. 176.

38. A. Kaltschmied, "Verjudung," *Bundesturnzeitung*, 21 March 1934, p. 125.

39. Cf. Ulrike Maria Gschwandtner, "Jüdischer Sport in einer antisemitischen Umwelt: Kontinuitäten antisemitischer Verhaltensmuster im österreichischen Sport des 20. Jahrhunderts exemplarisch behandelt am Beispiel des jüdischen Sportklubs 'Hakoah,' " MA Thesis, University of Salzburg, 1989, p. 16.

40. Cf. Pauley, *Eine Geschichte*, pp. 326–33.

41. Karl Haber, "Antisemiten kann man nichts beweisen," in *Hakoah—Ein jüdischer Sportverein in Wien 1909–1995*, Jüdisches Museum der Stadt Wien, ed. (Vienna, 1995), pp. 102–8.

42. Norbert Lopper, born 1919, quoted in Michael John, " 'Körperlich ebenbürtig': Juden im österreichischen Fussballsport," in *Davidstern und Lederball: Die Geschichte der Juden im deutschen und internationalen Fußball*, Dietrich Schultze-Marmeling, ed. (Göttingen, 2003), p. 249.

43. Cf. in particular Diego Cante, "Propaganda und Fussball. Sport und Politik in den Begegnungen zwischen den italienischen 'Azzurri' und den 'Weißen' aus Wien in der Zwischenkriegszeit," *Zeitgeschichte*, 25 (1999), p. 224.

44. Cf. ÖStA, BKA, Sgn. 22 in genere, Inneres, Zl. 318.263-35/22/Wien, G.D. 1–2.; Zl. 321.134-35/22/Wien, G.D. 1–2; Bericht der Bpoldion Wien vom 22. März 1935, contained in Bericht der Generaldirektion für die öffentliche Sicherheit an das BKA vom 27. März; Zl. 321.134-35/22/Wien, G.D. 1–2; Bericht des Leiters des Informationsdienstes im Generalsekretariat der V. F. an das BKA, Büro des Staatssekretärs of 21 March.

45. Baar, 50 Jahre Hakoah, p. 60.

46. Jüdischer Sport, 11 June 1925, p. 1.

47. Die Stimme, 29 September 1932, p. 12.

48. Cf. Illustriertes Sportblatt, 2 January 1926, p. 2.

49. Der Tag, 15 December 1926, p. 7.

50. Sport-Tagblatt, 17 November 1926, p. 3.

51. Hakoah, 19 November 1926, p. 5.

52. Cf. Bunzl, Hoppauf Hakoah, p. 60.

53. Walter Frankl, "Leichtathletik und Vereinspatriotismus," in: Bunzl, Hoppauf Hakoah, p. 87.

54. Eric Feuer, born in 1917, quoted in Michael John, "Aggressiver Antisemitismus im österreichischen Sportgeschehen der Zwischenkriegszeit. Manifestationen und Reaktionen anhand ausgewählter Beispiele," Zeitgeschichte 25, no. 3 (1999), pp. 214–15.

55. Hans Selinko, born in 1919, quoted in John, "Aggressiver Antisemitismus," p. 215.

56. Gschwandtner, Jüdischer Sport, p. 32.

57. Cf. Paul Nittnaus and Michael Zink, Sport ist unser Leben. 100 Jahre Arbeitersport in Österreich (Vienna, 1992), p. 76.

58. Cf. Bunzl, Hoppauf Hakoah, pp. 127–37.

59. Shulamit Volkov, "Antisemitismus als kultureller Code," in Shulamit Volkov, Jüdisches Leben und Antisemitismus im 19. und 20. Jahrhundert (Munich, 1991), pp. 13–36.

60. Volkov, "Antisemitismus als kultureller Code," p. 36.

61. Moshe Zimmermann, Die deutschen Juden 1914–1945 (Munich, 1997), p. 42.

62. Albert Lichtblau, "Antisemitismus-Rahmenbedingungen und Wirkungen auf das Zusammenleben von Juden und Nichtjuden," in Handbuch des politischen Systems Österreichs: Erste Republik 1918–1933, Emmerich Talos et al., eds. (Vienna, 1995), p. 470.

63. Marcel Prawy, "Ein Land wie eine Operette," in NEWS. Österreichs größtes Nachrichtenmagazin, no. 45 (7 November 2002), p. 182. Marcel Prawy, born in 1911, died in 2003 at the age of ninety-two.

64. Anton Pelinka, Zur österreichischen Identität: Zwischen deutscher Vereinigung und Mitteleuropa (Vienna, 1991); Susanne Breuss, Karin Liebhart, and Andreas Pribersky, Inszenierungen: Stichwörter zu Österreich (Vienna, 1995), pp. 19–29; cf. also Gerhard Botz, Krisenzonen einer Demokratie: Gewalt, Streik und Konfliktunterdrückung in Österreich seit 1918 (Frankfurt and New York, 1987), pp. 13–118.

65. Horak and Maderthaner, Mehr als ein Spiel, pp. 47–56.

66. Lichtblau, Antisemitismus, p. 456.

67. For examples, Bunzl, Hoppauf Hakoah, p. 95 (on a water polo match Hagibor Prag versus Hakoah Vienna); Pauley, Eine Geschichte, pp. 273–84 (chapter titled "Ein geteiltes Haus: Innerjüdische Politik").

68. Leon Botstein, Judentum und Modernität: Essays zur Rolle der Juden in der deutschen und österreichischen Kultur 1848–1938 (Vienna, 1991), p. 209.

69. Cf. *Drei Jahre Bund jüdischer Frontsoldaten* (Vienna, n.d.).
70. It is not only for Austria that this can be shown empirically, however, but also for parts of Germany. See Dirk Walter, *Antisemitische Kriminalität und Gewalt: Judenfeindschaft in der Weimarer Republik* (Bonn, 1999), and Cornelia Hecht, *Deutsche Juden und Antisemitismus in der Weimarer Republik* (Bonn, 2003).

9. Jews, Antisemitism, and Sports in Britain, 1900–1939

Tony Collins

B RITAIN IS THE birthplace of modern sports. Soccer, rugby, cricket, modern athletics, and many other sports can trace their genesis back to English public schools in the first half of the nineteenth century. But, just as important as the codification and organization of individual sports, these schools also helped to define the moral attributes of sport. The concepts of sportsmanship, fair play, and athleticism were defined and propagated by them. At the same time, in contrast to this ideal of sporting manhood, the traditional British stereotype of the Jew as physically weak, effete, and intellectual was also promulgated by many of the same proponents of the virtues of sports. Antisemitism—both in the definition of the Jew as an "other" against which British sport could define itself and in the exclusion or restriction of Jewish participation in sports—is an important if as yet largely unacknowledged aspect of the history of sports of Britain. This is a frustrating omission. While the study of Jewish sports history has been something of a blossoming field in continental Europe and North America over the past few years, almost no work has been done on the subject in Britain. Indeed, it may well be the case that the absence of work on the subject is the result of the continuing strength of this stereotype, which has led to the widespread but mistaken belief that there have been few, if any, "sporting Jews" in Britain.

Although antisemitism in nineteenth-century Britain was generally not as violent as in Eastern Europe or as politically flammable as in France or Germany, it was nevertheless deeply rooted. Jews were only granted full political emancipation, the legal right to be elected to local and national government, in 1858. At a cultural level, one only has to think of literary characters such as Shakespeare's Shylock and Charles Dickens's Fagin to see the ubiquity of the stereotype of the scheming, money-grabbing Jew in British culture.

Given the centrality of the image of the athletic body to nineteenth-century British sports, it is very important to note that the traditional stereotype was very firmly based on the supposed physical characteristics of Jews. At best they were seen as exotic, unmasculine, and alien. Thus, for example,

P. J. MacDonell worried that Benjamin Disraeli was "debauching" traditional English masculinity. At worst, they were portrayed, like Fagin, as being morally and physically ugly. To give just two of many examples: Lord Robert Cecil remarked on meeting Chaim Weizmann that he had a "repulsive body"; Joseph Chamberlain told the Italian Foreign Minister that the Jews were "all physical cowards."[1]

Such a view of the Jews was in stark contrast to the way in which the British elite saw themselves, especially in the latter half of the nineteenth century. Flowing out from the public schools, "Muscular Christianity" sought to create a new Anglo-Saxon ideal of the athletic male body, in which sports was a source of moral education for an enlarged Victorian social elite. The cult of games was based upon a form of British cultural nationalism that stressed physical virility and a moral code of honor based on "sportsmanship." In this context it is noteworthy that Thomas Arnold, the headmaster of Rugby School from 1828 to 1842 and the spiritual forefather of Muscular Christianity, was vigorously opposed to Jewish emancipation.[2]

Alongside this flowering of Muscular Christianity, from the early 1880s tens of thousands of Jewish immigrants fled Eastern Europe and settled in Britain. In 1882 the Jewish population of Britain was around 60,000. By 1914 it had grown to about 250,000, creating a sizeable Jewish working class, especially in the East End of London. Although Jews from Eastern Europe had begun to settle in Britain from the 1850s, the immediate cause of the successive waves of immigration from the 1880s was the widespread antisemitic pogroms throughout the Russian Empire following the assassination of Czar Alexander II in 1882.[3]

This influx was not necessarily welcomed by the leading sections of Anglo-Jewry. There were widespread fears that their position in British society would be undermined and antisemitism inflamed. Indeed, some called for immigration controls to restrict the flow. However, the main response was the creation of a huge number of working-men's clubs, youth clubs, schools, sporting organizations, and charitable movements. The goals of these organizations were to teach the new immigrants English values and cultural norms. Sports and the ideals of "sportsmanship"—the most English of value systems—were seen as vital components of this crusade to Anglicize the newcomers. In contrast to the idea of "Muscular Judaism," which Max Nordau had called for at the Second Zionist Congress in 1898 in order to demonstrate the vitality of the Jewish race, Anglo-Jewry wholeheartedly embraced the tenets of Muscular Christianity as a path toward assimilation.

The social and athletic organizations that were set up by Jews in Britain from the 1880s onwards were based on emphasizing the Britishness of British Jewry, not its Jewishness. Their goal was to create what was termed at the time "Englishmen of the Mosaic persuasion." In this they were following a pattern that had already been established by members of the elite of Anglo-Jewry, such as Sir Ernest Cassel and Baron Maurice de Hirsch, who as part of the process of gaining social acceptance among the upper echelons of British society had become racehorse owners and patrons of "the sports of kings."

An early example of the use of sports as part of the "acculturation" of immigrant and lower-class Jews was the Jewish Working Men's Club and Institute, which was founded in London in 1874. Its adoption of athletics dovetailed almost exactly with the first waves of Jewish immigration. It introduced athletics and drill in the 1880s, and cycling, soccer, and cricket by 1900. The club also started drill for women in 1894, which was followed by athletics in the early 1900s. This fascination for English sports was not confined to those who sought acculturation into British society; Theodor Herzl also hoped that all boys in the future Jewish state would learn to play cricket.[4]

As well as working men's clubs, scores of youth clubs were established in the 1880s and 1890s, especially in the East End, which by 1914 was probably home to about half of Britain's Jewish population. Clubs such as Stepney Jewish Lads Club, Whitechapel's Brady Street Lads Club, and the West Central Jewish Working Lads Club all placed great emphasis on sports, the latter being very successful in soccer. Indeed, such was the interest in, and importance attached to, sports of all types, that in 1899 the Jewish Athletic Association (which later changed its name to the Association of Jewish Youth) was founded in order to bring together and coordinate the sporting activities of Jewish youth clubs and schools. In developing such activities, these organizations to some extent anticipated the growing concern in wider British society about the "physical degeneration" of the male population. The failure to vanquish easily the Afrikaners in the Boer War, combined with disquiet about the unhealthy reality of urban, industrial working-class life, led to much discussion about the need to improve the physical fitness of British men and youths. The 1904 report of the Inter-Departmental Committee on Physical Deterioration highlighted the poor health of many recruits to the British army and recommended the integration of sports and physical education into the curriculum of state schools.

Sports therefore became a crucial aspect of the daily life of schools that had been set up by the Anglo-Jewish middle-classes, such as the Jews' Free School in London and Manchester Jews' School. They heavily promoted British sports and sought to emulate the ideology of British public and grammar schools. Indeed, it was possibly in these schools, which had been set up for the children of working-class Jewish immigrants, that the pressure to Anglicize was most intense. Most, if not all, of these schools banned the speaking of Yiddish by children. Some even forced Jewish children to adopt Anglicized names.[5]

One of the most important organizations set up at this time was the Jewish Lads' Brigade (JLB). Founded in 1895, it was explicitly based on the examples of the Boys' Brigade and Church Lads' Brigade, which had been founded by Anglicans seeking to bring Christian values to working-class youths in the cities. Uniforms, drill, and a quasi-military structure were an essential part of the trappings of these organizations and the JLB accepted this wholeheartedly. The middle-class Anglo-Jewish founders of the JLB saw its role as one of turning the immigrant Jewish youth into what they termed a "good Jew and a good Englishman." The JLB organized swimming, soccer, cricket, and athletics events as a means of bringing the English values of sportsmanship, fair play, and teamwork to its members.[6] There was, however, one marked contrast between the JLB and the Boys' Brigade and Church Lads' Brigade: Both of these organizations laid great stress on religious instruction. But the JLB consciously did not see itself as a vehicle of religion. There was no religious instruction, and contacts with synagogues were kept to a minimum. The tension inherent in its slogan of "a good Jew and a good Englishman" occasionally meant that the JLB was keener to emphasize its Englishness over its Jewishness. A highly illustrative example of this occurred in 1936 when, disturbed by their own boxing teams' domination of the Prince of Wales youth boxing tournament, the brigade temporarily withdrew from the competition because it feared its success would encourage antisemitism: "There was a danger in the Jewish clubs always being so successful, so much so that jealousy was perhaps created and non-Jewish clubs would not enter the competitions," explained the commanding officer of the Manchester JLB.[7]

Examples such as these underscore the fact that Jewish participation in sports at this time was far wider than traditional stereotypes allow. Given the paucity of the currently available quantitative evidence we can say very little that is definitive about the extent to which Jews played or watched sports.

There is a common, but largely mistaken, explanation for the apparent lack of participation in sports such as soccer, rugby, and cricket, which argues that the observance of the Sabbath clashed with sports that were played on Saturday afternoons, many of which were team sports.[8]

There are a number of problems with this assumption. First and foremost, a large proportion of the Jewish population was not especially observant in religious matters, a fact that caused some concern among the more orthodox members of the community. In the 1930s, Selig Brodetsky, the noted mathematician who was to become the first Zionist president of the Board of Deputies of British Jews, who lived in Leeds, complained that more Jews were interested in going to Headingley Stadium in the city to watch rugby league or cricket on a Saturday than in going to the synagogue. It is also the case that in the interwar years Southern Railways printed its timetables to Epsom station in both English and Yiddish because horse-racing was so popular with London Jews. It was during this period that Tottenham Hotspur soccer club became known for having significant Jewish support.[9] Even going back to the 1890s, significant numbers of Jews in Leeds went to watch rugby matches on Saturdays, so much so that the local team they supported, Leeds Parish Church, became known in the area by the antisemitic epithet of "the sheenies."[10]

Certainly by the 1920s there is widespread evidence that many Jews were not only watching but also playing sports on Saturdays. At the elite level, the professional Broughton Rangers rugby league club, based in the heart of Manchester's Jewish community, had a number of Jewish players, such as Lester Samuels and Reuben Gleskie, who played as amateurs so that they could compete on a Saturday afternoon with a clear conscience. A soccer team from Grove House, a Manchester Jewish youth organization, won the Manchester Combination Cup in the 1930s. Other branches of the JLB also played sports on Saturdays in the 1920s. Rosalyn Livshin's interviews with Jews who grew up in Manchester in the interwar years show that sneaking out behind the backs of observant parents to play sports on Saturdays was common among young Jewish youths of the time.[11]

Such was the appeal of sports to young Jews that many Jewish political groups used sporting activities as a means of recruitment. In 1934 an organizer of the British Young Zionist Clubs complained that most clubs did nothing but organize "dances, billiards and ping-pong championship contests, to the detriment of the supposed Zionist activities of the club." Young middle-class Jews were also highly active in school sports: one notable example being Arthur Gold, later to become a leading athletics administrator and chairman of the British Olympic Association, who won the Public Schools' Championship for the high jump in 1935.[12]

However, with the exception of boxers and Harold Abrahams, the thoroughly anglicized winner of the 100-meter gold medal at the 1924 Olympics, Jews were absent from the elite and professional levels of many sports. Antisemitism appears to have played an important role in blocking the participation of Jewish players at higher levels of sports—this was certainly the case in middle-class sports such as golf and tennis, where the exclusion of Jews from clubs was commonplace as early as the 1900s. Anyone looking at Golf Illustrated magazine, the sport's leading journal, from the pre–First World War period will be shocked at the casual virulence of the antisemitic cartoons that it published in its pages. Outright exclusion or the imposition of quotas on the number of Jews allowed to join golf clubs became commonplace; so much so that when the Nazis banned Jews from German golf clubs in 1937 the sports correspondent of Action, the newspaper of Oswald Mosley's British Union of Fascists (BUF), supported the ban but said that it would be unnecessary in Britain because "at many [golf] clubs the administration merely fails to elect them without giving reason."[13] Anecdotal evidence suggests that this informal exclusion still exists today. In response to this, Jews began to set up their own golf clubs, although none of these ever excluded Gentiles, and many also had Gentiles in leadership positions. The first of these clubs was the Moor Allerton club in Leeds, founded in 1920, followed by Whitefields in Manchester in 1921 and Potters Bar in North London in 1923. Another nine were founded in the main Jewish population centers following the Second World War.[14] A similar process took place in tennis, where the extent of exclusion seems to have been at least equal with that of golf, with explicitly Jewish tennis clubs being set up in London and Liverpool in the early 1930s.[15]

This may also have been the case with team sports. According to the Jewish Chronicle in 1935, there had only been four Jewish soccer players to have played the game professionally, despite the evident popularity of the sports at youth level. This was despite an attempt in the late 1920s to form an all-Jewish soccer team, the Judeans, to play professionally in the English Football League, which suggested that there was a sufficient number of Jewish players able to play at the top levels of the sport, although the plan did not come to fruition because of the problem of playing on Saturdays.[16] In cricket, only three Jewish players played first-class county cricket before

1939, and of around 1,400 clubs affiliated in 1939 with the Club Cricket Conference, based largely in the south of England, only one had an overtly Jewish name. A widespread, but apparently untrue, rumor that the Surrey and England batsman Percy Fender was Jewish was held by some to be the reason for his failure to become the captain of the England cricket team in the 1920s. [17] In 1930 the predominantly middle-class and amateur Rugby Football Union made a decision not to allow Jewish clubs to affiliate, ostensibly because such clubs would encourage others to play on Sundays, which was expressly forbidden by the RFU's rules. [18] The fact that Jewish sports clubs often played on a Sunday was one of a number of common rationales given for antisemitic exclusions. Some were based on the social mythology of antisemitism, such as the flat declaration of the Middlesbrough Motor Club that "Jews and Gentiles do not mix socially in numbers" or the claim in a history of golf clubs that Jews didn't drink enough alcohol to make their membership in a golf club profitable. The same historian of golf went on to voice the "concerns" of antisemitic golfers and suggest that the "flamboyant and luxurious tastes of Jewish golfers" would mean that "any Gentile club admitting Jews in large numbers would be likely to find life more difficult and more expensive." [19] More fundamentally, other objections were based on an attempt to defend the principles of Muscular Christianity and a corresponding belief that Jews were incapable of upholding the ideals of fair play. This appears to have been a widespread belief in certain sections of British society, and was articulated most strongly by Mosley's BUF:

> We look upon our games as something to enjoy, to keep bodily fit and treat them as just games. In the other [Jewish] way, they are treated partly as a business with "heads I win, tails you lose" motto. It does not matter how much time and money we Britishers spend in trying to make others adopt our mentality to athletics and games of any description, we cannot alter their racial characteristics. . . . They [the Jews] cannot understand the meaning of "a good loser. . . . Their mentality is exactly the same in business as in sports—to win at any price and to hell with the other fellow." [20]

One of the interesting features of this belief is that exactly the same prejudices were expressed toward working-class athletes when they began to enter soccer, rugby, cricket, and athletics in the 1880s and 1890s. This indicates that there was a considerable overlap between middle-class feelings of antisemitism and hostility toward the working classes. The Mosleyites presented the clearest, albeit ultimately genocidal, expression of the idea that traditional British middle-class sporting values were under threat from "outsiders." In 1936 this paranoia was given an added dimension when the BUF's *Action* began publishing a regular column entitled "The Sporting Jew" that railed against the "Jewish racket" that allegedly controlled boxing, wrestling, and horse-racing, and the "unsportsmanlike" behavior of Jewish supporters of Tottenham Hotspur soccer club for jeering at referees and being overly partisan toward their own side.

The success of Jewish boxers caused the Moselyites particular discomfort. Boxing was seen as a quintessentially English art that demonstrated the vigor and vitality of the Anglo-Saxon race—Mosley himself was a noted schoolboy boxer who was not above fighting with demonstrators at his public meetings, and the BUF organized its own boxing schools and contests— which meant that Jewish preeminence could only be explained as a conspiracy against British values of fair play. Boxing was the one major sport in which Jews achieved national and universally acknowledged prominence in the interwar years. It is difficult to overemphasize the importance of the sport in Jewish working-class culture. The combination of antisemitic prejudice and the practical problems faced by urban Jewish schools and youth clubs in obtaining fields and pitches on which to play sports meant that, in general, indoor sports were easier to organize and therefore more widely played by Jewish youngsters, thus establishing a tradition of success in boxing, chess, and table tennis (something that was to last until at least the 1970s, as is finely illustrated in Howard Jacobson's 1999 novel *The Mighty Walzer*).

By the end of the First World War it is clear that boxing had become established as the primary sport of choice for working-class Jewish youths. As early as 1889 Alf Bowman had won the British amateur heavyweight championship. But it was the 1920s and 1930s that were the Golden Age of Jewish boxing, best exemplified by the prominence of British Jewish boxers, such as world champions Kid Lewis and Kid Berg, numerous Jewish British champion fighters, and Jewish boxing promoters. Boxing competitions of all types dominated the sports coverage of the *Jewish Chronicle* during this period. At the youth level, Jewish success was even more conspicuous. Between 1921 and 1939, JLB boxing teams won the Prince of Wales Shield (the preeminent boxing tournament for British youth clubs) twelve times. In six of those tournaments, the final was contested between the London and Manchester JLBs.[21]

Why did boxing have such a strong hold in Jewish communities? Obviously a major reason was that it was easy for youth clubs and other groups to organize. But far more importantly, there was a long, preexisting tradition of Jewish success at the highest levels of boxing, stretching back to the 1780s and the emergence of the champion prizefighter Daniel Mendoza. [22] Mendoza has often been presented as the exception that proves the rule about the rarity of Jewish sporting champions. But in fact there were many others like him. As is attested to in Pierce Egan's classic work of the early nineteenth century, Boxiana, there were numerous Jewish boxers active between 1760 and 1820, notably Samuel Elias, and later his son, Aby Belasco, Barney Aaron, and Elisha Crabbe. A number of them also spanned the transition from bare-knuckle fighting to Marquis of Queensbury rules, including Young Barney Aaron, Asher Moss, and Israel Lazarus and his two sons. [23]

For Jews in Britain, therefore, boxing was historically a source of ethnic pride—similar to, but perhaps less pronounced than, West Indian pride in cricketing prowess as highlighted by C. L. R. James. [24] On a more practical level, it was also part of the day-to-day combat of antisemitism, both in terms of providing useful skills and bolstering self-confidence. Francis Place, the London radical and moral-force Chartist of the early 1800s, noted at the start of the nineteenth century that the success of Mendoza saw "the art [of boxing] soon spread among the young Jews and they became generally expert at it. The consequence was in a very few years seen and felt too. It was no longer safe to insult a Jew unless he was an old man and alone." [25] A similar attitude prevailed in the 1930s, as the Jewish Chronicle's boxing correspondent alluded in 1935: "The participation of Jews in the sports [boxing] has done more than cartloads of oratory and writing to combat any tendency toward antisemitism that might have been sown by unscrupulous and perverted devotees of the very un-English hate cult." [26] This boxing prowess stood in marked contrast to the traditional stereotype of English antisemitism and indicates that physicality and its expression was an important factor in Jewish working-class life, not least because it offered a valuable way in which to combat the threats of antisemites. At the end of the nineteenth century, this physicality was especially expressed through boxing, weightlifting, and, to a lesser extent, wrestling. As well as Alf Bowman's heavyweight championship victory in 1889, Edward Levy won the British amateur weightlifting championship two years later. It was also demonstrated by the career of Leeds rugby forward Edward Jacobson, who played representative rugby for Yorkshire twelve times in the 1890s and was presented with a specially commissioned medal to mark his sporting achievements by the local Jewish community in 1897.[27]

But perhaps another crucial reason for the popularity of boxing both for Jewish participants and proponents was that it was a sport that straddled both Jewishness and Britishness. Mendoza and the early Jewish boxers were prominent in the heroic age of British prize fighting, when bare-knuckle boxing became known both as the manly art and the noble art. The early-nineteenth-century sporting journalist Pierce Egan in particular helped to articulate the idea that boxing symbolized in sports the manly virtues that had led to Britain dominating large swathes of the globe: "Fair play is a Briton's motto: she would extend it to the extremities of the earth. No conse-quence what country, religion or colour. . . . Long may she be home for the exile—the defender of the oppressed—the best boxer—and arbiter of the world!" And, as Egan had recorded, Mendoza and his fellow Jewish pugilists were a key part of that heritage. As boxing's leading aristocratic patron, Lord Lonsdale, pointed out in 1935 in a message to young Jewish boxers, "a great many of the best boxers have been Jewish." For Jews seeking to use sports to assert their Britishness, boxing was practical proof that Jews were not outsiders but occupied a central place in British sporting culture.[28]

However, by the mid-1930s the axis of Jewish voluntary sporting activity had begun to shift away from its adoption of the nonreligious core of Mus-cular Christian values. The coming to power of Nazi, fascist, and other anti-semitic regimes in Europe, together with the rise of Mosley's fascist move-ment in Britain, had undermined the traditional Anglo-Jewish approach to antisemitism and assimilation, and provided space for the growth of a much more assertive attitude toward Jewish self-defense. In working-class areas, this led to a significant rise in Jewish involvement in the Communist Party (CP) and its activities, especially in the East End of London, where CP members were regularly elected as local councillors and which also elected Phil Piratin as one of only two communist members of parliament in 1945. Jewish CP members were prominent in the CP's sporting wing, the British Workers' Sports Federation (BWSF, which for a time had its headquarters in the predominantly Jewish area of Whitechapel in London's East End). Most notable were Jack Cohen, who in 1930 criticized the party for its lack of support for the BWSF's activities, and Benny Rothman, who in 1932 was jailed for four months for his leadership of the mass trespass on Kinder Scout in Derbyshire, when hundreds of walkers defied police to assert their right to walk on private land in the countryside.[29] As well as an increase in Jewish support for communism, the changing world and domestic political situation also helped the growth of Zionism. This was most exemplified by the newfound importance of the British Maccabi organization, which had only been founded in the mid-1920s. Although Maccabi steadfastly claimed to be nonpolitical, its close links with the Zionist movement and its belief in the unity of all Jews, not to mention the wide range of sporting and social activities it offered, gave it a wide appeal. By 1936 it was not only creating new local organizations but also gaining affiliations from other well-established Jewish sporting and social organizations, such as the Tottenham Jewish Tennis Club.

The difference between the old and the new attitudes toward Jewish identity and self-defense was encapsulated in two speeches made in November 1934. At the first, Lord Bearsted, a pillar of the Anglo-Jewish elite and a patron of the Stepney Jewish Lads Club for thirty years, told the club's annual prize-giving ceremony that "providing Jews were loyal citizens and exercised a beneficial influence, this would go far to refuting [antisemitism]. It was both futile and unwise to join in demonstrations and become involved in violence."[30] Although this may well have been aimed at youths attracted to the socialist and communist movements, its message seemed at odds with the increasingly dangerous world in which Jews now found themselves. In contrast, a week later, Sir Alfred Mond, a prominent Zionist and Maccabi supporter, told a meeting in London that "Maccabi would hold the Jewish people together, and would help instil into them a sense of discipline that was perhaps lacking at the moment. The three principles of the Maccabi were discipline, fortitude and faith."[31] For Jews seeking a commitment to protecting themselves and their Jewishness in an increasing climate of fear, this was at least a message of self-assertiveness.

In hindsight, although it was not at all clear at the time, the increasing importance of Maccabi and similar organizations marked the start of a transition in Jewish sports in Britain, in which the traditional sporting and social organizations of Anglo-Jewry either went into decline or moved away from the idea of being Muscular Christians in everything but religion. Following the end of World War II this emphasis came to dominate British Jewish sports organizations, helped by the impact of the establishment of Israel and the decline in the size of the British Jewish population, especially in the working class. Organizations like the JLB became bodies that sought to preserve Jewish culture and traditions, rather than bring British culture to Jews. From now on, the stress in Jewish sporting life, summed up in the Jewish Lads' Brigade slogan of being "a good Jew and a good Englishman," would most definitely be on being a good Jew.

What impact did this shift have on Jewish sporting activity in Britain? Undoubtedly participation in traditional working-class sports such as boxing and soccer declined. On the other hand, many Jews became prominent administrators, or, especially in the case of boxing, promoters and entrepreneurs. Membership of golf and tennis clubs increased. Most importantly, sports ceased to be seen as a vehicle for integrating Jews into British society, in large part either because Jews now saw themselves as a broadly accepted part of British society, albeit with the disadvantage of having to put up with greater or lesser levels of informal antisemitism, or because they no longer placed any importance on their Jewishness and had become thoroughly assimilated into mainstream British society.

Even so, there is still evidence of strong residues of past attitudes in British sports today. In particular, the antisemitism displayed at soccer grounds toward Tottenham Hotspur and its supporters is the direct successor to the activities of Mosley's fascists in the 1930s. Since the early 1970s soccer stadiums have been used as recruiting grounds by fascist groups, and it is not an uncommon sight to see and hear fascist salutes and chants from sections of supporters at matches. Elements of the old reluctance to assert Jewishness for fear of antagonizing antisemites can also be seen in the way in which the management of the Tottenham club have historically sought to downplay their links with North London Jewry. This same passivity was also demonstrated by the extreme reluctance in the 1970s and early 1980s of Leeds United, a club that at the time had a significant Jewish presence on its board of directors and which has traditionally drawn support from the local Jewish community, to distance the club from the large National Front fascist presence among its supporters.

There is much work to be done on the relationship between Jews and sports in Britain. For a variety of reasons, social historians of British Jewry and of British sports have generally ignored the subject. This is to be regretted because the uniqueness of the Jewish sporting experience in Britain— encompassing periods of large-scale immigration, significant involvement in working-class movements, apparent widespread assimilation into the middle classes, and links with the highest echelons of British society—gives the subject a relevance that can provide broader insights and signposts for the study of the interaction between sports and national, local, and racial

Ikey, Junr.: "Fader, I von two balls. Here, I make you a present of von."
Ikey, Senr. (after careful scrutiny): "Vat's der madder vid it?"

Antisemitism in British golf: a 1910 cartoon from Golf Illustrated, the leading British weekly golf magazine of the time.

identities, as well as uncovering a vital and important aspect of the social history of Jewish life in Britain over the past two centuries.

Notes

1. MacDonell is quoted in Rob Colls, *Identity of England* (Oxford, 2002), p. 167. Cecil and Chamberlain are quoted in Dan Cohn-Sherbok, *The Crucified Jew* (London, 1992), p. 187.
2. Lytton Strachey, *Eminent Victorians* (London, 2000 [Folio edition]), p. 180.
3. For background, see Todd Endelmann, *The Jews of Britain 1656–2000* (Berkeley CA, 2002); Geoffrey Alderman, *Modern British Jewry* (Oxford, 1998), ch. 3; and E. C. Black, *The Social Politics of Anglo-Jewry, 1880–1920* (London, 1988).
4. Harold Pollins, *A History of the Jewish Working Men's Club and Institute* (Oxford, 1981). For Herzl, see Ian Buruma, *Voltaire's Coconuts* (London, 1999), p. 193.
5. Rosalyn Livshin, "The Acculturalisation of the Children of Immigrant Jews in Manchester, 1880–1930," in *The Making of Modern Anglo-Jewry*, David Cesarani, ed. (Oxford, 1990).

6. Sharman Kadish, *A Good Jew and a Good Englishman: The Jewish Lads and Girls Brigade 1895–1995* (London, 1995).
7. Quoted in Kadish, *A Good Jew*, p. 126.
8. This view is expressed, for example, in Stan Shipley, "Boxing," in *Sport in Britain: A Social History*, Tony Mason, ed. (Cambridge, 1989), p. 99.
9. See John Efron, "When Is a Yid Not a Jew? The Strange Case of Supporter Identity at Tottenham Hotspur," chapter 14 in this volume.
10. Todd M. Endelmann, *The Jews of Georgian England, 1714–1830: Tradition and Change in a Liberal Society* (Philadelphia, 1979), p. 176.
11. For Broughton, see Graham Morris, *Rugby League in Manchester* (Stroud, 2003); and Rosalyn Livshin, "The Acculturalisation of the Children of Immigrant Jews in Manchester, 1880–1930," *Athletic News*, January 25, 1926, pp. 90–91.
12. *Jewish Chronicle*, December 28, 1934.
13. *Action*, 6 February 1937. For more on antisemitism during this period, see Colin Holmes, *Antisemitism in British Society 1876–1939* (New York, 1979).
14. Geoffrey Cousins, *Golf in Britain* (London, 1975), p. 141.
15. For tennis, see the memoir of Angela Buxton, "The 1956 Wimbledon's Ladies Doubles Champion," *Observer*, July 8, 2001.
16. *Jewish Chronicle*, March 15, 1935 and November 2, 1934.
17. *Jewish Chronicle*, November 9, 1934. The paper actually names only two, M. J. Susskind and Victor Rothschild, and omits John Raphael, who played for Surrey in the 1900s. Jack Williams, *Cricket and Race* (Oxford, 2001), pp. 40–43.
18. Rugby Football Union, *Committee Minutes*, October 3, 1930.
19. Quoted in *Jewish Chronicle*, January 12, 1934. Cousins, *Golf in Britain*, pp. 137–142.
20. *Action*, March 19, 1936.
21. See John Harding, Jack "Kid" Berg, *The Whitechapel Windmill* (London, 1987). Kadish, *A Good Jew*, p. 126.
22. For Mendoza, see George Eise, "Daniel Mendoza, A Jewish Bruiser in the Eighteenth Century Fancy" in *Physical Education and Sports in Jewish History and Culture: Proceedings of an International Seminar*, Ariel Simri, ed. (Wingate Institute for Physical Education and Sport, 1977).
23. David S. Katz, *The Jews in the History of England 1485–1850* (Oxford, 1994), pp. 361–63.
24. *Jewish Chronicle*, September 27, 1935.
25. Quoted in Katz, *Jews in the History of England*, p. 363.
26. *Jewish Chronicle*, September 27, 1935.
27. *Yorkshire Post*, May 5, 1897.
28. Pierce Egan, *Book of Sports* (London, 1832), p. 172. Lonsdale is cited in the *Jewish Chronicle*, September 27, 1935.
29. For the CP and the BWSF see Stephen Jones, *Sport, Politics and the Working Class* (Manchester, 1992), chapter 4, and Joe Jacobs, *Out of the Ghetto* (London, 1978), p. 39. For Rothman, see his obituary in the *Guardian*, January 25, 2002.
30. *Jewish Chronicle*, November 23, 1934.
31. *Jewish Chronicle*, November 30, 1934.

10. Nazi Ideology and the End of
Central European Soccer Professionalism, 1938–1941

Rudolf Oswald

It is tragic that by being loyal to a task . . . we Germans in particular mean
the maintaining of previous styles, methods and principles. But in fact, just
the faithful pursuit of a duty often . . . requires a change of the methods, and
sometimes even a change of the principles.

GUIDO V. MENGDEN, 1955, in an obituary
on the Catholic sports official Prälat Ludwig Wolker

D ISCUSSING THE EXCLUSION of Jews from sports under the Third
Reich, German historians almost entirely focus on the short period of
the so-called Gleichschaltung (enforced conformity). The expulsion of Jewish
athletes and officials from bourgeois clubs and federations in the first half
of 1933 has formed an essential part of German sports history for more than
two decades now.[1] What scholars thus far have not considered, however,
is the continued racial persecution in sports after 1938 in occupied and
dependent territories, as well as Nazi-allied countries. With regard to soccer, this discrimination was justified by postulating a Jewish responsibility
for the partly ruinous state of central European professionalism—a sports
phenomenon of the interwar period—which typified soccer in countries
belonging to the former Austro-Hungarian Monarchy, but which during
the twenties and thirties caused the most vehement arguments in Germany.
While this debate remained free from any antisemitic connotation until
1938, the situation changed with the beginning of aggressive foreign policy
against Austria and Czechoslovakia. Focusing particularly on the events in
Vienna and the German-speaking parts of Bohemia (Sudetenland) in the
spring of 1938, this unexamined turn toward antisemitism in the German
debates about professionalism shapes the topic of the following paper.[2]

Amateurism within Bourgeois German Soccer during the Twenties
In Germany, the question of whether one might make a living out of playing soccer had been discussed by organizers of soccer associations since
the end of the nineteenth century. The main institution for supporting the
game, the bourgeois German Soccer Association (Deutscher Fußballbund,
DFB), had propagated rigid anti-professionalism since its foundation in

1900.[3] Until the First World War, however, the idea of amateurism was not based upon an established and explicit ideology—a fact that changed in the aftermath of the German defeat in 1918. The forced abolition of compulsory military service as a term of the Versailles Treaty seemed to make it necessary to find a new suitable form of physical education for young men—and the most appropriate compensation for it seemed to be sports.[4] This new function of sports also increased the social status and value of soccer, which on the one hand freed it and other sports from a long tradition of having to justify themselves against gymnasts (i.e., the Deutsche Turnerschaft, DT), but which on the other hand opened a general debate about the social function of the game. In the DFB and the bourgeois trade press, this new discourse extolling the civic and social virtues of soccer rapidly became dominated by a culturally pessimistic attitude toward the commercial aspects of the sports. These concerns centered on the notion of a "community of the people" (Volksgemeinschaft), an idea that at the time of the Weimar Republic influenced the political thought not only of far right-wing groups, but also of centrist, bourgeois groups as well.[5]

Since the beginning of the twenties, bourgeois sports papers had spoken of soccer as a proper "physical training for the whole people," as a future "program to harmonize the social organism," or in a more comprehensive sense, as a means to rebuild "the broken-down community of the people."[6] Following the contemporary discourse on hygiene, DFB officials further understood the "people's body" (Volkskörper) as "suffering from a disease," against which the "people's sport" (Volkssport), soccer, was thought to be the best remedy. But these officials also feared that this process of recovery was threatened from within the sport itself, especially by players who took financial advantage of displaying their "artistry" (Artistentum). The argument was that, in order to get as much money as possible out of soccer, the so-called "professionals" would produce mass audiences, and therefore would promote the passive consumption of sports by the fans, who would then be inspired to improve their own health by playing themselves.[7] Although the usual paying practices in Germany at that time—illegal payments to players for changing clubs, or excessive accounts of expenses[8]—did not fit the definition of true sports professionalism, alleged "pros" nevertheless were treated like overpowering enemies of German soccer and therefore of the "people's body." Players who violated the strict rules of the DFB statute designed to prevent professionalism (Amateurstatut) were regarded as "contamination," as "pus, which rampages in a sick body," or as "mangy elements," against which "extermination" was sometimes required.[9]

The Antisemitic Turn of the Discourse in Spring 1938

On the surface, the attacks by bourgeois sports organizers on commercial sports during the twenties would seem to foreshadow the rhetoric of the Third Reich. But there remained an important difference: unlike some Nazi authors who wrote about the topic, [10] DFB ideologues never identified professionalism, the "element that damages the *Volksgemeinschaft*" as "Jewish." [11] After 1933, critics of professional sports continued to evoke the "national community" and the medicalized rhetoric of degeneration, but did not adopt antisemitism in their attacks until 1938. The so-called *Selbst-Gleichschaltung* of the DFB in 1933, which best describes the response of the association and its regional subdivisions (*Landesverbände*) to the Nazi takeover, led not only to the abolition of federal and democratic structures in German soccer, but also to the exclusion of Jewish officials, members, and players from federations and clubs within only a few months. For the time being, this rapid discrimination therefore knocked the bottom out of an accentuated antisemitic agitation against professionalism. The continued debate on amateurs versus pros can also be ascribed to the ingratiating behavior of leading DFB officials toward the new regime, which enabled the most rigid advocates of amateurism, like the chairman of the association, Felix Linnemann, or the executive manager of the Western German Sports Association (Westdeutscher Spielverband, WSV), Guido von Mengden, to continue their careers after 1933.[12]

Only with the annexation of Austria in March 1938 were the right conditions provided for an ideological turn of the discourse. In countries succeeding the Austro-Hungarian Empire, National Socialism met with a culture of soccer that was considerably different from the German context. The so-called "Danubian Soccer" (Donaufußball) had not only its own style of play—the Scottish "short-pass"[13]—but also a legalized and in most cases a bankrupt system of professionalism. And to an extent unknown in Germany before 1933, clubs in Vienna, Prague, and Budapest had Jews as players, officials, and financial backers. In the context of totalitarian power politics from 1938 onwards, a culturally conditioned disapproval of professionalism now joined with racial hatred. Led by some Viennese dailies, which could fall back on a long tradition of antisemitic polemics in the Austrian trade journals in the interwar period, racism rapidly made its way into the soccer-related publications of the Third Reich.[14] And finally, even some high-ranking exponents of the former bourgeois sports adopted an anti-semitic argumentation as suitable for promoting their own ideals.

The End of Professional Soccer in Vienna

The first victim of the racist turn of the discourse was Viennese soccer, which since the early thirties had remained in a state of permanent financial crisis. The introduction of a professional league by 1924–25 had resulted on the one hand in increasing incomes for the larger Viennese clubs, but on the other hand had also resulted in exorbitant wage claims on the part of the few stars. Whereas the sponsors, in order to save the "aces" (*Kanonen*) for the club, tried to fulfill their demands, most of Vienna's nearly three hundred pros had to scrape by with scantier earnings. In addition, the clubs suffered from high taxes and from expenses for advertising and for maintaining the playing fields. Thus, after some years of professionalism, a number of clubs teetered on the brink of bankruptcy.[15] Finally, in March 1938, this precari-ous financial situation of Viennese soccer was presented to the public as a surface argument for liquidating the whole system.

Though in large part the reintroduction of amateurism must be ascribed to the pressure to unify Austrian and German soccer,[16] official phraseol-ogy nonetheless stressed the necessity of ending "the trend toward one-sided showmanship" and the need for bringing "all the people's comrades (*Volksgenossen*) . . . back to physical exercise."[17] But now, the "pro" was no longer blamed for damaging the "people's community." In contrast to bour-geois sports officials, Nazism now regarded professional players as "misled victims of a liberalist bad spirit,"[18] and in the case of Vienna, made "Jewish managers" responsible for the negative consequences of professionalism. First affected by this new type of campaign were some urban clubs, above all Wiener Austria, the favorite club of the Viennese coffeehouse-culture, whose managing committee consisted almost exclusively of Jews; then the Zionist club Hakoah,[19] winner of the first professional championship; and finally, the management of the Austrian Soccer Association (Österreichis-cher Fußballbund, ÖFB). Chiefly attacked were the recently deceased Hugo Meisl, former secretary-general of the ÖFB and coach of the famous "*Wun-derteam*,"[20] who was considered responsible for the establishment of the professional league, Josef Gerö, chairman of the local Viennese Soccer Fed-eration (Wiener Fußballverband), and Emanuel "Michl" Schwarz, president of Wiener Austria.[21]

The Viennese edition of the *Völkischer Beobachter* defamed this circle of soccer officials as a "Jewish clique" that, assisted by a Jewish-controlled press (*Systempresse*), would have pursued the "deterrence of the . . . masses" from active sports by glorifying the "unattainable artistic feats of professional and specialized athletes."[22] With the "invasion of Jewry" into Viennese soccer, the Nazi paper remarked in retrospect a year later, "the original meaning of physical exercise" would have "degenerated into a circus show, the 'final expression' of which would have been 'professionalism.' "[23] The actual reproach lay in the claim that in promoting professionalism, the "Jewish managers" were solely interested in making profit.[24] Therefore, according to the *Völkische Beobachter*, it was not the wage claims of the stars or the municipal fiscal policy that would have brought the clubs to the brink of ruin, but the "Jewification of the sporting entrepreneurship."[25] Modeled on traditional antisemitic agitation, but modified in shape, the phrase the "greedy Jew" in soccer was also present in other Viennese dailies. The NS *Telegraf*, for instance, accused the management of Wiener Austria of criminal business methods,[26] while the *Wiener Neueste Nachrichten* denounced the officials of the Viennese Soccer Federation around Josef Gerö as "Jewish protectors" of "parasites."[27]

According to the logic of the *Völkischer Beobachter*, which was by this time one of the decisive voices within the sports discourse, it was obviously too late "to heal" "Danubian Soccer" and to maintain the system of professionalism. At the end of March 1938, the paper stated that "circumstances in Austrian sports" had "become intolerable"; bringing back the "people's community" to physical exercise would now require a resolute "reamateurization" of the pros.[28] The demand was swiftly complied with: on April 22, 1938, Reich Sports Leader (Reichssportführer) von Tschammer und Osten decreed the reintroduction of amateurism to Viennese soccer, July 1 saw the termination of the players' contracts, and finally, during the summer, most of the "Aryan" pros were supplied with "usual" jobs.[29] But the debate on Viennese professionalism by no means ended with that—and it remained antisemitic.

From the fall of 1938 onwards, the agitation focused on the aggressive atmosphere of the capital's soccer fields. Suddenly, the notorious and often violent behavior of the Viennese fans was explained as the result of the methods by which "the Jews" had popularized professionalism. This grotesque discourse on Danubian Soccer reached its climax in June 1939 in an article by Guido von Mengden, in which he justified the exclusion of Jews from municipal sports grounds in October of the previous year.[30] Actually thought of as an answer to the fierce reactions among Viennese fans after Admira Wien had lost the championship final of 1939,[31] von Mengden's comment makes clear the racist turn of the professionalism and hygiene discourse in soccer: "The principle of professionalism inevitably has left its marks on the people. Professionalism is business—and business demands commercial methods, it demands advertising, stars, scandals and sensations. For years, this poison has been injected into the people with . . . true Jewish cleverness. In the eyes of the masses therefore, soccer must have become more a Circensian than an educational function."[32]

But by the time von Mengden made this statement, those blamed for the financial disaster of Viennese professionalism had already fallen victim to the "people's community." At the end of March 1938, after a wave of discrimination unprecedented in the sports sector, there were no more Jews in Viennese soccer: the Gestapo had dissolved Hakoah and confiscated its property, the managing committee of Wiener Austria had been removed from office, Michl Schwarz had been arrested, and more than seventy Jewish referees had been expelled from the referee's faculty (*Schiedsrichterkollegium*) of the ÖFB.[33]

The expulsions of officials were typically justified as combating an alleged "Jewish conspiracy," which purportedly had caused the financial distress of the clubs. For example, the *Wiener Neueste Nachrichten* remarked: "During the last years, soccer was treated in the worst way. A certain kind of 'coach' [*Betreuer*] has brought it to the brink of ruin. A host of parasites . . . has immodestly behaved as if they owned the sport. Jewish profiteers, called managers, have tugged and pulled at its viability."[34] Not surprisingly, the author concluded, "[t]hese parasites . . . have to disappear."[35]

But the expulsion from federations and clubs only marked the beginning of the demanded "disappearance." While the majority of Jewish players and officials, such as the management of Wiener Austria, were able to emigrate, thirty-seven members of Hakoah were murdered in concentration camps.[36]

The "Cleansing" of German-Bohemian Soccer
At the same time that Austrian dailies were still cynically commenting on the exclusion of Jews from Viennese soccer, the German-speaking parts of Bohemia faced similar events. Under pressure from the movement of Konrad Henlein (Sudetendeutsche Partei), the German Soccer Federation in Czechoslovakia (Deutscher Fußballverband in der Tschechoslowakei,

DFV)[37] announced at the end of April 1938 that it would join the Educational Federation of the German-Bohemian Ethnic Group (Erziehungsverband der sudetendeutschen Volksgruppe)—which concealed nothing but Henlein's own racial *Turnerschaft*.[38] For professionalized German-Bohemian soccer, this brought forth two immediate consequences. First, being modeled on *Turner* tradition, the "source" of a "true and real *Volksgemeinschaft*,"[39] the Educational Federation flatly rejected sports as a means of making money; and second, as an association that defined itself as "racial" (*völkisch*), the organization demanded the expulsion of the numerous Czech and Jewish DFV members. Discrimination against "non-Aryans" as well as the fight against symptoms of professionalism were both consequences of the nature of the *Turnerschaft*, but they were of necessity not dependent on each other. Nonetheless, the German trade press argumentatively linked both issues— and again a financial distress of the soccer clubs, said to have been caused by the legalization of professionalism, provided the starting point of all reflections.

In 1925, Czechoslovakia had introduced a professional system in soccer. At the end of the thirties, there existed roughly five hundred contracts with individual players, of whom approximately one third belonged to the DFV. But the new system presented the German clubs, chiefly in the industrial areas of North Bohemia, with a fatal dilemma: if they agreed to pay high wages, they burdened themselves excessively, and if they maintained their lower salaries, their best players went to clubs in Prague, Vienna, or Budapest. Thus, sports, too, developed the structural problem typical for the countries of the former Austro-Hungarian Empire. Clubs from the Hungarian province, for instance, suffered from the dominance of the capital, as did the Austrian and Czech clubs with respect to their own. But instead of discussing the facts, the press of the Third Reich constructed—as in the case of Vienna—a Jewish responsibility for the situation. Jewish sponsors, not structural problems in the organizations, were supposed to have caused the ruin of the clubs. To teams wanting to buy stars, Jews gave loans, as the story went, with usurious interest rates. The pros themselves, by contrast, were again declared victims: exploited by Jewish officials, they were forced to sign with Prague clubs.[40]

The campaign, now led by the most popular German sports paper, the *Kicker*, was mainly aimed at those clubs of the Sudetenland whose managing committees had Jewish members.[41] Thus, the enormous debts of DSK Gablonz were traced to financial machinations of "Jews," who "in the years 1935–1936" were claimed to have "nested" in the club.[42] This reproach was further directed against the Brüxer Sportbrüder, the "management" of which, according to the *Kicker*, consisted "down the line of Jewish and Marxist elements."[43] In order to verify the alleged exploitation of players by "Jewish club managers," critics sometimes quoted former pros. In October 1938, for example, Kugler, the right-winger of the Teplitzer FK, made the following statement: "The experiences I had during my employment as a player under contract were not even the best and most pleasant ones. . . . I despised . . . completely playing under contract, because all of these contracts were drafted in a Jewish way of doing business, that means 99 percent in favor of the club."[44]

Although the authenticity of such interviews may be doubted, the genuineness of the quotations may not have concerned the fans a great deal.[45] Kugler was a star, whose remarks the supporters of the Teplitzer FK certainly found more interesting than a sharp denouncement of professionalism by the party press.

By mid-June 1938 the fate of German-Bohemian professionalism was sealed. The DFV officially returned to amateurism. No new contracts were approved and current ones were no longer renewed.[46] But the *Kicker*, again by linking anti-professionalism with antisemitism, already had called for the end of the system by the beginning of May, after the DFV had announced its entry into Henlein's Educational Federation. According to the paper, "foreign elements" had made their "way into several top clubs by means of money," and had thus "caused heavy damage within the soccer movement of the Sudetenland."[47] Logically, the *Kicker* came to the conclusion that German-Bohemian sports should undergo a "process of cleansing," through which amateurism should be reestablished. The case of the Brüxer Sportbrüder gives an idea of what form that "cleansing" would take: fans and players organized a boycott against the club's matches until finally the Jewish members stepped back voluntarily.[48] If, however, a club refused more persistently to make way for a "racial" leadership, then it was excluded from the DFV and "left to the care of the Czechoslovak national federation"[49]— which meant nothing less than exclusion from organized soccer. The most prominent victim of this kind of exclusion became DFC Prague, home club of many German-Jewish citizens in the Czechoslovak capital, whose management in October 1938 found itself compelled to dissolve the club.[50] As the *Reichssportblatt* announced, after the Munich Pact, which ended "Jewish obstructionism" in German-Bohemian soccer,[51] there was already most likely not a single Jew left in the sports world of the Sudetenland.

In the months following the establishment of the Protectorate of Bohemia and Moravia, the debate on professionalism was extended also to Czech clubs, and the bourgeois Slavia Prag became the main target of the German trade press.[52] But the discussion was about phantoms now: growing antisemitism in the remaining parts of Bohemia had led to the expulsion of Jews from sports organizations even before German troops occupied the country.[53]

Conclusion

In the spring of 1939, one year after Jewish sports officials had been blamed for the first time for the disastrous state of central European professionalism, antisemitism had become a constant feature within the discourse on amateurs versus professionals in Germany. The paradigm of a "Volksgemeinschaft in Leibesübungen," derived from the cultural criticism of the twenties, had been merged potently with Nazi ideology, and in the years to come the racist way of dealing with the problem was employed at every opportunity. Such was the case in July 1939, when, in the course of antisemitic waves in Hungary, Jewish officials and referees were expelled from the national soccer federation—and the Kicker could not grasp the fact that despite these measures professionalism would continue.[54] Such was also the case in August 1940, when, after the invasion of France, the crisis of French professionalism was exaggerated—and the Secretary for Physical Exercise, Jean Zay, a Frenchman of Jewish origin, was held responsible for it.[55]

Besides von Mengden, other major exponents of the former bourgeois German soccer also seemed to now have an interest in agitation against Jewish sponsors.[56] In 1941, for example, Ernst Werner, the long-standing editor of the Berlin Fußball-Woche, recalled an old scandal about professionals in the twenties, which he now viewed as "Semitic contrived,"[57] while, in a series of articles during the spring of 1943, the former national coach Otto Nerz generally regarded the "Jewified" German soccer of Weimar as the cause of earlier symptoms of professionalism: "Particularly with respect to the matter of professional players, the Jews and their enslaved made life a perfect hell for the . . . leadership [of German sports]. During the crisis before 1933, the danger of Jewification was also acute in soccer. The big clubs were heavily indebted, and in many cases the creditors were Jews. The tendency toward professional soccer was intense and the state at that time was not able to support the sports leadership, because it was itself enslaved to the Jew." [58]

But now, one decade later, amateurism seemed to be advancing throughout Europe: The Czech soccer federation restricted the system of fixed salaries in 1939, Hungary and France both liquidated professionalism the following year, and the Swiss association finally prohibited playing for money in 1941. [59] The editor of the *Kicker*, Hanns J. Müllenbach, apparently had reason for cheering, "One island [of professionalism] after the other disappears, and it won't be to the disadvantage of soccer." [60] But it seemed not to be a cause for concern that as a result of this triumphant advance the alleged exploiters of central European sports had to emigrate or to "resettle." On the contrary, Nerz concludes: "One nation after the other is shaking off the yoke of the Jew. In the end there will be left a Europe free from Jews with sports free from Jews." [61]

Notes

1. See, for example, Hajo Bernett, *Der jüdische Sport im nationalsozialistischen Deutschland 1933–1938* (Schorndorf, 1978); idem, "Der deutsche Sport im Jahre 1933," *Stadion* 7, no. 2 (1981), pp. 225–83. The discrimination against Jews within organizations of the German Soccer Association (DFB), however, first received attention only on the occasion of the centennial of the federation in 2000; see, for example, Arthur Heinrich, *Der Deutsche Fußballbund: Eine politische Geschichte* (Cologne, 2000), esp. pp. 140–45.
2. Hajo Bernett has also failed to notice this change in content of the debate; see, for example, Hajo Bernett, "Die nationalsozialistische Sportführung und der Berufssport," *Sozial- und Zeitgeschichte des Sports* 4, no. 1 (1990), pp. 7–33. Unaware of the sources, the recent approach of a cultural and social history of soccer views the year 1933 as the true break within the discourse; see Fabian Brändle and Christian Koller, *Goal! Kultur- und Sozialgeschichte des modernen Fußballs* (Zurich, 2002), p. 90.
3. See Heinrich, *Der Deutsche Fußballbund*, p. 76.
4. Heinrich, *Der Deutsche Fußballbund*, pp. 100–102.
5. See Hans-Ulrich Thamer, "Volksgemeinschaft: Mensch und Masse," in *Erfindung des Menschen: Schöpfungsträume und Körperbilder 1500–2000*, Richard van Dülmen, ed. (Vienna, 1998), pp. 375–79.
6. For the quotations, see H. Seibold, "Sport und Schule," *Fußball* 10 (March 10, 1920); Eduard Sütterle, "Vom Geiste des Fußballsportes," *Fußball* 11 (August 17, 1921); Heinrich, *Der Deutsche Fußballbund*, p. 89. The interpretation of the class-crossing structure of a soccer team as a "model for the Volksgemeinschaft" was one of the main topics within the bourgeois debates. It still can be found in the trade press of the mid-thirties; see, for example, "Zum Opfertag des deutschen Fußballs," *Kicker* 16 (November 19, 1935).
7. On the ideological foundation of amateurism within the DFB, see Heinrich, *Der Deutsche Fußballbund*, pp. 88–92, as well as the programmatic article written by the later chairman of the federation, Felix Linnemann, "Viel Lärm um Nichts," *Fußball* 10 (August 18, 1920).
8. Contemporaries therefore spoke of "fictitious amateurism" (*Scheinamateurismus*).

9. For the quotations, see "Gedanken, die dazu gehören," *Fußball* 11 (June 15, 1921); "Für oder gegen Profis?" *Fußball* 10 (September 7, 1920); "Vom Spielfeld verwiesen," *Fußball* 11 (September 27, 1921); "Weihnachten 1921," *Fußball* 11 (December 20, 1921).

10. See, for example, Bruno Malitz, *Die Leibesübungen in der nationalsozialistischen Idee* (Munich, 1933), esp. pp. 39–42. Though often quoted, this pamphlet by the former sprinter is nonetheless not representative of the debate during the first years of the Third Reich.

11. The absence of antisemitic argumentation generally accentuates the dividing line between bourgeois and National Socialist sports theory; see Hans Joachim Teichler, *Internationale Sportpolitik im Dritten Reich* (Schorndorf, 1991), pp. 43–44.

12. Having gained even more power by the Führerprinzip, Linnemann destroyed plans for a professional league in the summer of 1933 and ordered stricter rules for amateurism that fall; see "Interessengemeinschaft Deutscher Berufsfußballclubs," in *Denkschrift über die Notwendigkeit einer Bereinigung der Verhältnisse im deutschen Fußballsport durch Trennung von Amateur- und Berufssport* (Stuttgart, 1947), p. 6; and "Neue Amateur-Bestimmungen des DFB," *Kicker* 14 (September 5, 1933). The relative independence of DFB-officials after 1933 has so far been ignored by sports historians. Thus, they are puzzled by the fact that professionalism within other sports, like boxing or cycling, was not a matter of contention; see Brändle and Koller, *Goal!*, p. 90; Bernett, "Die nationalsozialistische Sportführung," p. 24.

13. See Michael John, "Österreich," in *Fußball, soccer, calcio: Ein englischer Sport auf seinem Weg um die Welt*, Christiane Eisenberg, ed. (Munich, 1997), p. 74.

14. See Michael John and Dietrich Schulze-Marmeling, " 'Haut's die Juden!' Antisemitismus im europäischen Fußball," in *Fußball und Rassismus* (Göttingen, 1993), pp. 136–37.

15. See Roman Horak and Wolfgang Maderthanner, *Mehr als ein Spiel: Fußball und populare Kulturen im Wien der Moderne* (Vienna, 1997), pp. 134–37; John, "Österreich," pp. 68–69.

16. Sometimes the *Kicker* addressed the true nature of the problem; see, for example, "Zum letzten Male: Österreich-Deutschland," *Kicker* 19 (March 29, 1938).

17. "Sport am Scheideweg," *Völkischer Beobachter* (March 21, 1938, Vienna edition).

18. Bernett, "Die nationalsozialistische Sportführung," p. 24.

19. On Hakoah, see John Bunzl, "Hakoah Vienna: Reflections on a Legend," chapter 7 in this volume.

20. The *"Wunderteam"* referred to the Austrian national team, which was regarded as the best team in continental Europe during the early thirties. It consisted entirely of Viennese professionals.

21. The Viennese dailies were masters of the indirect attack. Names were rarely quoted, but paraphrases made it quite plain who was intended.

22. "Sport am Scheideweg" (see n. 17).

23. "Ein Jahr Leibeserziehung in der Ostmark," *Völkischer Beobachter* (March 12/13, 1939, Vienna edition).

24. See "Wie wird das Fußballprogramm der Ostmark?" *Völkischer Beobachter* (June 25, 1938, Vienna edition).

25. "Sport am Scheideweg" (see n. 17).

26. See "Sekretariat geschlossen: Austria-Leitung nicht vertrauenswürdig," NS *Telegraf* (March 16, 1938), in "Wien am Mittag."

27. Rudolf Kastl, "Sport-Tagebuch," *Wiener Neueste Nachrichten* (March 13, 1938).

28. See "Wiens Sportler und Turner empfangen den Reichssportführer," *Völkischer Beobachter* (March 28, 1938, Vienna edition).

29. "Einer neuen ruhmreichen Zukunft entgegen?" *Völkischer Beobachter* (July 20, 1938, Vienna edition); M. J. Leuthe, "Abkehr vom Berufsspielertum," *Kicker* 19 (June 28, 1938); "Die Wiener Profis arbeiten," *Kicker* 19 (August 16, 1938); Bernett, "Die nationalsozialistische Sportführung," p. 24; John, "Österreich," p. 77.

30. See "Für Juden verboten," *Völkischer Beobachter* (October 7, 1938, Vienna edition).

31. In view of the sensational 9–0 defeat against Schalke 04, the fans of Admira suspected the game of having been manipulated. Additional anger was caused by a heavy assault on Fritz Szepan, which almost led to the death of the German star; see Matthias Marschik " 'Am Spielfeld ist die Wahrheit gewesen.' Die Wiener Fußballkultur in der Zeit des Nationalsozialismus: Zwischen Vereinnahmung und Widerstand," in *Österreichische Zeitschrift für Volkskunde* 50, no. 99 (1996), pp. 193–94; "Schalke eine große Meisterelf," *Kicker* 20 (June 20, 1939). The final of 1939 was the cause for numerous riots between German and Viennese fans in the following years; see Marschik, " 'Am Spielfeld ist die Wahrheit gewesen,' " p. 194.

32. Guido von Mengden, "Schlusswort zu neuem Anfang," NS-Sport 1 (June 25, 1939).

33. See John, "Österreich," pp. 75–76; "Auswirkungen der Säuberungsaktion," NS Telegraf (March 16, 1938), in "Wien am Mittag."

34. Rudolf Kastl, "Sport-Tagebuch," *Wiener Neueste Nachrichten* (March 13, 1938).

35. Kastl, "Sport-Tagebuch."

36. See Karl-Heinz Schwind, *Geschichten aus einem Fußball-Jahrhundert* (Vienna, 1994), p. 112; John, "Österreich," pp. 76–77.

37. According to the "principle of nationality," the Czechoslovak Soccer Federation during the interwar period was divided into several subdivisions. Separate organizations existed for Czech, Slovak, German, Hungarian, and Jewish clubs; see *Beckmanns Sportlexikon* (Leipzig, 1933), pp. 2287–88. Between 1929 and 1936, the most successful club of the DFV, the Teplitzer FK, played in the Czechoslovak national league.

38. See "Die sudetendeutschen Sportler und der völkische Zusammenschluß," *Kicker* 19 (April 26, 1938); Lutz Koch, "Europa-Fahrtenbuch," *Kicker* 19 (May 3, 1938).

39. Artur Keser, "Heimkehr," *Reichssportblatt* 5 (December 6, 1938).

40. See "Sudetengau," *Kicker* 19 (October 25, 1938).

41. The beginning of the antisemitic mode of the debate in the *Kicker* can be dated almost exactly to the beginning of May 1938. Why it did not happen with the "annexation" of Austria cannot be explained from the available sources.

42. "Aus der Stadt des falschen Goldes," *Kicker* 20 (March 21, 1939).

43. "Großer Säuberungsprozeß im Sudetenland," *Kicker* 19 (May 3, 1938). During the "Sudetenkrise," the term "Marxist" was used by the German press as a synonym for "Czech."

44. "Schattenseiten des ehemaligen sudetendeutschen Profitums," *Kicker* 19 (October 25, 1938).

45. With regard to the research into the involvement of top players with Nazi politics, this question first arose with the analysis of a contemporary portrait of Ernst Kuzorra and Fritz Szepan—the two stars of Schalke 04; see Heinz Berns and Hermann Wiersch, *Das Buch vom deutschen Fußballmeister—Szepan und Kuzorra: Die Geschichte zweier Mannen und einer Mannschaft* (Wattenscheid, 1936). There, Kuzorra is quoted as speaking in Nazi platitudes, whose form does not go well with his own—obviously limited—

stylistic capabilities; see Siegfried Gehrmann, "Fritz Szepan und Ernst Kuzorra—zwei Fußballidole des Ruhrgebiets," in *Sozial- und Zeitgeschichte des Sports* 2, no. 3 (1988), pp. 69–70; Dietrich Schulze-Marmeling, *Der gezähmte Fußball: Zur Geschichte eines subversiven Sports* (Göttingen, 1992), pp. 120–21.

46. See "Zum Amateurstandpunkt zurückgekehrt," *Völkischer Beobachter*, June 22, 1938 (Munich edition).

47. "Großer Säuberungsprozeß im Sudetenland" (n. 43).

48. See "Großer Säuberungsprozeß im Sudetenland" (n. 43).

49. "Zum Amateurstandpunkt zurückgekehrt" (n. 46).

50. See "Sudetendeutscher Brief," *Kicker* 19 (June 28, 1938); F. Richard, "Tagebuch," *Fußball* 29 (March 21, 1939).

51. Wolfgang Menzel, "Heimkehr," *Reichssportblatt* 5 (November 1, 1938).

52. See F. Richard, "Tagebuch," *Fußball* 29 (March 21, 1939).

53. See Livia Rothkirchen, "The Jews of Bohemia and Moravia: 1938–1945," in *The Jews of Czechoslovakia: Historical Studies and Surveys*, vol. 3, Avigdor Dagan, ed. (New York, 1984), p. 14.

54. See "Doch Profis," *Kicker* 20 (July 18, 1939).

55. See "Der französische Sport nach dem Zusammenbruch," NS-*Sport* 2 (August 25, 1940).

56. Despite his early declarations of devotion to the regime, Felix Linnemann did not adopt antisemitism in order to fight professionalism. As late as the early forties, he remained true to the argumentation that had dominated until 1938; see Felix Linnemann, "Wird die Berufsspieler-Frage im Fußball ein Problem?" *Kicker* 21 (November 12, 1940).

57. Ernst Werner, "Ein Leben mit Fußball," *Reichssportblatt* 8 (August 15, 1941). Werner had already used antisemitic stereotypes during the twenties, which made him an exception within bourgeois German soccer at that time; see Erik Eggers, "Lücke in der Mannschaft," *Jüdische Allgemeine*, August 15, 2002. *Fußball-Woche* was one of the official papers of the DFB.

58. Otto Nerz, "Europas Sport wird frei vom Judentum," *12 Uhr Blatt*, June 4, 1943.

59. See "Telegramme," *Kicker* 20 (June 6, 1939); Hanns J. Müllenbach, "Glossen," *Kicker* 21 (July 23, 1940); "Auslands-Notizen," NS-*Sport* 3 (July 6, 1941); see also Brändle and Koller, *Goal!*, p. 84.

60. Müllenbach, "Glossen."

61. Nerz, "Europas Sport wird frei vom Judentum."

Exiles, Survivors, and the Transformation of Jewish Identity

11. Soccer and Survival among Jewish Refugees in Shanghai

Albert Lichtblau

RESEARCH ON EXILES has mostly concentrated on the output of creative intellectuals and artists who have left behind works of enduring importance. More recently, however, there has been increasing attention devoted to average people in exile, and thanks to a number of different research approaches we know a great deal about the conditions of life in different places of exile. One of the last resorts for those who escaped from National Socialism was the Chinese city of Shanghai with its International Settlement and its French Concession.

Exile researchers place the number of Jewish refugees from Nazi Germany and Austria in Shanghai at about 18,000, while some estimates range between 20–25,000 and even 30,000. Approximately 10 percent were Orthodox Jews, and the proportion of converts and individuals in so-called mixed marriages was about 13 percent. The overwhelming majority of refugees in Shanghai maintained a secular lifestyle.[1] It is estimated that over a third of the Shanghai refugees came from Austria.

Scholarly literature and autobiographical works have shed a great deal of light on the management of everyday life under the conditions of expulsion, the loss of social status, raging warfare, and concern about fates of relatives and friends still in the clutches of the Nazis. The fact that the Japanese—allies of the National Socialists—exercised colonialist power over Shanghai was an additional burden in the lives of Jewish refugees, particularly after the entry of Japan into the war and the ghettoization of the Shanghai refugees.

Sports activities are mentioned in most accounts of exile in Shanghai, but usually only as a secondary issue. I became aware of this subject above all in the course of conducting oral history interviews, in which soccer was repeatedly mentioned. Since sports had played an extremely important role in the lives of German and Austrian Jews prior to National Socialism, I went about investigating what remained of this in exile. The fact that the Jewish soccer team Hakoah could win the Austrian championship showed the absurdity of the antisemitic cliché of the unathletic, weak, and lazy Jew and filled even those Austrian Jews who were not particularly enthusiastic about sports with pride. Thus, prior to the emergence of National Socialism in Germany and Austria, sports had enabled Jews to assert themselves in their confrontation with an increasingly antisemitic environment. Sports not only promoted internal cohesiveness and endowed its practitioners with self-confidence and power, they also lent a positive aspect to a Jewish identity that was faced with strong antisemitic pressure. In interviews with refugees who found asylum in Shanghai, I noticed that enthusiasm for soccer had been brought along into life in exile. However, in contrast to the way things had been in Austria and Germany, this was not so much a matter of competition with soccer teams representing other ethnic or religious groups, nor was it an expression of self-assertion in confrontation with non-Jewish society; rather, this was above all the continuation of a practice in everyday culture that had been transferred from Europe to the Far East.

Sports in exile was closely connected to the struggle for survival. Like other forms of cultural expression—such as associations, cafés and restaurants, cinemas, dancing halls, or virtual sites of congregation like newspapers and radio broadcasts—soccer offered a tightly knit communication network to which individuals could turn in the case of crises or existential emergencies. The extent to which these social networks in the sports world were used even before National Socialism, during exile in Shanghai, and even afterwards will be illustrated using the example of Leo Meyer, Shanghai's most outstanding soccer player.

Shanghai is just one example, since enthusiasm for soccer could also be observed in other places of exile where this sport was not otherwise popular. In New York, Jews founded their own league, the Eastern District Soccer League.[2] In Sosua, in the present-day Dominican Republic, where Jewish refugees had to build an agricultural settlement from scratch, laying out a soccer field had high priority for them. Soccer offered a thread of continuity with life before expulsion, which was experienced as a biographical break. The culture of everyday life—be it eating, music, language, values in getting along with others on a daily basis, or even relations with the opposite sex— was thus an important form of adhesive that helped to seal this breach. In Shanghai, the continuation of practices that the émigrés had brought with them was so extensive because only a few had prospects for a long-term stay, and integration into the local culture made little sense in the context of a "life in the waiting room."

The experience of exile in Shanghai was certainly among the most difficult—because of the distance, the cultural differences, and the physical stress that resulted from the tropical climate. It is often overlooked that the refugees had entered a tense situation in which fighting had taken place. In 1937 Japanese military units bombed a section of Hongkew in which Chinese lived, and which on May 18, 1943, became the area of the de facto ghetto for the refugees from the Nazis. Massive destruction and civilian casualties were the result of this attack.[3]

The Jewish League

Europeans had introduced the sport of soccer into China long before the First World War. Matches were already played in Shanghai in 1879; the Shanghai Football Club was founded in 1887, and the Shanghai Football Association in 1910. The sport, which was initially considered a European phenomenon, increasingly attracted Chinese sports enthusiasts, and in addition to the teams made up of Europeans living in Shanghai, teams with Chinese players were soon established. During the 1926–27 season, there were already three Chinese teams playing in the Shanghai League.

In 1931, the soccer section of the Chinese Amateur Athletic Association was recognized by FIFA. Nevertheless, the clubs led by Europeans living in Shanghai remained organized within the London Football Association. The Chinese national soccer team participated—albeit without success—in the 1936 Summer Olympic Games in Germany.[4]

In the Shanghai League a single Jewish all-star team, the Jewish Recreation Club (JRC), played against Chinese and other European clubs. The JRC had been founded by Russian Jews in 1912, but it was not until 1933 that the JRC's soccer team was promoted to the first division of the Shanghai League. Several of its best players were refugees from the Nazis, including Leo Meyer and Horst (later Robert H.) Winokur.

It is said, however, that the European teams played unwillingly against Chinese clubs, since there were repeated disturbances and attacks on the referees. Fred Fields, the publisher of the exile newspaper *Sport*, recalls such incidents. When asked about his favorite reminiscences concerning soccer, he related anecdotes about not only the victory of "our side" over an all-star team of Englishmen living in Shanghai, but also a match between a Jewish and a Chinese all-star team, which was won by the Jews. In their rage, the Chinese fans got out of control and attempted to set fire to the stands.[5]

As more and more Jewish refugees from Germany and Austria arrived in Shanghai, the JRC made an effort to help. In December 1938 the JRC's executive committee held a meeting on the subject of "Sport for the Emigrants," and on April 23, 1939, the first soccer match between two teams consisting entirely of refugees was held at Kinchow Place. The two teams were combined by the JRC and nominated for the third division of the Shanghai League. This provided an impetus, and the Jewish refugees soon established their own league. This Jewish League began playing during the 1940–41 season with eight teams. It was divided into three divisions, and there was also a youth league with teams of school children. Matches were initially played at a field on Kinchow Road, which later had to be abandoned because it was needed for a school. The JRC then found a new playing field on Chaoufoong Road, where play began on November 16, 1941.[6]

Teams and Championships

The most successful team of the Jewish League was the AHV (Alte Herren Verein, or Old Men's Club). Most of its members were older players who had had already been active in the sport in Germany and Austria. Some had already retired from soccer and began playing again in Shanghai. The AHV won the Jewish League championship in 1941–42, 1943–44 and 1944–45. The first championship of the 1940–41 season was won by a team named Embankment; in 1942–43, Barcelona became the champion of the Jewish League. Its name was derived from a café and restaurant of that name in Chusan Road 21 that offered Viennese cuisine and whose owner supported the team financially.[7] The name Embankment came from the Embankment Building, in which the reception and registration bureau for arriving refugees was located.[8] The Shanghai Jewish Chronicle team was also named after its sponsor and was renamed Blue White in 1946. And of course, one name could not be absent in Shanghai: that of the legendary Zionist Austrian sports club Hakoah. However, Hakoah's Shanghai soccer team included not only Austrians and Viennese, but also German refugees. Another team was called Wayside after the street in Hongkew on which the housing facility for the poorest of the refugees was located. It provided accommodations for those who found hardly any work with which to provide for their families or themselves. With virtually no money, they took to the field in uniforms that had been sewn by their mothers and wives. Robert H. Winokur was a goaltender and played for several teams, including Wayside. Asked which matches were really hotly contested, he cited those between AHV and the "kids" who played for Wayside. "And when we went out and played against the AHV and we beat them, that was a big thing. Unbelievable, you know. How could those kids beat the AHV?"[9]

174

Other teams included United and BNZ (Brith Noar Zioni, also Maccabi). The so-called Häusler team was supported by a well-known jelly manufacturer, [10] and Al Cock was named after a street on which another housing facility was located.

Sports under Difficult Conditions

Weather in general and wartime summers in particular in Shanghai were extremely hot in comparison to Europe, and the immigrants suffered accordingly. In July, temperatures ranged between 61° and 105° Fahrenheit. For that reason, according to Fred Fields, the games were scheduled for late in the day. The Shanghai Jewish Chronicle reported that during a cup match involving the Embankment team the playing field was so wet and slippery "that the players spent more time on their behinds then on their feet." [11] The Jewish League's playing field had no grass cover at all; holes had to be bored into the field to help the water drain and allow play to continue despite the wet conditions. [12] Improvisation was of utmost importance for the European soccer players in Shanghai. Some had brought their soccer shoes with them from Europe, others found such footwear in Shanghai, and still others improvised. For example, a Viennese shoemaker manufactured soles for soccer shoes from worn-out tires. [13]

A unique feature was the mini-soccer championship played on half of a regulation field with smaller goals, a lighter ball, seven players, and shorter playing time. This made it possible to keep playing during the hot and humid summer after the end of the regular season. What better way for soccer fanatics to spend a pleasant Sunday afternoon?

The Jewish League's playing field was located in Hongkew, the neighborhood in which the refugees had been ghettoized by the Japanese occupation army since 1943 and where they lived under extremely difficult conditions. During the war, Japanese bureaucrats ruled in brutal fashion over the refugees crowded there. [14] The high-handedness of a certain Kanoh Ghoya, who referred to himself as the "king of the Jews," was even once directed at the soccer players. An article that appeared in Aufbau, the exile newspaper that was published in New York, reported that Ghoya once closed the soccer field and summoned the league officials to his office. As often happened, he slapped their faces. Play was suspended for several weeks, and when it began again some of the joy that players and fans had previously felt was missing. [15]

Recreation and Stabilization

The enormous differences between the lifestyles of the European refugees and the local population, the local dialect that was difficult for many refugees to learn, the abject poverty, the uncertainty as to what the future might bring, the worries about friends and relatives back in Europe, the occupation of the city by the Japanese, the ghettoization, and the war placed an enormous burden on the refugees' everyday lives. The game of soccer assumed an important position in the refugees' physical and mental stabilization. Responding to the question of what was actually so important about sports in Shanghai, Fred Fields said that it was first and foremost a diversion from the distress of everyday life. Alfred Zunterstein, who was not only a soccer player but also a well-known boxer in Shanghai, recalls that it was something like therapy. Sports allowed the refugees to think about something besides their daily cares and gave their nerves a rest. For Fred Fields, sports was also an "ersatz homeland."[16] According to Winokur, the function of sports in exile in Shanghai was to reduce tension. That is also how Alfred Lambert saw it: "It was wonderful. It was something new for us. We worked during the week and on Sundays we played soccer."[17] Parodying a German-Catholic expression, Kurt Duldner said, "Soccer was the Amen at the end of the Sunday prayer."[18]

Whether as players or spectators, those living under extreme mental pressure were provided with a sort of outlet. Shouting was accepted and even welcome when it came to cheering on the home team or loudly decrying a referee's decision. This provided a ritualized form of expression for pent-up aggressions and kept people from "eating their hearts out" or taking out their hostilities on others.

Relations between the Sexes

"What was I supposed to do? Sit home and twiddle my thumbs?" For Ann Bernfeld, who lived in Shanghai as a young woman, as well as many other young people, soccer was a means of recreation and a cultural activity like going to the theater or comedy clubs.[19] Her father, who had played in Vienna for the city's WAC and in Wiesbaden in Germany, had already retired as an active soccer player. But in Shanghai, he started playing again for a senior team. [20] After the games, Ann Bernfeld, like many other fans and players, got together in one of Shanghai's cafés or nightclubs.

Poverty massively undermined men's feelings of self-confidence. Soccer was a countervailing strategy that enabled young players to enhance their attractiveness to young women. Otherwise it was tough for young men—not only because of the surplus of men, but also because they were hardly in a position to offer material security and a future to women.[21] For Kurt Duldner, it was clear that there was a connection between sports and picking up women: "All the ladies we were after were there. . . . Young ladies were all that was important to us."[22] The clubs organized events featuring live dance music, and this gave young players the opportunity to meet women. Winokur also confirmed that this was not just a matter of playing games; it was also a big part of social life. "We always had a wonderful party. If we won we had a party. If we lost we had a party."[23]

The good athletes benefited from the fact that they were in good physical shape. Their feelings of self-esteem were enhanced since they had better chances with women, a fact also confirmed by Fred Fields in an interview. Good athletes also were more likely to get jobs as waiters and cashiers; thus, they could earn more, and this in turn further increased their attractiveness. They could also make a name for themselves and impress others with their commitment and enthusiasm. Grete Winokur was a native of Vienna who met her husband, a native of Berlin, in Shanghai. Her eyes literally shone with fervor as she related how female fans stood behind the goal her future husband was guarding and cheered him on with calls of "Horsti, Horsti!"[24]

Jewish Identity

Hakoah in Vienna was considered a Zionist club even though athletes who were not Zionist oriented were members. In Shanghai, the accentuation of Jewish identity played a role in exile soccer only to the extent that the league in which most players were active was an exclusively Jewish one. Persecution and expulsion forced those who had had only a loose connection to their Jewish ethnicity in Germany and Austria to become more cognizant of their roots. Many exiles in Shanghai were living in or had been born into so-called mixed marriages. Robert Winokur was the son of a Russian-Jewish POW from World War I who married a non-Jewish woman from Berlin. The son knew nothing of his father's Jewish descent—he had even been a member of the German nationalist Jahn Turnverein (gymnastics association). When the Nazis took power, he and his friends wanted to join the Hitler Youth. It was a tremendous shock for the ten-year-old to find out that this was impossible on account of his father. In Shanghai, on the other hand, he fully identified with his Jewish companions. As a prizefighter, he boxed under the name "Killer Winokur," and photos from those days show a tough looking, handsome young man with a Star of David on his shorts. In response to the question whether it made a difference to him if he played for a soccer team in the Jewish League against other Jewish teams or for the JRC in the Shanghai League against a non-Jewish team, his answer was clear. Playing for the JRC meant playing with more pride, because they were representing their group in a contest against the others: "You want to beat them, because they are richer, they have better clothes, better shoes, they had better equipment, better fields, and you came out of nowhere and we tried to beat them. And so you take a little pride, if you could do it. So it's a little bit more incentive." [25]

Among the other sports in which refugees competed in Shanghai, first and foremost was boxing, the sport that corresponded closest to the ideology of "Jewish musclemen" and the Zionist conception of Jews capable of defending themselves. Nevertheless, among those we interviewed, ideological considerations hardly played a role. Several of them were both soccer players and boxers. Winokur was even amateur welterweight champion of Shanghai, although it must be mentioned that there were hardly any Chinese boxers in his weight class. The JRC founded a boxing team in 1939. [26] Boxing and soccer were masculine domains, but other sports were also open to female sports enthusiasts and were offered by the JRC and by the school that the Jewish philanthropist Horace Kadoorie had endowed for refugee children. Chess, handball, ping-pong, tennis, field hockey, and track and field were other sports played by the emigrants.

Information Network

Sports fans stayed well informed about local sporting events by reading the various exile newspapers. One weekly, *Sport*, provided extensive coverage of all games. Fred Fields—known as Ferdinand Eisfelder in those days—was one of its publishers. He had been born in 1919 in Emden, Germany, and grew up in Berlin, where he was a boy reporting on soccer for newspapers like the *Israelitisches Familienblatt*. He was also an active soccer player for Tennis Borussia, the Berlin sports club that ultimately had to change its name to Jüdische Sportgemeinschaft. In 1938 he made his way alone to Shanghai, a trip via Naples, Bombay, and Hong Kong that lasted twenty-three days. His uncle Louis Eisfelder ran the legendary Café Louis on Bubbling Well Road. Opened on February 11, 1939, it was famous for its pastries and homemade chocolates as well as for the so-called Berliner Weisse, a mixture of raspberry syrup and weak Shanghai beer. [27] Upon arrival, Fred Fields profited from a family network. At first he worked for his uncle in Café Louis and then got a job as an editorial assistant and proofreader for the *Gelbe Post*, the intellectually oriented newspaper.[28] He then switched to the *Shanghai Jewish Chronicle*, the city's leading German-language exile newspaper, which was published by Ossi Lewin, a native of Vienna. When the war broke out, Fred Fields was promoted to night editor thanks to his technical insights. But to survive he also had to find other sources of income. For example, he worked for a chemical plant and managed stage productions in the Eastern Theater, a movie palace with a seating capacity of nine hundred.

Fred Fields started out as a sports reporter in Shanghai. He published the *Sport* newspaper together with Blacky Schwarz, a pal from Vienna. In our interview, Fred Fields confirmed many of the above-mentioned hypotheses about the function of sports in exile. Publishing a sports newspaper was not just a matter of enthusiasm for athletics; it was a matter of survival. Despite his many jobs, Fred Fields was under constant financial pressure, and he lived in a tiny room in the *Shanghai Jewish Chronicle* building. As a publisher of *Sport*, he hoped to increase his income through advertising revenues, but he could hardly keep his head above water in the face of stiff competition from other exile newspapers. To increase sales, he even peddled copies himself in the cafés on Sunday. One is struck by the fact that many different cafés advertised in *Sport* and the *Sportkalender*. For example, Café Klinger described itself as meeting place for all athletes, and Café Barcelona announced its totally new entertainment program. Salo Natowic's Elite Liqueurs also aimed its ad campaign at sports enthusiasts to get them to visit their bar at 169 Chusan Road.[29]

In its two years of publication, ninety-five issues of *Sport* appeared. The second anniversary issue drew a connection between its founding and the opening of the Chaoufoong soccer field in November 1941. The creation of this new athletic facility was really one of the great achievements of the emigrants. At the dedication, all Jewish agencies were represented, all the sports clubs took part in the procession, track and field competitions were held, and at the end there was a big soccer game. So it was just natural that a program would be printed for the spectators. This program received an enthusiastic reception and fans expressed the wish for a publication that would keep them up to date on sporting events. So Fields decided to bring out a regular weekly sports newspaper. And that was the beginning of *Sport*, which went on to become a widely read publication.[30]

Ersatz Family and Mutual Aid

Fred Fields came without a family. His parents stayed behind and were killed by the Nazis. He agreed without hesitation that sports had been a sort of replacement family for him, and he added that the managers of the soccer teams also helped their players in certain cases. In times of need, personal contacts and a flow of information are indispensable. And when things became absolutely critical, athletes helped one another. Robert Winokur told about a friend whose apartment had been destroyed by a fire: "He lost all his clothes [and] shoes. He came home, there was everything gone. Well, we got together and you gave him a coat and I gave him shoes and you underwear . . . a lady bought some linen and we furnished him."[31]

In response to the question of who the most outstanding players were, one name is always mentioned: Leo Meyer.[32] During an interview, he characterized himself in these terms: "I wasn't a gentlemanly soccer player. I was hard, you know!" With that style of play he did not make himself popular, but he certainly did win the respect of all those he played with.[33] Born in 1911 in Langenfeld near Leverkusen in Germany as a son of a cattle dealer, Leo Meyer had only one ambition since his early childhood: to play soccer. Until the rise of National Socialism, he had played right wing for Solingen-Ohligs. Under the Nazis, he switched to Maccabi Düsseldorf and did not manage to flee to Shanghai until 1939. And sports helped. Leo Meyer was already a well-known soccer player and he immediately got a job as physical education teacher at the Kadoorie School. He was also able to earn a little money on the side with gymnastics instruction for "rich women." He remained an active soccer player during his time in Shanghai, playing for Hakoah and JRC. During our interview, he mentioned with particular pride that after the war he was the only Jew nominated for the Shanghai Interport, the all-star team made up of players from all Shanghai clubs. Together with Chinese and European players, he participated in games in Hong Kong and Macao.

At the end of the war, the refugees began to leave Shanghai. Only a few saw bright economic prospects there. With the Communists' takeover of power in the end, even those who had actually wanted to stay left Shanghai. There were even farewell parties and matches for well-known and popular soccer players.[34] Goaltender Winokur went first to San Francisco and then to Los Angeles. Upon arrival in San Francisco, he was welcomed by soccer enthusiasts who persuaded him to join Hakoah San Francisco, which was also connected with a job offer. Half the team was made up of former Shanghai players.

In 1947, Leo Meyer also left Shanghai and found his next place of asylum in New York, where the soccer social network continued to function for him as well. He was immediately able to play for the Jewish soccer team New World Club. Although this was not a professional club, the players also got jobs with one of the sponsors. Since he did not like working as a butcher, he switched to the Hakoah team in New York. The job he got this time with the shoe company that sponsored Hakoah did not involve a great deal of work. Once again, he was one of the best players in the league and was named to the all-star team. This time he was playing in the EDSL, the Eastern District Soccer League.

The Continuation of a Tense Relationship: Vienna against Berlin

There was an intense competitive relationship between many of Shanghai's cafés. The German-style Café Louis was legendary, as was the Fiaker Restaurant at Joffre Avenue, which was run like a genuine Viennese Kaffeehaus. Café Klinger at 85 Wayside opened its doors on May 28, 1938, with a menu that was limited to Wiener Schnitzel, apple strudel, and dumplings with prune mousse filling. [35]

For Europeans, the living conditions in Shanghai were catastrophic, and this alone made these cafés and restaurant extremely attractive meeting places. The lifestyle that had been transferred from Europe to East Asia led some to refer affectionately to Shanghai in those days as "Little Berlin" and "Little Vienna." In his depiction of the social class structure in the emigrant community, David Kranzler categorized those who succeeded in starting up their own businesses as the most successful group. According to him, this group included those who had been responsible for establishing "Little Vienna." [36]

The fact that the experience of expulsion had done little to wipe out prejudices that the emigrants had brought with them was reflected most clearly by the perceptions that these exiles from Germany and Austria had of one another and which they repeatedly mentioned during the course of interviews. But it went further: even the differing styles of play of Austrian and German soccer players were maintained in exile.

Leo Meyer also recalled that Austrians and Germans did not get along well and seldom developed close friendships. Whereas some regard the Viennese style as technically oriented and speak of graceful dribbling, Leo

Meyer said that the Viennese were, in fact, more aggressive: "I wanted to win, too!" Fred Fields, on the other hand, did not find the differences all that significant. Nevertheless, what immediately came to his mind was the so-called Prager Gässchen, the style of play that had been adopted by Slavia Prag, in which players used short passes to fake out their opponents' defense. For him, the Germans played a faster and harder brand of soccer.

Kurt Duldner played on Embankment's second team. Even to this day, the eyes of some former Shanghai soccer players—his as well—begin to glow when they recall the highpoint of the season: the tensely awaited match between Vienna and Berlin. The intercity tournament had a long tradition in Europe and had already been played for the thirtieth time in Vienna in 1938. [37] In Shanghai as well, this game was hotly contested, but according to Kurt Duldner, it never led to violence.

This is not the appropriate place to elaborate on causes of the animosities between Austrians and Germans. Nevertheless, the extent to which these attitudes had been adopted by the Jewish population of both countries and continued in exile was remarkable. If we proceed under the assumption that many Jews of both countries harbored patriotic feelings toward their homelands, then the experience of expulsion had merely disturbed these basic attitudes but did not destroy them. When during the interviews we specifically inquired into these issues, the responses indicated that the tensions between the two groups existed but were not that strong. German emigrants repeatedly described their Austrian counterparts as very clannish. Perhaps this perception is based on the fact that the overwhelming majority of the Austrian refugees had lived in Vienna, whereas the Germans came from many different regions of the country and for this reason alone had less in common with one another than the Austrians. And this was another reason why sports was very important: individual soccer teams brought together members of groups who actually did not get along that well, like many Germans and Austrians. [38]

Some of the social networks among Shanghai émigrés still exist, and their members still keep in touch with one another. [39] When they met for a reunion at the Concord Hotel in Kiamesha Lake, New York, in 1985, the now-aged men could not let such an occasion go by without playing a soccer game. And which match-up seemed to be the most attractive? Of course it was Vienna versus Berlin! Just like in the old days, there was a shortage of equipment and uniforms, so it was decided that the Berliners would play in undershirts and the Viennese would play topless. As always, Leo Meyer gave

上海香港
埠際足球
秩序册

上海市體協會足球委員會出版
上海市體育記者聯誼會編行

三十六年五月
和國幣二千元

Printed by THE MERCURY PRESS

Leo Meyer (behind Chinese characters) played for the Shanghai Interport team,
here during a match in Macao. Courtesy of Leo Meyer.
(Editors' efforts to track other rightsholders were unsuccessful.)

it his all and played without regard to injury to himself or his opponents. Nevertheless, the game ended in a narrow victory for the Viennese. The article in the *New York Times* about the game reported: " 'It was a sport rivalry that was akin to that of the Yankees and the Red Sox and the Giants and the Jets,' said Leo Meyer, a Berliner, who was known to many present as 'one of the best soccer players in Shanghai.' For fun, the soccer rivalry was revived Wednesday afternoon on a football field near the hotel. For forty-five minutes, two older, less agile teams of Berliners and Viennese fought a spirited battle. Final score: Vienna 1, Berlin 0."[40]

Although the game was meant above all to be fun, the competition was played out in the usual no-holds-barred fashion. Some players were even injured so badly that they had to leave the field of play. Fred Fields was reduced to crutches for weeks. Robert Winokur forgot about his advanced age, leaping through the air to keep shots out of the Berliners' goal just like in the old days. But this spirited play exacted a high price: Winokur broke his shoulder. Nevertheless, as he said with a grin, the Viennese did not score until after he had been sent to the sidelines. This episode is another indication of the fact that soccer was not only important to the emigrants because of its numerous social and survival functions; it was also a serious sport that they pursued with tremendous enthusiasm.

Notes

I am thankful for suggestions provided by Helga Embacher and Michael John, and especially the interviewees Ann Bernfeld, Jerry Breuer, Kurt Duldner, Horst Eisfelder, Fred Fields, Ralph Hirsch, Alfred Lambert, Kurt Maimann, Leo Meyer, Robert H. Winokur, and Alfred Zunterstein.

1. See Georg Armbrüster, Michael Kohlstruck, and Sonja Mühlberger, eds., *Exil Shanghai 1938–1947: Jüdisches Leben in der Emigration* (Berlin, 2000).
2. See Helmut Kuhn, "Der Tiger der Thora," *Aufbau*, January 7, 1994, pp. 8–9; and Helmut Kuhn, *Fußball in den U.S.A.* (Temmen, 1994).
3. See Stella Dong, *Shanghai: The Rise and Fall of a Decadent City* (New York, 2001).
4. "Fußballsport im Fernen Osten," *Gelbe Post*, December 1, 1939, p. 7. Shanghai was considered one of the most important soccer towns in China. The international matches against Japan were especially popular, and were usually won by China. At the 1936 Summer Olympic Games, China lost its only match to England. See Richard Henshaw, *The Encyclopedia of World Soccer* (Washington DC, 1979), pp. 130–31.
5. See Bill Murray, *The World's Game: A History of Soccer* (Chicago, 1998).
6. See *Almanach-Shanghai* (1946–47), pp. 73–74, 76 (published by the Shanghai Echo). In 1946 soccer was once again played on Kinchow Road.
7. On the Barcelona restaurant see James R. Ross, *Escape to Shanghai: A Jewish Community in China* (New York, 1994), p. 25.
8. Ernest G. Heppner, *Shanghai Refuge: A Memoir of the World War II Jewish Ghetto* (London,

1995), pp. 40–41. The players quartered in the Embankment Building named their team after it (interview with Robert H. Winokur, August 23, 1999).

9. Interview with Winokur, December 17, 2002.

10. The company's ad in the 1945 *Sportkalender* stated, "H. Haeusler's Jam was always the best and it still is!"

11. *Shanghai Jewish Chronicle,* December 29, 1941, p. 6.

12. Interview with Kurt Maimann, March 4, 1997.

13. Interview with Jerry Breuer, September 25, 1998.

14. Heppner, *Shanghai Refuge,* pp. 113–15, 132–34; Ross, *Escape to Shanghai,* pp. 205–7.

15. *Aufbau,* March 29, 1946, p. 24.

16. Interview with Alfred Zunterstein, May 27, 1995.

17. Interview with Alfred Lambert, May 8, 1996.

18. Interview with Kurt Duldner, May 28, 1995.

19. For a description of the emigrant theater scene in Shanghai, see Michael Philipp, *Nicht einmal einen Thespiskarren: Exiltheater in Shanghai 1939–1947* (Hamburg, 1996).

20. Interview with Ann Bernfeld, October 14, 1995.

21. Among Shanghai refugees from Austria and Germany, there were approximately three thousand more men than women. See Helga Embacher and Margit Reiter, "Geschlechterbeziehungen in Extremsituationen. Österreichische und deutsche Frauen im Shanghai der dreißiger und vierziger Jahre," in Armbrüster, Kohlstruck, and Mühlberger, eds., *Exil Shanghai,* p. 133.

22. Interview with Kurt Duldner, May 28, 1995.

23. Interview with Robert H. Winokur, December 17, 2002.

24. Interview with Grete Winokur, December 17, 2002.

25. Interview with Robert H. Winokur, December 17, 2002.

26. Ross, *Escape to Shanghai,* p. 74; *Almanach-Shanghai* (1946–47), pp. 70ff.

27. See Horst Eisfelder, "Exil in China: Meine Zeit in Shanghai," in Amnon Barzel, ed., *Leben im Wartesaal: Exil in Shanghai 1938–1947* (Berlin, 1997), pp. 82–99.

28. See Paul Rosdy, *Adolf Josef Storfer: Shanghai und die Gelbe Post* (Vienna, 1999) ("Beilage zum Reprint der Gelben Post").

29. See *Sport* [Shanghai], May 24, 1945, p. 4.

30. See "2 Jahre 'Sport'-Sportplatz," *Sport,* November 20, 1943, p. 1.

31. Interview with Winokur, December 17, 2002.

32. A documentary was made of Leo Meyer's return to Shanghai, in which he not only tells about his earlier life, but also plays soccer with Chinese kids. See Diane Perelsztejn, *Escape to the Rising Sun,* 95 min. (Brussels, 1990). See also Ross, *Escape to Shanghai,* pp. 74–75.

33. See Ross, *Escape to Shanghai,* pp. 74–75, 185–86.

34. For example, Shanghai émigré newspapers on February 16, 1948, reported that the mini-soccer game that was to have been held in honor of Robert Winokur and three other players was cancelled on account of bad weather. Instead, his farewell ceremony featured dancing and tea (private archive of Robert H. Winokur).

35. "Restaurant Klinger—Good-bye," in *The Shanghai Herald,* April 12, 1946, p. 8.

36. David Kranzler, "The Miracle of Shanghai: An Overview," in *Exil Shanghai,* p. 37. See also David H. Kranzler, *Japanese, Nazis, and Jews: The Refugee Community of Shanghai, 1938–1945* (New York, 1976).

37. See *Neues Wiener Tagblatt,* November 20, 1938, p. 6.

38. See *Shanghai Jewish Chronicle*, September 11, 1942, p. 8.

39. Former Shanghai refugees stay informed about each other with newsletters such as *Bulletin* (Association of Former Residents of China) or *The Hongkew Chronicle*, which Max Kopstein and Curt M. Pollak founded in 1981. The Internet also provides this group with a means of global communication. See, for example, http://www.rickshaw.org.

40. Lena Williams, "800 Refugees at Reunion Recall Life in the Ghetto of Shanghai," *New York Times*, September 6, 1985.

12. Sports in the DP Camps, 1945–1948

Philipp Grammes

A morbid phenomenon which is very difficult to eradicate has crept in to affect the Jewish spectators. Sport has become a business, a gambling contest, mere hooliganism, and various terror methods are used to ensure victory. . . . Every game in Feldafing ends in a fight, and not only in Feldafing but elsewhere too.[1]

JEWISH SPECTATORS FIGHTING soon after the Holocaust: In Germany of all places, barely a year after the end of the Third Reich, Jewish sports clubs were competing against each other, fighting, boxing, playing soccer, Jews against Jews—in their own leagues and followed with great interest by a large group of supporters (who, as we have seen above, did not always treat each other gently). Between 1945 and 1950, on German soil, "which is soaked with our blood,"[2] European-Jewish diaspora life flourished one last time. Around a quarter of a million Jews, mainly of eastern European origin, were living in West Germany, in barracks and workers' housing estates, on farms and in former slave-labor camps. They had survived the Nazi terror and were now "Displaced Persons" (DPs)—or She'erith Hapletah, as they called themselves.[3] They were not able or did not want to return to their old homes in Central and Eastern Europe, since there had recently been pogroms against those Jews who had survived in hiding or in exile in Russia. Nor could they go to Palestine or the United States, as the policy of the British Mandate and the strict American immigration regulations denied them entry. Hence they were forced to wait in the assembly centers that had been set up by the occupying authorities, most of them located in southern Germany.

In this state of temporariness they developed their own Jewish culture, in modern Germany hitherto unknown.[4] The She'erith Hapletah established organs of self-administration and elected political leaders, they started up schools and published Yiddish newspapers, they built up their own infrastructure with kosher cooking and Jewish libraries, they organized theater productions and cultural evenings. And they played a great deal of sports. They played in their own clubs and in supraregional leagues and they fought for trophies and championship titles. Sports was an occupation and a distraction in the fight against the monotony of camp life—and it was also

187

blown up ideologically, as training for the struggle in and for their own nation in Palestine.

Historians have recently begun to examine the history of She'erith Hapletah more intensively, and they have investigated and at least outlined the self-administration organs and structures in the camps, as well as their theaters and schools. Cultural activities, and in particular those of the theater groups, are generally considered to have been decisive factors for the education, identity-formation and self-conception of the She'erith Hapletah. Sports, however, have been relegated to the fringe; yet sports must surely have been at least as important to the She'erith Hapletah as theater, schools, and other cultural institutions: Sports clubs, training groups and league teams provided considerably larger groups of people with an occupation and fulfillment than did the theater groups (which is not to detract from the value of the latter, of course).

It is therefore high time to examine more closely the development of sports and the role they played in the Jewish DP camps. The focus will be on the American-occupied Zone, since it is there that most of the Jewish DPS were quartered and the sports scene there was the most diverse.[5] Because for the most part the self-administration organs of the She'erith Hapletah did not attach much value to sports, in the archives there are hardly any documents from which the sports scene can be reconstructed. It is mainly from the She'erith Hapletah camp newspapers that we gain an insight into the competitions and championships. In the match reports and sports columns of these papers the whole spectrum of teams, different sports, and clubs is revealed.[6]

The Emergence of the She'erith Hapletah in the American Zone

In the first months after liberation sports were out of the question. For the Jews it was a matter of bare survival at first, and later of searching for surviving relatives and friends, as well as setting up their own DP camps. The majority of the approximately fifty thousand surviving Jews spent the first months following the end of the war in assembly centers close to the places from which they had been liberated, along with the DPS of other nationalities. They were forced to live together with Poles, Ukrainians, or Latvians, some of whom had collaborated with the Nazis and among whom there were also former "Kapos" (i.e., overseers) from the concentration camps. In view of this situation, and after massive Jewish protests, the American authorities started setting up camps that were exclusively for Jews. The camps in Feldafing, Föhrenwald, and Landsberg am Lech were established between the end of April and the middle of June 1945, but it was only after the report by U.S. Special Ambassador Earl G. Harrison in August 1945, condemning the plight of the Jews in the American zone, that they were made into camps for Jews alone.[7]

While the occupation authorities were changing their policy on Jewish DPs, the latter were also increasingly taking matters into their own hands. In Landsberg, located in southwest Bavaria, for instance, a camp committee met for the first time at the beginning of September, which was then officially confirmed in a democratic vote on October 21, 1945.[8] According to its first report, the aim of the committee was to represent the camp residents in the Jewish and non-Jewish world outside, to organize the administration of the camp, and to raise the material and cultural standard and the morale of the Jews in Landsberg.[9] To this end, a "cultural department" was established as a separate institution, which was to organize school education and specialist training and to arrange theater and song evenings, and which also produced the *Landsberger Lager-Cajtung*, the Yiddish-language publication of the Landsberg Jews. Later the self-administration branched out to establish a tribunal, a health department, a rabbinate, an economic department, and others. All the other big Jewish DP camps in the American zone also organized themselves along the lines of the Landsberg model.

A national committee of the liberated Jews had already been set up in July 1945. Around forty representatives from different camps assembled in Feldafing to elect the Central Committee of Liberated Jews in Bavaria, which chose Munich as its base.[10] The central committee subsequently created a number of central institutions, which were based on the structures in the individual camps. Thus only shortly after the central committee was constituted, the cultural department was created, followed by the public relations department in August 1945, the economic department in September, and the health department and rabbinate in October.[11] These structures remained in place when the Bavarian central committee was extended to include the Jewish representatives from Hessen and Baden-Württemberg, becoming the Zentralkomitee der befreiten Juden in der amerikanischen Besatzungszone in Deutschland (Central Committee of Liberated Jews in the American Occupation Zone in Germany) at the end of January 1946.

The self-administration in the camps and at the zone level formed the institutional framework in which the very diverse activities of the She'erith

Hapletah could develop. For example, the cultural departments soon established schools and libraries and organized theater and song evenings. The U.S. military authorities welcomed the Jewish self-administration, but did not give it active financial support. And likewise the committees were given rooms and facilities by the UN refugee organization UNRRA, which ran the camps, but no money. American-Jewish aid organizations such as the American Joint Distribution Committee (AJDC) thus played an important part; with the help of their networks in the United States they were able to provide aid in the form of necessities like clothes and shoes, but also books, typewriters, and other equipment. Without their help the newspapers would not have appeared, nor would schools have opened—and the sports clubs would have been without balls and other sports equipment.

Sport Is Taken Up Again

With the forming of self-administration, which culminated with the first congress of the liberated Jews in the U.S. zone from January 27–29, 1946, in Munich, the Jewish DP camps were consolidated, and something like an everyday life came into being—though under very particular conditions.[12] One manifestation of this was the establishment of Jewish sports teams: Now that their physical survival was ensured, and the prospects of emigration held little promise as a result of the world political situation, the DPs began to reflect on their roots—one part of which was, after all, a lively interest in sports. It is not possible to ascertain when the first teams played against each other, as the first DP newspapers, which went on to become a forum for camp sports, did not appear until early October 1945.[13]

The first match report in the *Landsberger Lager-Cajtung* announced that Ichud Landsberg had beaten Maccabi Turkheim 7–0 at soccer on October 28, 1945, and that over two thousand spectators had watched the game.[14] One week later, when Landsberg beat Maccabi Feldafing 1–0, apparently as many as three thousand spectators were present.[15] Yet by then there were already more sports being played than just soccer: the same article reports that Landsberg had lost against Feldafing in table tennis.

In October 1945, then, there were already individual Jewish sports clubs that played against each other. The commitment of single individuals must have been the decisive factor, however, since the self-administration institutions had only just started to tackle the area of sports and organize it for the broader masses. On October 24, for example, the administration in Landsberg established its own sports department.[16] This new sports department had sections for basketball, volleyball, boxing, track and field, gymnastics, table tennis, and soccer.

This dual structure, with the Jewish sports clubs on the one hand and the sports institutions on the other, was not limited to Landsberg. In the beginning especially, sports clubs and the official instances of the self-administration were frequently established and run in tandem. It was not until February 1946, when the official Center for Physical Education (center far fizisze dercijung) was founded at the health department in Munich, that some kind of structure was brought into the maze of all the various competences. [17] The center immediately requested progress reports from the sports clubs, took over the supraregional coordination, and helped to supply equipment. Nevertheless, in many camps the dual structure of clubs and official committee-departments remained in existence.

The Year 1946: Championships, Sports Festivals, and Scandals

While there were competitions between Jewish teams in 1945, as described above, these were generally friendly matches, where apart from honor there was nothing to be won. It was not until the following year that leagues were established, and in soccer especially, the fight for a zone-wide championship title began. This came about above all as a result of radical demographic changes, which led to several new camps and Kibbutzim being set up, and with them an increase in the number of Jewish sports clubs and teams. Pogroms, and the desire to emigrate to Palestine, had triggered off a wave of the remaining Jews fleeing Poland, so that in 1946 the number of Jewish DPs in the American zone rose from about 40,000 to over 145,000. [18] The great speed of this development can be seen if we take the camp in Bamberg (northern Bavaria) as an example. Established on December 19, 1945, by the end of the year there were already 800 Jews living there. Only half a year later, by the end of July 1946, their number had more than doubled to 1,665. [19] At the first conference of the Jewish sports clubs in the U.S. zone, on April 21 in Landsberg, the representatives from Bamberg were in a position to report that thanks to the help of UNRRA, they had established a sports club. [20] The situation was similar in other camps: the arrival of Polish refugees led to the creation of several new sports clubs.

It is worthwhile taking a closer look at the conference of the sports clubs. Through the comments of the individual participants, much is revealed about the state of sports among the She'erith Hapletah at the time. Thus the representatives from the central committee, for example, reported that in the U.S. zone there were now 5,740 athletes organized in clubs, which bore names like "Hakoah," "Bar Kochba," or—the most popular, with one third being so named—"Maccabi"; there were nine different clubs registered in the Munich district alone. Afterward, the representatives of the individual clubs gave their progress reports: Feldafing (near Munich) reported that besides Maccabi there was now a workers' sports club, Hapoel, that 750 athletes altogether were registered, and that there was a lack of equipment and clothing; Zeilsheim (near Frankfurt) complained that they were receiving no help from UNRRA, so they were helping themselves and also providing their friends in Lampertheim with assistance in setting up a club there. Stuttgart complained about their own camp committee, which had been disregarding the interests of the athletes; Schwabach (near Nuremburg) was proud to report that half of their eighty residents were members of their Kadimah sports club—though they were short of everything they needed, which is why the local German club was helping them out; Föhrenwald (near Munich) boasted of its "splendidly equipped" gymnasium, but on the other hand they lacked soccer and athletics equipment, and so on and so forth.

The Landsberg representatives were the last to report, and their account highlights the stark differences between the standards of the different clubs: while other clubs were happy to have three dozen participants and a gymnasium that was just about in working order, Landsberg reported an impressive 800 active athletes in the camp itself, with another 600 in the surrounding Kibbutzim. They had sections for soccer, tennis, basketball, table tennis, chess, bicycle-racing, and even motorsports—only the "fitness exercises" were in need of improvement, owing to a lack of coaches.

In view of this imbalance, the director of the Center for Physical Education, Dr. Boris Pliskin, promised at the conference to provide as much help as possible. He said there was no money, but they would start up a course for coaches and appeal for more support for the sports clubs from UNRRA and the aid organizations. He would also make contact with teams abroad. When asked if it would not be a good idea to cooperate with German athletes, Pliskin relied: "We should not associate ourselves with German teams, nor should we play against them, and not against other DP teams either. We should try to get by through our own efforts and not allow any German coaches."[21] Here a lengthy debate unfolded, the outcome of which was that the conference agreed that in exceptional cases, German coaches could be taken on until the center sent Jewish ones.

It was not only in the question of disassociation from other nationalities that this first conference of the Jewish sports clubs was a pathbreaking one; it was also here that the Verband der jüdischen Sport-Klubs in der amerikanischen Besatzungszone (Association of Jewish Sports Clubs in the U.S. Zone) was constituted, which from this point on was to organize the leagues and championships of the She'erith Hapletah, under the auspices of the Center for Physical Education. The conference also represented a first step toward professionalization—many of the sports functionaries in the camps and clubs were enthusiasts who not only lacked equipment, but also the necessary specialist knowledge. An impression of this can be gleaned from the following dialogue between Pliskin and a representative from Feldafing, which the AJDC director at the time, Leo W. Schwarz, recounted in his memoirs:

> [Functionary:] "We could prepare the field, but before we requisition American machines to put it in shape, we have to measure the length and width of the arena. I'll take care of that. Don't worry."
> [Pliskin:] "I'm not worried. But there's no need to make a special excursion to the field. It's hundred meters long and fifty wide."
> "Where did you get this information?"
> "What do you mean 'where'? Any athlete worth his salt knows how large a soccer field should be." [22]

The size of the soccer field was a problem quickly solved, but the complaints about the lack of equipment were to be a lasting issue. The matter was remedied to some extent by donations from the United States, and these did not come only from Jewish aid organizations: "Many of the soccer and basketballs and boxing gloves had been contributed by the American Catholic and Protestant organizations." [23] Here, too, it was the central associations in Munich that organized the distribution of the donations.

The associations thus created the conditions under which the sports activities of the She'erith Hapletah were able to flourish, leading to the following announcement in the Landsberger Lager-Cajtung at the end of May 1946: "The sport season is in full swing. In almost every Jewish Center sports competitions are taking place weekly." [24] According to Schwarz, there were over forty sports clubs active in the U.S. zone at the beginning of 1946. [25] By July 1946 there were already sixty-four clubs, with around 7,800 members—and the number continued to rise. [26] Yet the majority of DPs who actively pursued sports were not even included in this figure. They were not club members, but took part in the range of sports that were open to all, taking gymnastics classes, and so forth. Sports in the DP camps had become a mass phenomenon.

Along with the growing number of athletes and clubs, the wish of the DPs to compete with each other also grew. At first there were single friendly matches, in soccer especially, then later tournaments were organized, and ultimately zone-wide championships. Some of these sports events will be exemplified in what follows.

On July 6 and 7, 1946, a "boxing championship of all Jewish sports clubs in the American zone" took place in Zeilsheim near Frankfurt. In fact only four clubs took part in this, the first boxing championship of the She'erith Hapletah.[27] This low level of participation explains why the DP press hardly devoted any space to the event.[28] The Zeilsheim camp paper *Unterwegs* reported that the director of the cultural department greeted those present and emphasized how important sports were.[29] There was no mention of the names of the athletes and no report on the fights. Incidentally, the fact boxing was the very sport in which the functionaries enjoyed an especially prominent role is borne out in the bon mot by the Bamberg editor Chaim Goldzamd, who made this nasty remark about the sports column in his paper *Undzer Wort*: "A sports column (particularly boxing) specially for the committee members."[30] The cup for this first boxing championship had been donated by the Zeilsheim UNRRA director. "In addition the winners of the finals received a package with sportswear."[31]

The first track and field championships of the She'erith Hapletah in the U.S. zone took place in Landsberg on September 15–16, 1946. The sports field there was ceremonially opened immediately before the competition. The contests were in the Olympic disciplines, although the *Landsberger Lager-Cajtung* mentions women participants only for the hundred-meter sprint.[32]

There were only a few reports on other sports to be found in the DP press, in which soccer predominated massively. However, there do appear to have been championships in other sports as well. The *Landsberger Lager-Cajtung* mentioned a "league match" in basketball, for example, between Landsberg and Feldafing on August 19, 1946—although the league evidently cannot have been very big, as both Landsberg and Feldafing had two teams playing in it.[33] There are similarly sparse indications that there were leagues and championships in table tennis and volleyball, too.[34]

It was the soccer competitions that met with the greatest interest on the part of the spectators and the press. As described above, there had already been friendly matches between Jewish DP teams in 1945. In the end, what provided the impetus for building up a proper soccer league was the Passover tournament from April 18 to 22, 1946, on which occasion Ichud Landsberg had gathered together the best Jewish teams in the American zone. The cup was donated by the Landsberg UNRRA director A. C. Glassgold, who said in his opening speech: "My wish for you, dear athletes, is that the next time you compete with each other it may be next year in Eretz Israel!"[35] Then the players paraded past the rostrum with their team flags. The following qualifying matches were watched by more than three thousand spectators. By the third day, of the twelve teams that had been playing in the tournament only Landsberg and Feldafing were unbeaten, and they fought it out in the final in front of five thousand spectators. In the second half, though, the match was broken off "owing to the unsporting behavior of the Feldafing players toward the referee."[36] After much heated discussion, the match recommenced the following morning: "Landsberg played offensively and were technically and tactically better than the Feldafing team, but yet again the match was broken off, this time because the referee was unable to control the game. The tournament was therefore left unfinished and there was no victor."[37]

Nevertheless, the Pessach tournament in Landsberg was the spark that triggered off the foundation of the She'erith Hapletah soccer league in the U.S. zone. The tournament had proved that there were enough teams that could play the game well enough, and what is more, on more or less the same level. The great interest on the part of the spectators, too, was further confirmation for the association officials to set up a league. The DPs were craving sports—not only in order that they could actively participate, but also as a channel for their longings and energies.

Until the middle of 1946, then, the soccer matches between the different camps and clubs were above all friendly games, serving as a platform for contact and solidarity between the groups, and as such were praised by the newspapers for their good atmosphere. With the establishment of their own soccer league, the competition among the She'erith Hapletah took on a completely different character: now the battle for the championship was at the forefront. This certainly enhanced the attractiveness of the games, but at the same time it also led to a greater degree of unsporting behavior on the part of the players and spectators.

The top league of the She'erith Hapletah was made up of the nine best teams in the U.S. zone. Three other clubs had proved themselves in the Landsberg Pessach tournament to be too weak for this top league. They played with several other smaller clubs in the second league, the so-called "A-Klasse."[38] The top league got under way, accompanied by great spectator interest, on July 13, 1946. At the match between Landsberg and Feldafing, for instance, there were four thousand spectators.[39] The highlights were above all the matches between the very top teams:

> The match aroused great interest in Stuttgart. All the Jews in Stuttgart were present at this soccer event. . . . Landsberg started off with strong attacks, and already in the 37th minute Urbach (Landsberg) headed a goal from a corner from the outside-right Mundek. At the end of the first half it stood at 1–0 to Landsberg. . . . Stuttgart started to attack very aggressively, with the result that goalkeeper Helfing got a bad eye injury and center-right Urbach was hit in the foot and couldn't play on at first. . . . It seemed as if Stuttgart wanted to win with sheer might. But the Landsberg defense is in a class of its own. They let nothing get past them, and even in the final minute Urbach managed to head the ball over the goal. . . . The match ended in a 1–1 draw.[40]

The smaller teams could not keep pace with this level. In 1946 Ichud Landsberg won the soccer championship in the U.S. zone, followed by Feldafing and Stuttgart. Ichud Landsberg's triumph can be ascribed on the one hand to the better general conditions: Landsberg was one of the biggest and oldest Jewish DP camps. The club had 853 members, 210 of them active athletes.[41] Landsberg could already boast soccer teams before many of the other camps even existed. The main factor behind their success, however, was the sheer quality of their players. Unlike the other teams, which often recruited newcomers to the sport, the Ichud team was made up exclusively of men who had been active soccer players before the war—often on Jewish teams, like the midfielder Goldberg, who had played for Maccabi Warsaw. The undisputed star of the team was the right winger, Mundek Schulsinger, aged thirty-seven, who had been a professional soccer player with Gwiazda Warsaw before the war and had also played for the Polish workers' eleven.[42] In the match reports he is often highlighted as the best player.

The 1946 soccer season ended with a festive celebration in Munich. Within the space of a year, a professional operation had been formed from the diverse improvised clubs, soccer pitches, and leagues. As the Center for

Physical Education proudly announced, at the end of 1946 there were ninety-five Jewish clubs in the American zone, with around fifteen thousand active DPs.[43] This professional operation had not only brought forth successful clubs and zone-wide championships, however, but had also changed the attitude of the She'erith Hapletah toward sports in general and toward the teams in particular. In any case, what now arose was a phenomenon that is a matter of course in professional sports, but which does come as quite a surprise in view of the special solidarity of the Jewish DPs: unsporting play, spectator riots, and cheating started to occur increasingly:

> The Regensburg sports club had a German referee. When he saw that things were going badly, he only blew the whistle on the other side's fouls. The other thing that was striking is that certain Regensburg Jews even stooped to using obscene language. The climax at this match came when one Regensburger ran around with a knife in his hand, threatening anyone who had dared to express the hope that Straubing would win. The game had to be abandoned because of physical attacks by the Regensburg side.[44]

This report basically contains the whole gamut of scandals that the sports of the She'erith Hapletah had to offer. It was often the referees who were a cause of aggravation. Many of the accusations in the DP press that the referees were biased could well be explained by the fact that these press reports were usually written by players or officials from one of the teams involved. Yet in the beginning especially, the referees did indeed often lack the specialized knowledge needed to manage a match smoothly, which is why some matches had to be broken off—the Passover tournament in Landsberg described above is one example. Just how emotionally fraught the soccer matches were altogether is borne out by the numerous riots and incidents among the spectators and the players. These did not always involve knives, though; according to the *Jidisze Cajtung*, reporting on the game between Hakoah Hof and Maccabi Marktredwitz, "Hof cannot countenance the fact that Marktredwitz holds the initiative; Hakoach has a bad attitude toward Maccabi, and as a result, a Maccabi player was punched by one of the Hakoah players. The Hof fans behaved badly too; they crowded together as an organized group behind the Marktredwitz goal in order to distract the goalkeeper—they really put on a shocking display."[45]

The match was stopped twenty minutes before the end after the Marktredwitz players left the field in protest. Yet that was not the end of the affair:

Hakoah Hof made an official complaint about the accusations that had been made and disputed the fact that it had been their fans who had been so rowdy. Marktredwitz then countered again in the *Jidisze Cajtung* a couple of issues later: "The people who congregated behind the 'Maccabi' goal were indeed definitely from Hof, since, as has already been reported, there was a typhoid epidemic in Marktredwitz at the time, so only the players were allowed to travel to Hof."[46]

Furthermore, the newspapers reported that now and then teams kept the money from the entrance tickets for themselves, although these proceeds were normally divided up between both teams. This was certainly one source of trouble, but it caused nothing like the consternation brought about by what the associations called an "offence against national pride": the inclusion of non-Jewish players in their teams. One official from Amberg, for example, accused the club from Cham of having included "Yugoslavian murderers" in its team, to which Cham retorted in its defense: "We have been accused of having Yugoslavian murderers playing for us— yet the truth of the matter is that we had one single Yugoslavian."[47]

In the end, such breaches of the rules and unsporting behavior did not cause more than an angry stir in the 1946 season. There were no arbitrational proceedings or disciplinary tribunals which could have imposed and enforced sanctions. The press was thus the only outlet through which people could give vent to their annoyance: "Instead of friendly games they should rather be called hostile games. . . . Would it not be better to disband the sports clubs, given that they cause us more damage than they benefit us? It is simply a huge disgrace to make enemies of each other just because one side did not win a game."[48]

Luckily, nothing came of this suggestion. In the new season, other ways and means were tried out to impose more discipline on the players and spectators.

The Year 1947: The Heyday of DP Sports

Around a hundred clubs in the U.S. zone launched themselves into the 1947 season, playing friendly and championship matches in almost a dozen different sports. A few new clubs were founded in 1947 as well, but on the whole the sporting scene was consolidated now.[49] The structures of the associations were firmly in place and the leagues had been established. After the great flood of Polish Jews in the previous year the population of the camps now remained constant. A normality of sorts had entered camp life, especially since the hope of a chance to emigrate in the near future had not been fulfilled, as the world political situation had stagnated.[50] The tendency toward professionalization that had manifested itself in 1946 continued to increase. The leagues became more differentiated, zone-wide championships took on the form of major events, and last but not least, the founding of a dedicated sports magazine, *Jidisze Sport Cajtung*, reflected the heightened status sports now enjoyed. In short, in 1947 the sports of the She'erith Hapletah was at its peak.

The "biggest sports event of 1946/47" took place from the end of January 1947 in the Zirkus-Krone-Bau (Circus Krone Arena) in Munich: the boxing championship of all the American-zone Jewish sports clubs.[51] "Drums rolled. The hall was filled with light. Applause thundered as two ten-year-old boys from Landsberg . . . stepped into the ring and gave a neat round of exhibition boxing which was declared, fittingly, a draw."[52] The championship was a major social event, as is borne out by the presence there of high-ranking representatives of the military administration and the central committee. The competition reached its climax at the finals on the last evening. The Zirkus-Krone-Bau was "completely full, packed with guests, fans, boxers, and regular spectators. Hundreds of people had to stay outside because there wasn't enough space. There were around 2,000 spectators at the finals."[53] Both Jewish and German journalists and photographers reported on this event. The newly fledged zone champions achieved considerable popularity; "victory banquets" were held for them in the various camps for weeks after the event, at which they proudly presented their trophies.[54] For many boxers the championship in Munich meant a kind of return to normality after the long, dark years of the Holocaust. "It was evident that many of the boxers were not novices. Several of the boxers had held amateur and professional records before the war."[55] This goes far to explain the high standard of the Jewish boxers: "Some former Polish champions are the coaches of the Jewish future champions and have very good results."[56] The makeshift nature and the necessity to improvise that had marked camp sports, at least in the beginning, should not hide the fact that the sporting achievements of the She'erith Hapletah were indeed something they could rightfully boast about.

More evidence of this is the "sensational boxing match against negroes" which took place in Munich in October 1947.[57] At this event a selection team of the She'erith Hapletah fought against a selection of the American occupying forces, which even had reinforcements from the Berlin garrison. This tournament revealed that the Jewish boxers were an equal match to the

Americans in every respect. In the end the Americans just won narrowly, 8–6, which was celebrated as a victory in the *Jidisze Sport Cajtung*: "Our boxers have demonstrated their high level and we can say with pride that the Jewish fists are a match for anybody."[58]

Similar competitions between Jewish clubs and teams of the occupying forces took place quite frequently in many places, and in Landsberg even on a regular basis. While the Americans were often better at boxing, the Jewish teams often emerged as the winners in other sports.[59] Yet it was not only the American forces who were welcome opponents: in August 1947 a select boxing team from the U.S. zone fought against a selection of Jewish boxers from Austria.[60] In December 1947 the soccer team Maccabi Munich traveled to Berlin to play against various Jewish DP teams.[61] Such matches against other Jewish DP teams or against the Americans were very important to the She'erith Hapletah, as they demonstrated that the She'erith Hapletah could hold their own against other nations. In the humiliating situation of camp life, such representative games helped to restore confidence and were a source and a sign of strength.

The soccer league in the U.S. zone reached its peak early in 1947 as well. What had started off in 1946 in a somewhat makeshift fashion was now in 1947 governed by clear rules regarding its composition and for qualification. The top league was enlarged considerably as a result: the best teams from the A-Klasse fought for promotion to the top league in playoffs in February and March 1947. They were joined by Maccabi Munich, whose membership in the top league was decided on by the Center for Physical Education.[62] The number of teams in the top league was thus increased from nine to twenty-two. In order to ensure that the competitions would nevertheless run smoothly, at a meeting on April 26, 1947, the Center for Physical Education decided to split the league up into a northern and a southern division.[63] There were ten teams in the northern league, and twelve in the southern.

These newly constituted leagues fast became magnets for spectators. In the smaller towns there tended to be between five hundred and a thousand spectators, while big, successful clubs such as Landsberg or Zeilsheim drew crowds of up to five thousand at times. It was these two clubs, too, that dominated their leagues virtually unchallenged. They had the most consistent players and the most experience, whereas the teams at the bottom end of the table had to fight against a problem that the *Jidisze Sport Cajtung* noted: "In the first round we saw a number of brilliant players, but unfortunately they have only few talented teammates and so they often lose."⁶⁴ According to the paper, the weaker teams were still profiting from the league, though, as their level had risen considerably. At the end of the season Ichud Landsberg, rather unsurprisingly, was the old and the new soccer champion of the She'erith Hapletah in the American zone. A championship was planned for 1948 as well, and in December 1947 and January 1948 the teams at the top of the A-Klasse fought in the playoffs for promotion to the top league.⁶⁵ However, in the end there was to be no new champion in 1948, owing to the mass emigration to Israel and the closing of the DP camps.

In view of the mass of matches that had had to be abandoned and the unsporting incidents, all of which threw a shadow over the noble ideal of sports propagated by the central committee, at the beginning of the 1947 season the Center for Physical Education implemented a number of measures designed to induce the spectators and the players alike to stick to the rules. For example, a refereeing seminar was started, which even went on to have its own representative in the association of sports clubs.⁶⁶ The most important measure, however, was probably the founding of a disciplinary committee, which from then on was to introduce and monitor regulations and to impose sanctions.

In April 1947 the new committee took up its work with a vengeance. For "playing with and against Germans," for instance, four soccer players were each suspended for two months; "all the players expressed their deepest regrets, admitted that they were at fault, and solemnly swore that it would not happen again." ⁶⁷ The committee imposed the same punishment for similar offences in table tennis and boxing. In another disciplinary action, two members of the administration were disqualified for the rest of the season for "the willful use of a Christian player." One player was prohibited from coaching a German team. On the other hand, the protest of one club that the opposing team had used a Christian player was rejected, "because the player is half-Jewish and has been acknowledged by the rabbinate and the regional association in Regensburg." ⁶⁸ The punishment for hitting an opponent was disqualification for a month, and the coach of a boxing team was disqualified for the rest of the year for hitting a referee.

Since in the previous season it had not only been the players but also the spectators who had behaved so badly, the Center for Physical Education now planned draconian punishments for all kinds of unsporting behavior. The referees in particular were given special protection: should the referee be hit by a spectator, the club management of the home team would be held responsible—the match could be broken off, with the opposing team being granted a victory, and the pitch could be closed down for up to a year. Similar measures were to be imposed if spectators should invade the pitch or cause a disturbance on the sidelines.[69]

Even with such an arsenal at their disposal, the effect of the disciplinary committee's decisions left much to be desired at first. The *Jidisze Sport Cajtung*, for example, mockingly wrote that the first half of the season had ended on a lucky note, "since there were no fatalities, no serious injuries either, and the few dozen players who had been hit or had suffered minor injuries cannot seriously be seen as a cause for consternation."[70] In fact the unsporting behavior did continue: "The disciplinary committee had many difficulties to deal with, these basically being undisciplined players and functionaries and often wild spectators as well. They have decided to tackle all breaches of discipline more forcefully, and we hope that the second half of the season will proceed more calmly."[71] This wish was to remain unfulfilled: in spite of clear rules and draconian sanctions, the sports associations did not get the problem of rampaging spectators and players under control to the last.

The Year 1948: Athletes Are Mobilized

In November 1947 the partition of Palestine was resolved by the UN; in May 1948 the British Mandate ended and the state of Israel came into being. The Jewish DP camps were gradually closed down and the residents emigrated to Israel in droves. Whereas there were still 165,000 Jewish DPs in Germany in April 1948, five months later there were fewer than half of this number left—and the trend continued apace.[72] This being the situation, the Jewish sports scene collapsed.

Although the associations were well aware of the imminent end of the British Mandate and the new prospects for emigration that this would entail, the 1948 season got underway as if nothing had happened—planning for the new season was carried on vigorously. At the beginning of March the league matches in soccer were started, and at the beginning of April a new innovation was introduced. Until then, every fifth weekend had been free of matches; now all fifty-two teams from the first and second leagues were to play in a cup competition on these weekends.[73] This competition was due to start on April 10, 1948; yet even for this first weekend, the *Jidisze Sport Cajtung* reported "weak participation."[74] Many clubs automatically reached the second round because their opponents had not appeared. It is doubtful whether any second-round matches were played at all—at any rate, the cup competition no longer received a mention in the DP newspapers.

With the founding of the state of Israel on May 14th, 1948, and the invasion by the neighboring Arab states that followed hard on its heels, in sports, too, more important issues took the limelight. The superior military might of the Arabs made the stocking up of the Israeli army an immediate necessity; this also set off a wave of excitement in the self-administration area in the U.S. zone.[75] The sports associations now appealed for the mobilization of the athletes: "We athletes must prove that we are the spearhead of the nation. All athletes must join in the campaign for mobilization in this historic hour, and be the first to volunteer!"[76] As a consequence, whole teams together volunteered for the army and left Germany.[77] The championships thus lost their lifeblood. The 1948 boxing championship in the middle of April, for example, which the organizers had intended to be equally impressive as in the year before, only lasted two instead of three days. The signs of disintegration are documented in the Jidisze Sport Cajtung: "Despite intensive efforts, the attempt to bring together a large number of participants and thus gain a more representative overview of our boxers was unsuccessful. Some of the boxers have already joined up and left the country, others are in special training courses for recruits, and the remaining few dozen who actually came to Munich were unable to impress, being badly prepared and having but little fight in them."[78]

The disintegration of the soccer leagues is not so precisely documented. The last league table for the southern league that appeared in the Jidisze Sport Cajtung showed how things stood on April 18.[79] In the June issue the Jidisze Sport Cajtung then announced that the championship had been "stopped temporarily." It was intended that a youth championship would be initiated in its place.[80] It is improbable that this ever got off the ground, though, in view of the rapid bleeding of the whole sport system that was taking place.

Not all the clubs were disbanded abruptly, however. In December 1948, for instance, Undzer Weg reported that Maccabi Munich had sent a delegation to the Maccabi world congress in Tel Aviv.[81] Yet this was actually the last report on DP sport to appear in that newspaper. It is not possible to reconstruct from the DP press when the last club was disbanded. In any case, with the end of the camps, the short flourishing of Jewish sports in postwar Germany also came to an end.

The Status and Function of Sports in the DP Camps

They had escaped from the Holocaust, they were just regaining their strength after an unimaginable ordeal, they were prevented from emigrating to the land of their dreams, they were held in camps that, at least in the early days, were reminiscent of the concentration camps they had survived, they were imprisoned in despair and monotony—this was the situation of the Jewish survivors in Germany from 1945 to 1948. Therefore, one would hardly expect the existence of such a diverse sports scene as that of the She'erith Hapletah in the American zone. Yet the 175 sports clubs, around a dozen different sports, several zone-wide leagues, and thousands of spectators are an expression of the immensely important functions that, of all things, sports had in the social system of the DP camps.

Sports Provides an Outlet

"Physically weak, mentally destroyed, morally bereft, apathetic, resigned—that is the picture of the She'erith Hapletah when they were catapulted down from the heady heights of liberation into the dark depths of the DP camps." [82] Once freed from the concentration camps, they had hoped to be able to emigrate to countries like Palestine or the United States straight away. Nothing came of this. Instead they found themselves stuck fast in the hated Germany—and these shattered hopes remained with them for more than two years. This situation of temporariness wore away at their morale and gave rise to aggressions, which were intensified still further by the narrow confines and social constraints in the camps.

At the same time the camp residents cannot be regarded as a homogenous group. First of all there were their different origins. There were Jews from the Baltic states, Poland, Hungary, Romania, Greece, and other countries. They differed from one another with regard to their traditions, their dialects, and their social status in the camp. Baltic Jews often took on leading positions and considered themselves to belong to the intelligentsia, while Polish Jews, who after all did make up the bulk of the camp population, had little say in such matters. These social differences led to friction, as did the various political positions. The camp committees were dominated by Zionist groups, which is why most of the sports clubs, and the press as well, tended to be Zionist oriented. Non-Zionist parties and associations hardly had a voice at all—hence the intense rivalry between the supporters of the diverse political factions. Thus when sports clubs of opposing political orientation met, the matches soon turned into the "hostile games" mentioned above.

Probably, though, most of the players did not care too much about the political leanings of the club leadership. We therefore need to look for the psychological causes of the outbreaks of violence on and around the pitch. Inside the camps there were several trials in which Jews accused other Jews of collaborating with the National Socialists: Former inmates often recognized block orderlies and "Kapos" from the concentration camps, who were then charged at once; this led to a heated atmosphere of suspicion and mutual mistrust in the camps—the DP newspapers are full of cases in which the camp police and occupation troops were able to intervene just in time to prevent residents taking the law into their own hands and lynching the accused. In this respect, too, sports might have functioned as an outlet through which the DPs could channel their aggressions in a "permitted" fashion.

For the committee members, however, such incidents were not to be tolerated at all, standing as they did in opposition to the Zionist ideology of the "new man." Many appeals and complaints in the DP newspapers are concerned with the enormity of Jews fighting Jews: "On the sports field, feel solemn, feel Jewish, feel at home, feel you are all brothers of one clan, of one crippled but forbearing family. . . . Unfortunately they [the players] lack the feeling of brotherly love and sympathy toward all members of what is left of the small Jewish sport family after the annihilation." [83] This can be partially explained by the brutalization of manners brought about by the inhuman life in the concentration camps. [84] On the other hand, though, sports was actually the only possibility the DPs had to reduce their frustration and aggression levels—and the fact that their Jewish brothers were hurt in the process was only of secondary importance.

Sports Provides an Occupation

There was another big problem in the DP camps that also gave rise to aggressions: There was hardly any work or meaningful way of occupying time; even the Jewish holidays sank into monotony. "The third Passover festival on unclean German soil. . . . One holiday resembles the other. Each holiday is worse than the other—all our days are enshrouded in a dreary melancholy, a gnawing grief—we are strangers in a strange land!" [85] Sports provided a means of occupation in this monotonous situation—not only in clubs and fixed teams, but also in the open training sessions that large numbers of DPs took advantage of.[86] In Landsberg and elsewhere, gyms and sports equipment were available at fixed times for the use of anyone who was interested.

In this context sports took on another important function: the temporary state experienced by the DPs offered few opportunities for structuring daily life. It was unimportant if it was a Monday or a Wednesday, morning or evening. The DPs therefore lacked the necessary framework to organize their everyday lives. Here sports could provide structure: regular training sessions during the week and league matches on the Sabbath and on Sunday were temporal fixtures in an otherwise aimless and structureless condition.

Sports Creates a Sense of Community

The concentration camps had not only devastated the Jewish DPs physically; their cultural foundations had also been destroyed. Their pride in their Jewish traditions and origins had suffered under the Nazi ideology that saw Jews only as subhuman creatures. As the "propaganda poison" still had its after-effects, the political leaders of the She'erith Hapletah saw it as one of their major tasks "to eradicate the crippled psychological aberrations that the concentration camps tried to instill in us, such as feelings of inferiority and self-hate."[87] Sports was one means of achieving this.

There were the names of the sports clubs, for example. Names like Maccabi, or Bar Kochba established a link to glorious times. On the one hand, the Jewish clubs that had existed in Europe before the war, and that still existed in Palestine, bore such names. On the other hand, many of the names referred to Jewish resistance in the past—Simon Bar Kochba, for instance, had led a Jewish revolt against the Romans. In naming their clubs after historical models, the DPs were deliberately positioning themselves in their Jewish tradition.

Playing matches against Polish, American, or Swiss teams also contributed to the DPs' identification with the Jewish people. This is borne out by the newspaper reports. It was not only Landsberg camp residents playing soldiers from the occupying forces; at the same time they were very conscious of the fact that it was Jews versus Americans—and if, or rather, because, the Jews came off so well, this served to strengthen the sense of belonging to the Jewish people. After the humiliations of the Nazi terror, these competitions and the way they were perceived certainly had an element of "now we count for something again."

As far as identity is concerned, the rejection of all competition with German teams is also interesting. The abhorrence of the nation of their murderers undoubtedly played the biggest part in this, perhaps also sometimes the fear that a defeat could be regarded as being symbolic and revive old reflexes. But the concept of an enemy was also being created here, which reinforced the Jewish athletes' group identity, drew a clear dividing line that emphasized the sense of belonging to the Jewish people, and thus generated great integrative power. That this process was a deliberate one is borne out by the fact that it was the associations that prohibited such competitions and imposed drastic sanctions for violations of the ban, while the "simple" athletes did not seem to consider contact with the Germans to be such a bad thing. At any rate, sports was a tried and tested and exceedingly popular means of strengthening the sense of self-identification with the Jewish nation.

Sports Was Training for the Struggle in and for Eretz Israel

> The thrust of our work in the field of physical education must strictly take the direction of preparing our youth for the hard tasks they will face in the time ahead. Through physical training we must educate our youth in a spirit of strength, heroic courage, health, and general physical readiness.[88]

The education and training of the people is a factor that pervaded virtually all the activities and statements of the self-administration. On the one hand, the Zionist conception of humanity played its part in this, according to which not only was an independent state to be created in Eretz Israel, but also a new, well-educated, culturally advanced people with moral integrity. This ideal was the polar opposite of the mental and physical destruction from the years in concentration camps. Sports was thus first and foremost a means for the physical restoration of the people. On the other hand, though, it was also played up ideologically as a weapon for the (military) struggle in Palestine.[89] The committee members' penchant for boxing can also be seen against this background; they regarded boxing as a "national defense sport for Jews."

> "Through boxing, a person's physical condition and strength is developed first of all. Then he develops speed, stamina, cold-bloodedness, pugnacity, the will to win, and, best of all, heroic courage. . . . If we take all of this into consideration in connection with the situation we find ourselves in after the great catastrophe which has befallen our people, we cannot but draw the conclusion that boxing must take on the character of a mass sport, because for us boxing is so important for self-defense."[90]

Although the idea of preparation in the struggle for Palestine was more of a subliminal one at first, with the UN partition resolution in November 1947 it was openly declared to be the most urgent function of sports. According to Boris Pliskin, for example, president of the association of Jewish sports clubs, writing in the *Jidisze Sport Cajtung*: "We need to create a mighty liberation legion, which should join together with the heroic Haganah [*one of the Jewish resistance groups in Palestine*] which stands watch over the birth of our nation. We must be strong, courageous, disciplined, and ready when the call [to battle] comes."[91] And again, two months later, in the face of the Arab threats: "Only somebody who is strong and energetic will be able to confront the danger; only a vigorous, physically fit Jew can optimally defend our honor, our home, and our lives."[92]

The whole extent to which sports was blown up ideologically can be seen in the reaction of the DP officials to Israel's war of independence: "Today the time has come for Jewish athletes: what we planted in our bodies on the sports fields must now burgeon with the strength our people needs, with stamina, ambition, and the will to fight."[93] Thus, from the perspective of the sports associations it was completely obvious that the athletes should be the first to register to join up—and many teams did indeed emigrate in their entirety to Israel. Whether these "simple" athletes had regarded their competitions in the preceding years as practice to be prepared for the emergency when it came is questionable. Having a meaningful occupation, reducing aggression and gaining self-confidence must surely have been at least just as important.

Yet it is still true that in the DP camps, the cultural activities had altogether greater prestige with the officials of the self-administration, which is why cultural activities took up an above-average amount of space in the DP press, while "profane" sports were regarded at best as a fringe activity. With culture and education one could put on a show and make one's mark. In contrast, at worst sports could mean nothing but trouble, when the players and athletes misbehaved yet again. What is more, the very fact that sports had a much greater appeal to the broader masses than cultural activities did may have made some of the committee members suspicious of sports. Thus in the committees and newspapers of the She'erith Hapletah sport was only of marginal importance, while inside the camps and assembly centers themselves it became a mass movement.

And who can say? Perhaps the fragile construction that was "camp so-

Maccabi children's center for displaced persons. Bad Reichenhall, ca. 1946.
Courtesy of the American Jewish Joint Distribution Committee.

ciety" would not have managed to get through two and a half years on the hated German soil so peacefully if it had not been for sports: as an outlet for mourning and anger, as a goal for wishes and yearnings, as a vehicle and expression of Jewish pride and Jewish identity.

Translated from the German by Nicholas Jacob-Flynn

Notes

1. *Jidisze Cajtung* no. 117 (July 4, 1947), p. 9.
2. This expression comes from the Bamberg weekly paper *Undzer Wort* no. 1 (March 12, 1946), p. 1.
3. It is not known how the Biblical term *"Shee'rith Hapletah"* ("the rest . . . that were escaped," I Chronicles 5, 43) first entered the language of the Jewish DPs. The first recorded use comes after July 1945, when Rabbi Klausner published the first lists of survivors under this very title. See Yehuda Bauer, "The Initial Organization of the Holocaust Survivors in Bavaria," *Yad Vashem Studies* 88 (1970), pp. 127–57, here p. 127.
4. Michael Brenner, *After the Holocaust: Rebuilding Jewish Lives in Postwar Germany* (Princeton NJ, 1997), p. 3.
5. Of course, there were also Jewish sports clubs in the British zone, but—perhaps with the exception of Belsen in northen Germany—they could not match either the number of different sports played or the professionalism of the clubs in the U.S. zone. What is more, there has not been that much research regarding the history of the British DP camps.

6. Up until the end of 1946 there was a Yiddish-language newspaper in every sizeable camp. After the occupation authorities introduced compulsory licenses for the Jewish press, six regional newspapers remained, of which four were wound up at the end of 1947. Only *Undzer Weg* (the newspaper of the central committee in Munich) and the *Jidisze Cajtung* survived. These two, the biggest DP papers, as well as the *Jidisze Sport Cajtung*, which was established in 1947, are the main sources of this article. For the development of the DP press, see Philipp Grammes: " 'Ein Beweis, dass wir da sind!' Die jiddische Wochenzeitung 'Undzer Wort'—Kommunikationsstrukturen und -interesse von Displaced Persons," MA thesis, University of Munich, 2004, pp. 28–46.

7. For the history of the camps mentioned, see Juliane Wetzel, "Jüdisches Leben in München 1945–1951: Durchgangsstation oder Wiederaufbau?," Ph.D. Dissertation, University of Munich, 1987, pp. 241–62; cf. also Angelika Eder, "Flüchtige Heimat: Jüdische Displaced Persons in Landsberg am Lech 1945 bis 1950," Ph.D. dissertation, University of Munich, 1998, pp. 94.

8. Irving Heymont, "Among the Survivors of the Holocaust—1945: The Landsberg DP Camp Letters of Major Irving Heymont, United States Army," in *Monographs of the American Jewish Archives*, no. 10 (Cincinnati, 1982), pp. 12, 62.

9. Tetikajts-baricht fun der farwaltung, *Landsberger Lager-Cajtung* no. 2 (October 20, 1945), p. 7.

10. Bauer, "Initial Organization," p. 149.

11. Wetzel, "Jüdisches Leben," pp. 178–95.

12. On the congress in Munich, see Leo W. Schwarz, *The Redeemers: A Saga of the Years 1945–1952* (New York, 1953), pp. 80–88.

13. *Dos fraje Wort* (Feldafing) began to appear on October 4, the *Landsberger Lager-Cajtung* on October 8, and the central organ *Undzer Weg* (Munich) on October 12, 1945.

14. *Landsberger Lager-Cajtung* no. 4 (November 4, 1945), p. 8.

15. *Landsberger Lager-Cajtung* no. 5 (November 12, 1945), p. 6.

16. *Landsberger Lager-Cajtung* no. 3 (October 28, 1945), p. 6.

17. The foundation of the Center for Physical Education was announced in *Undzer Weg* no. 22 (March 1, 1946), p. 8.

18. Wolfgang Jacobmeyer, "Jüdische Überlebende als 'Displaced Persons,' *Geschichte und Gesellschaft* 9 (1983), pp. 429–44, here p. 436.

19. *Undzer Wort* no. 4 (April 5, 1946), p. 2; Jim G. Tobias, *Vorübergehende Heimat im Land der Täter: Jüdische DP-Camps in Franken 1945–1949* (Nuremberg, 2002), p. 40.

20. The conference was reported in the *Landsberger Lager-Cajtung* no. 26 (April 26, 1946), p. 8.

21. *Landsberger Lager-Cajtung* no. 26 (April 26, 1946), p. 8.

22. Schwarz, *The Redeemers*, p. 140.

23. Schwarz, *The Redeemers*, p. 140.

24. *Landsberger Lager-Cajtung* no. 30 (May 24, 1946), p. 6.

25. Schwarz, *The Redeemers*, p. 140.

26. *Landsberger Lager-Cajtung* no. 37 (July 12, 1946), p. 7.

27. *Landsberger Lager-Cajtung* no. 39 (July 19, 1946), p. 9.

28. In the whole of the literature, and also according to the contemporary witness Schwarz, the boxing championship in Munich in 1947 is described as the "first Boxing Championship of all the sport clubs in the zone," Schwarz, *The Redeemers*, p. 206.

29. *Unterwegs* no. 5 (August 15, 1946), p. 3.

30. *Undzer Wort* no. 50 (March 21, 1947), p. 5.
31. *Unterwegs* no. 5 (August 15, 1946), p. 3.
32. *Landsberger Lager-Cajtung* no. 52 (September 25, 1946), p. 43. It is not clear whether the paper omits the women for reasons of space or whether they really did only compete in this one discipline. Yet it must be said that the papers did not mention women participants in the 1947 championships either. See *Jidisze Sport Cajtung* no. 11 (October 1947), pp. 2–6.
33. *Landsberger Lager-Cajtung* no. 51 (September 13, 1946), p. 7. There must have been striking differences in the levels of the basketball teams in the U.S. zone: Ichud Landsberg beat Leipheim 100–2! *Landsberger Lager-Cajtung* no. 49 (August 30, 1946), p. 12.
34. E.g. *Landsberger Lager-Cajtung* no. 22 (March 15, 1946), p.10.
35. *Landsberger Lager-Cajtung* no. 26 (April 26, 1946), p. 8.
36. *Landsberger Lager-Cajtung* no. 26 (April 26, 1946), p. 8.
37. *Landsberger Lager-Cajtung* no. 26 (April 26, 1946), p. 8.
38. The A-Klasse was organized according to the administrative districts and it was above all the teams of the smaller DP centers that played in it. As the DP newspapers only rarely mention the A-Klasse in 1946, it is not until 1947 that their system can be reconstructed completely.
39. *Landsberger Lager-Cajtung* no. 39 (July 19, 1946), p. 9.
40. *Landsberger Lager-Cajtung* no. 41 (July 26, 1946), p. 7.
41. *Landsberger Lager-Cajtung* no. 37 (July 12, 1946), p. 7.
42. There are biographies of the Ichud players in *Jidisze Cajtung* no. 59 (November 15, 1946), p. 9.
43. *Jidisze Cajtung* no. 64 (December 13, 1946), p. 9.
44. *Landsberger Lager-Cajtung* no. 40 (July 23, 1946), p. 3.
45. *Jidisze Cajtung* no. 55 (October 25, 1946), p. 9.
46. *Jidisze Cajtung* no. 61 (November 29, 1946), p. 9.
47. *Jidisze Cajtung* no. 64 (December 13, 1946), p. 9.
48. *Jidisze Cajtung* no. 58 (November 8, 1946), p. 8.
49. At the end of 1947 the Center for Physical Education put the number of clubs at 175— almost 80 more than at the beginning of the year. *Jidisze Sport Cajtung* no. 16 (January 1948 A), p. 2.
50. Great Britain had already delegated the forming of a resolution in the Palestine question to the UN, but the commission there did not reach a decision until the end of 1947. Meanwhile Britain tightened its refugee policy, forcibly intercepting and diverting illegal refugee ships, and set up refugee camps on Cyprus. This led to great despair among the She'erith Hapletah, particularly in mid-1947. It was not until the UN decided on the plan for partition, in November 1947, that an end to camp life was finally in sight.
51. *Jidisze Cajtung* no. 71 (January 10, 1947), p. 10.
52. Schwarz, *The Redeemers*, p. 207.
53. *Jidisze Cajtung* no. 78 (February 4, 1947), p. 7.
54. Schwarz, *The Redeemers*.
55. Schwarz, *The Redeemers*.
56. *Our Way* (English Edition of *Undzer Weg*) no. 1 (November 25, 1947), p. 16.
57. *Jidisze Sport Cajtung* no. 11 (October 1947 B), p. 10.
58. *Jidisze Sport Cajtung* no. 11 (October 1947 B), p. 10.
59. In January 1948, for instance, a team selected from the occupation forces lost 0–4

against the newly founded ice hockey team of Hapoel Munich (*Jidisze Sport Cajtung* no. 17 [February 1948 A], p. 7).

60. The Austrians won 9–7 (*Our Way* no. 1 [November 25, 1947], p. 16).
61. *Jidisze Sport Cajtung* no. 15 (December 1947 B), p. 7.
62. *Jidisze Cajtung* no. 76 (January 28, 1947), p. 3.
63. *Jidisze Cajtung* no. 101 (May 6, 1947), p. 6.
64. *Jidisze Sport Cajtung* no. 9 (September 4, 1947), p. 2.
65. *Jidisze Sport Cajtung* no. 20 (April 1948 A), p. 7.
66. *Jidisze Sport Cajtung* no. 10 (September 26, 1947), p. 9.
67. *Jidisze Cajtung* no. 99 (April 25, 1947), p. 6.
68. *Jidisze Cajtung* no. 99 (April 25, 1947), p. 6.
69. *Jidisze Cajtung* no. 101 (May 6, 1947), p. 6.
70. *Jidisze Sport Cajtung* no. 9 (September 4, 1947), p. 2.
71. *Jidisze Sport Cajtung* no. 9 (September 4, 1947), p. 2.
72. See Brenner, *After the Holocaust*, p. 40.
73. *Jidisze Sport Cajtung* no. 20 (April 1948 A), p. 8. The cup was donated by Reuben Rubinstein, the editor-in-chief of the official central organ *Undzer Weg*.
74. *Jidisze Sport Cajtung* no. 21 (April 1948 B), p. 5.
75. See Schwarz, *The Redeemers*, p. 282. On this aspect see also Gideon Reuveni, "Sports and the Militarization of Jewish Society," chapter 3 in this volume.
76. *Jidisze Sport Cajtung* no. 21 (April 1948), p. 2.
77. *Jidisze Cajtung* no. 204 (May 25, 1948), p. 6.
78. *Jidisze Sport Cajtung* no. 21 (April 1948), p. 3.
79. *Jidisze Sport Cajtung* no. 21 (April 1948), p. 7.
80. *Jidisze Sport Cajtung* no. 23 (June 1948 A), p. 5. After this issue the newspaper ceased publication.
81. *Undzer Weg* no. 234 (December 21, 1948), p. 4.
82. *Undzer Wort* no. 85 (December 5, 1947), p. 1.
83. *Jidisze Sport Cajtung* no. 4 (June 25, 1947), p. 2.
84. The first Landsberg camp commandant, Irving Heymont, also reports of the difficulty the camp residents had in breaking with the manners of the concentration camps and getting reaccustomed to a normal life. See Heymont, *Among the Survivors*, p. 5.
85. *Undzer Wort* no. 52/53 (April 4/11, 1947), p. 1.
86. Sports officials estimated the proportion of the She'erith Hapletah who were actively involved in sports as being 50 percent (*Landsberger Lager-Cajtung* no. 37 [July 12, 1946], p. 7).
87. *Undzer Wort* no. 1 (March 12, 1946), p. 1.
88. *Undzer Wort* no. 20 (August 2, 1946), p. 10.
89. An example of this is the sports award, created at the beginning of 1947, which bore the name "HAMLU," which stands for the Hebrew phrase, Be ready to work and to defend.
90. *Jidisze Cajtung* no. 55 (October 25, 1946), p. 9.
91. *Jidisze Sport Cajtung* no. 13 (November 1947 B), p. 2.
92. *Jidisze Sport Cajtung* no. 16 (January 1948 A), p. 2.
93. *Jidisze Sport Cajtung* no. 23 (June 1948 A), p. 2.

13. Soccer and Antisemitism in Hungary

Victor Karady and Miklós Hadas

ALTHOUGH HUNGARIAN SOCCER teams were marked by differences between their social clientele from the very early days of their existence, the team identity of the more important squads was the product of historical development. It was shaped gradually by a specific "heritage" linked to the sociological characteristics of a team's founders and early fans and by the image the team achieved through its style and playing strategy. In addition, it was shaped by the position the team occupied among its rivals in competition as an effect of these criteria—a position that has tended to retain a certain historical permanence.

As early as the beginning of the twentieth century we note the existence of a "Jewish" club—the VAC (Fencing and Athletics Club)—and of an allegedly "Christian" and "bon genre" club of more genteel origins—the MAC (Hungarian Athletics Club). Though this was not necessarily explicit, the MAC did not admit Jewish members. But the elements making up the identity of the two future top teams whose rivalry was to define championships for the first half of the twentieth century, the MTK (Hungarian Physical Education Circle) and the FTC (Franzstadt Gymnastics Club), are not based on such a sharp and simple opposition.

The MTK was started in 1888 and financed by members of the Jewish middle class—particularly, so people say, by textile merchants—from the central districts of Budapest (sixth and seventh districts). Its founders were young, liberal-minded sportsmen who wanted a nonexclusive club based on performance in sports that were considered new at the time, such as swimming, cycling, and rowing, rather than on the so-called "noble" disciplines (preferred by the sons of the gentry)—gymnastics, fencing, and horseback-riding. The MTK tended to attract Jewish sportsmen, though this was by no means exclusive. One of the conflicts with its rival, the FTC, in the 1920s was in fact an accusation of having "stolen" an ethnic German player by the name of Schlosser. The president of the MTK in its glory days—which stretched from World War I to the Nazi years—was Alfred Brüll, a charismatic and dominating personality viewed as one of the "decadent" figures of the cultured Jewish middle class and interested in sports among many other things. He is said to have had homosexual inclinations, a rumor that enhanced his image as a touchy boss and gave the team an ambiguous reputation that was well suited to feed antisemitic stereotypes. In any case, the MTK was a team that irritated some others because of its overly "bourgeois" character. Until 1918, it hired most of its coaches from England, the Mecca of world soccer in those days.[1]

Even the name of the MTK reveals its desire to assert its links to Magyarized Jewish circles characterized by nationalistic, assimilating tendencies. Its acronym is the abbreviation of purely Hungarian terms chosen from a vocabulary established by eighteenth- and nineteenth-century linguistic reformers; it evokes a "universal Magyarism" free of any "local" or exclusive form of patriotism. Later on, as a professional team, the MTK changed its name to Hungária, the name of the Budapest boulevard where the team's stadium had been erected as a rival structure to the capital's first modern stadium, built in 1911 by its rival, the FTC. The MTK inaugurated its new, larger (seating twenty thousand spectators, a considerable number at the time), and technologically more advanced venue in 1912. When Hungarian soccer became a professional sport in 1926, the stadium's location provided the team with an irreproachably "national" name—a name with a clearly demonstrative function in these difficult times for those who were excluded from the Christian mainstream. The "Magyar" image sought by the team can also be seen in the names of the players, who were both Jewish and gentile: MTK players had mostly Hungarian or Magyarized names—55 percent for the pre-1914 years, for instance—while other major teams still tended to be made up of non-Hungarian players.[2]

The FTC—even then a rival of the MTK—had a totally different background. Even its name revealed the awkward, somewhat pretentious ambition of people with humble origins: the spelling of the word "club" in the Latin way with a "c," and the reference to an inner suburb of Pest immediately identified the FTC with a specific social context in the capital. Franzstadt was a transitional district between the chic business and shopping quarters of the city center and the proletarian suburbs further south. At the time, its population was mostly lower-middle and middle class—skilled workers and other intermediate social groups (transport workers, hairdressers, café and cabaret owners, low-level company employees, etc.), often of ethnic German (Swabian) origin. The diminutive used by both fans and opponents to describe the team—Fradi—explicitly recalls the German name for the district as it was used at the turn of the twentieth century and is still recognized today (Franzstadt) rather than its official Hungarian name (Ferencváros). Nevertheless, it was hardly a coincidence that the jerseys worn by the players (green and white stripes) displayed two of the three colors of the Hungarian flag. [3] Contemporaries confirm that the founders considered this a way of reminding people that Fradi was actually more "national" than its rival with the "M" for Magyar in its name. Right from the start, the team's clientele constructed an image of authenticity based on the reference to the urban territory of its origins. Fradi was the team that "plays with its heart" and not, as was hinted about the rival team, "with its head." This early opposition between the "little people" or people of the heart on the one hand, and the rational, calculating "bourgeois" on the other would never disappear in the minds of Fradi fans. Perhaps it is this opposition that, in the decades to come, allowed the Fradi self-image to consolidate into a moralizing, indeed political image of nonconformity and rebellion. Though it may remain diffuse, this self-image manifests itself in stadium behavior patterns: Fradi supporters are "those down below," "good people," "decent Hungarians," people who "think well" and will not submit to the powerful or the mighty.

Fradi is seen as being a "Christian" team. Yet, during the interwar period with its explicit political doctrine of a "Christian course" (in contrast to the previous "liberal" period which was now spurned by the right and associated by the left with rather nostalgic memories), this ideological position long remained devoid of any truly sectarian character. The team did not shy away from hiring Jewish top players such as Brodi or Bukovski, players whose names did not seem out of place until the advance of right-wing radicalism. It should also be noted that, "Christian" as Fradi may have been, it had fewer players with Hungarian names than the MTK—only 45 percent for the period prior to 1914. Before the Great War, Fradi became the MTK's main declared rival in the struggle for the top of the first division in the championship classification system. It is a consequence of the political situation and of the development of fascism that this rivalry, initially limited to sports, later deteriorated into conflicts between "Jews" and antisemites. By the end of 1919, during and after the White Terror period—years dominated by the MTK, who managed to win every championship between 1913 and 1925—some of the matches between the two teams degenerated into fistfights between MTK fans and the Fradi Magyar faction.

The ideological structures that consolidated the position of the teams within the sporting context probably made such an evolution inevitable, and matters could only get worse when the vast array of institutionalized anti-Jewish laws came into force as of 1938. Some of the new stipulations

involved state control, expropriation or forced "Aryanization" of compa-
nies, newspapers, and other agencies financed by "Jewish capital." Around
1939, a representative of the far-right government was appointed MTK manager to implement the Aryanization of the club. The team was dissolved in
1940, along with another first-division "Jewish team" called—for obvious
reasons—National (Nemzeti). As for Fradi, it took advantage of the situation to add to its championship trophies while continuing its drift to the
right in the ideological spectrum of the time. It is not surprising that in 1944,
under German occupation, its presidency was personally taken over by the
sinister pro-Nazi minister of the interior, Andor Jaross. (Jaross, who was
hanged after Liberation for his participation in crimes against humanity,
was one of the main organizers of Jewish deportations from the Hungarian countryside.) The representatives of the short-lived power structures
installed by the Nazi occupiers could probably not resist the temptation
of associating themselves with the leading team of the day as a means of
enhancing their doubtful prestige. Little did it help. As soon as the MTK was
dissolved, its leaders passed the word that fans should shift their support to
Vasas (metalworkers)—a rather mediocre team at the time but a politically
nonconformist choice in view of the team's roots in the Social Democratic
trade union movement. In fact, Vasas soon made it to the first league, and
its performance improved to the point that it was even able to defeat Fradi.
Perhaps it was to punish Vasas that, during the last years of the war, the
team was forced to change its name to Kinizsi; within a matter of months,
it initially had to take the name National Sport Circle of Metalworkers, then,
more simply, Vasas-National, before becoming Kinizsi.

All of this should not lead to the immediate and undifferentiated conclusion that Fradi had simply drifted right as a consequence of the general
shift of public opinion toward Fascism prior to and during World War II.
Admittedly, Fradi and its fans fulfilled many of the conditions for a shift
toward right-wing radicalism. Starting with the 1939 elections, Franzstadt
did indeed vote more strongly for the pro-Nazi Arrow Cross party than any
other inner suburb of Budapest. And many of the Fradi fans—most of them
administrative employees or skilled workers in big industry—must have
shared a generally widespread admiration for "German technology" as promoted under the Third Reich. Perhaps the Franzstadt ethnic Germans were
more likely to share this sentiment than others. But the far right, with its
egalitarian propaganda, also attracted voters among people of more humble circumstances, many of whom felt they had been let down by Social

Democracy. This basic tableau of the ideological orientation of Fradi fans is not complete without a mention of the populist nationalism of the capital's lower classes. Here were people of modest origins, often recent arrivals to the city and of non-Hungarian ethnic roots, who were not always willing to follow the official revanchist irredentism of the "upper-class" Hungarian gentry: they professed a nationalism of "little people" opposed to the existing social hierarchy and to the Jews, whom they saw as representing something both "bourgeois" and "foreign." As a result of this double-edged populism among Fradi fans, the team did not really take on an extreme-right image during the Fascist years, all the less so as right from the early years of the century its fans had never been limited to residents of the ninth district. Indeed, even before professional teams began operating in 1926, a rather dichotomized field of partisan preferences had established itself around the MTK-Fradi rival pair. Among the reasons for this polarization was the fact that few other districts of Budapest (with the exception of Ujpest, which would play an important role in the Communist years) had teams strong enough to attract fans from outside their own districts. So, for instance, the fans of Kispest (which would be renamed Honved during the Communist regime) tended to give their preference to Fradi. In addition, a certain number of soccer fans from outside Budapest also supported Fradi for lack of competitive teams of their own to support.[4]

From the Communist Takeover to the 1956 Regime Crisis

State power under the new regime generalized the principle of political manipulation of soccer and other sports: more and more openly, the new authorities misused sports to mobilize stadium masses for their own ends, engineering the feats of major teams in a system of auto-intoxication at home and in its propaganda outside the country. From then on, the overall reorganization of the teams and the selective allocation of privileges to some of them was also dictated by explicitly political choices. There was no area in any way relevant to soccer that did not somehow depend on highly political, arbitrary decisions: authorizations were even needed for a team to be upgraded to the first division or to be allowed to win a championship. As illustrated by an anecdote involving the secretary-general of the Communist Party, the regime was in no way hesitant about defining sports as a political matter of utmost importance.[5] It would be interesting to have more precise evidence and more detailed observations to determine the exact degree of autonomy teams were able to maintain on the field in spite of the political control weighing down on them, and to understand the symbolic value of the fans' support for their chosen teams. In the early days of the Stalinist regime, all the teams were brutally transformed and attached to a particular economic sector, administrative authority, or territorial body. These transformations were pushed through as part of an attempted unification explicitly intended to cut the teams off from their roots by remixing their material foundation and the symbolic field where they had positioned themselves and by way of an authoritarian intervention "from above" in the soccer market that, ultimately, tended to determine the power relationships that prevailed in the stadiums. It is therefore interesting to look more closely at certain significant details of this redistribution of financial and symbolic resources in order to understand the margin of liberty left to the teams out on the playing field.

After its incomplete misalliance with the radical right, it is easy to understand that, after Liberation, Fradi was in turn seriously threatened by dissolution. While the new regime had allowed the resurrection of earlier victims such as the MTK and Vasas (under different conditions), there was a real sword of Damocles hanging above Fradi in the new authorities' first months in power. And though it was ultimately not banned, Fradi was now truly a "broken" team. Its best players had been moved to other teams, it was forbidden from winning championships (until the post-Stalinist era, in 1959, and with a single exception in 1949), and its punishment included a change of name imposed until 1956. As well as being the name for one of the two great beer brands, its new name, Kinizsi, had a militarist tinge: it was a common name for barracks and other military installations.[6] We have also seen that it was the name assigned to the team of the metalworkers' union, Vasas, during the Fascist years. Nazis and Communists would seem to agree on giving the same extremely "national"-sounding name to banned, nearly destroyed teams; in both cases the regimes seemingly made sure not to destroy the teams completely, well aware of the need not to go overboard in the frustration imposed on the teams' fans. In 1949 or thereabouts, the presidency of the main Budapest teams was distributed to Communist dignitaries; Fradi, however, was put into the hands of Ferenc Münnich, minister of the interior for a brief period (like his pro-Nazi predecessor some years earlier) and chief of the Budapest police. This insignificant bureaucrat, a man of no personal stature whatsoever and a conformist down to his fingertips, was perhaps not a random selection as the new head of Fradi: at the time he was one of the few ethnic German party cadres, and in addition he had kept his original name.[7] By placing him in charge of Fradi, the Communist authorities were ensuring a kind of formal continuity of the symbolic association of the weakened team with the Franzstadt of pre-Communist years. Now under state control, the team found its new leaders in the top echelons of the food industry, the weakest link in the entire process of Socialist industrialization. This patronage could do no better than to plunge Fradi down into honorable mediocrity within the first division, denying it the possibility of sufficient resources to attract top-class players that might have propelled the team back up to the position its fans had never lost hope it would achieve.

In contrast to Fradi, the MTK was blessed with the discreet and relatively tolerant support of the new regime. Rapidly reestablished under its former name, the team was nevertheless not the Communists' favorite, probably because it had retained a slightly too obvious "Jewish" image. Its new sponsor was the textile industry trade union, here again ensuring a certain continuity. After the change in statute, the new MTK president was István Vas, the official in charge of the planning commission and one of the more important outsiders among party leaders. Vas was a man known for his "humanist weaknesses"—something totally exceptional at this level of Communist hierarchy. For instance, he consistently refused to deny or even to pretend to deny his Jewish origins, as was otherwise the rule among Jewish party cadres. Indeed, at a time when this was not explicitly forbidden, he is known to have dared display slightly pro-Zionist sympathies. He is also reputed to have had ties with the American Joint Distribution Committee, a Jewish aid organization for survivors of the Nazi concentration camps that was later banned in Hungary. The temporary presence of such a personality at the head of the MTK was the clearest but not the only sign of a reinforced symbolism of continuity in this "Jewish team." In the 1950s—the harshest years of the Stalinist period—the team was given the name Bastya (bastion) as a culmination of its enforced conformity with the regime's dominant set of symbols. The name Bastya evokes a figure of speech used by the secretary-general of the party calling for Hungary to play the role of a "powerful bastion" in the "struggle for peace and against imperialism." The symbol had an even greater weight if we recall that Bastya was already reputed to be the team supported by the Authority for the Defense of the State (the feared AVO), which was responsible for the "proletarian" police terror. It was even officially called Bastya-VL, an abbreviation for "red banner." In view of the largely deserved reputation of AVO as a party organ in the hands of Jewish officials, it is easy to see that what was at play here was a modernized version—perhaps involuntary, and otherwise perversely so—of the traditional "Jewish" image of the MTK. Be this as it may, MTK–Bastya–Red Banner was allowed to win championships alternating with Honved, the regime's favorite team.

As for the Fradi-MTK rivalry, it had not died—neither on the field nor among the fans. Fradi continued to attract mass support from an urban popular class that was devoted to soccer, while the MTK served as a repository for the tenacious nostalgia of a clientele brutally decimated by the Holocaust. But while Fradi was forced to languish at the bottom of the division, MTK-Bastya was allowed to win competitions. Apart from a few exceptions, the Fradi-MTK rivalry was no longer involved in determining top rank—in other words, between teams that are at the top of the list (rangado is the Hungarian expression)—but only in matches between teams nearer the middle or bottom of the first division. Still, the matches occasionally did witness incidents that showed that the ideological conflicts underlying fan reactions in the stadium were still very much alive. It is therefore hardly surprising that this ideological hostility was also expressed in a roundabout way via intermediate teams. In 1948 the authorities closed down the Fradi stadium for six weeks to penalize the team for antisemitic heckling against Vasas during a Vasas-Fradi match. But ideologically Vasas had always been a left-wing team, which explains why, at the turning point of total takeover by the Muscovite Party group, this manifestation of antisemitism may have actually been an anti-Communist protest directed against Vasas.

The favors of the new regime first went to teams of its own creation—above all Honved and Ujpesti-Dozsa—and to others that, like Vasas, could look back on a "leftist past," or that, like Csepel, could be supported for its image as a "proletarian team" conforming with Communist discourse, whatever their recent past (in this case Nazi).

Honved was clearly the regime's favorite. The team was the successor of a former squad at the bottom of the first division, Kispest, and its home territory was a middle-class suburb of company employees—Fradi supporters in Fradi's heyday as a great national team. Kispest had been expropriated and allocated to the minister of defense. The name Honved (defender of the fatherland) was a programmatic moniker. It evoked the war of independence against Austria, where the name was used for the first time to designate the national armed forces. Here, it illustrated the successful efforts of Hungary's Communist leaders (nearly all of Jewish origin in the Stalinist period) to skillfully hide their hand: by flaunting the "national" references of the government's favorite team, they wove undeniable and seldom denied emotional links between the masses of Hungarian soccer fans and the new authorities whose sponsorship had allowed the rise of so many talented players who would make up the Golden Team, the national eleven of the 1950s. Indeed, Honved—with players like Puskás, Kocsis, Czibor, Bozsik, Grosics, Budai, Lóránt—was the backbone of the great Hungarian team that for a while dominated world soccer. (The other national team players— Hidegkuti, Lantos, Zakariás—came from the MTK.) Honved members are said to have enjoyed privileges otherwise inaccessible not only for normal citizens but even for higher-placed cadres in these years of Stalinist austerity when the standard of living had declined for the majority of Hungarians. Puskás and his companions, some of them virtual illiterates, could be seen strutting around in officers' uniforms, being welcomed with great pomp by dignitaries, invited as guests of honor to the grand international rituals organized by the regime, and given dachas, bonuses, stays at luxury training camps (guarded by police), and so forth.

Honved repaid the regime's investment well. The Golden Team won the 1952 Olympics and beat England 6–3 on English soil in 1953, something not yet achieved by any continental team. The year 1953 also saw the dedication of the Budapest People's Stadium, the regime's most important sports facility and in fact one of the largest stadiums in Europe at the time. And finally the 1954 World Cup against West Germany, where the national team earned the enthusiastic support of the public even as it lost the final match. Disappointment gripped the whole country, to a point where criticism of the coach sparked spontaneous protests in the streets of Budapest, something hitherto totally unthinkable in a Communist country. This atmosphere of genuine mourning among Hungarian soccer fans was contrasted by the triumphal mood in victorious West Germany: on one side the frustration in the face of a major defeat and on the other the first occasion for the new Germany to assert its new-found power in an international competition of symbolic importance.

To promote new possibilities for competition at the top of the first division—which was restricted to teams approved by the authorities—the regime did not neglect other teams that now moved up and took their place among the "democratic clubs." One of these is Ujpesti-Dozsa, a team steadily left behind in the third division throughout the 1950s. The team's name combines at least two important sociohistorical references: formerly an independent municipality, Ujpest was another industrial suburb of Budapest characterized by the long-standing presence of a strong Jewish community, but especially by masses of workers living in large housing estates built at the time of the Communist regime or earlier. Dózsa was the leader of the most important revolt of the serfs against their feudal masters in the early sixteenth century. Because of this, he found a place on the historical pedestal of official imagery. Ujpesti-Dozsa thus had a triple reference: populist, "left-wing," and "Jewish," able to strike an emotional chord among the "left-wingers" of the day on alternative and very different registers. In addition, Dozsa was made the official team of the national police force, taking its place in the international "family" of teams supported by the interior ministries of the people's democracies. The letter "D" on its emblem linked it to the Dynamo teams in Moscow, Kiev, East Berlin, and Bucharest.

At this point, the regime effected a general reorganization of the entire symbolic field of soccer by introducing Socialist names for most first-division teams. From then on, we frequently see provincial teams with names such as Metalworkers, Miners, Builders, Honved, Progress, Locomotive, Forward, and Concord. Even an old team like Csepel was renamed Csepel-Metalworkers. The symbolic ideology of Csepel, another team promoted by the Communist regime, in fact retained a number of much blunter elements. It was the old team of the "red zone" of Budapest, and the city's Communist authorities made sure to give official backing to the legend identifying the team as a "proletarian side" despite its ideologically murky past and its temporary association with Fascism. As for Vasas, renamed Vasas-Budapest and thus leader of the tribe of "Vasas" (metalworker) teams around the country—it was allowed to occupy an honorable position but nothing more in the championships. Linked to the Social Democratic movement that was forcibly absorbed into the party in power in 1948, Vasas-Budapest fell from the second or third places it had held between 1945 and 1948 to positions lower on the scale of major teams (between fourth and seventh places) during the triumphal Stalinist years of 1949–56.

The Post-1956 Years: Soccer in "Real Socialism"

The power structures trying to consolidate as best they could after the Hungarian uprising were forced to adopt a pragmatism that had little in common with the brutality of the initial variant of Communism, which was now publicly spurned. Over the next three decades, the authorities drew the larger part of their legitimacy from a kind of before-and-after contrast. The reorganization of soccer that the new authorities undertook soon after taking power shows how clearly they understood the need to make use of the symbolic value of the teams. Action was particularly urgent in view of the fact that some old favorites were now seen as traitors: most of Honved and many other well-known players had taken advantage of the weeks of the uprising to turn their backs on their golden ghetto and "choose freedom."

The remodeled system drew on several aspects of earlier arrangements, for instance by giving teams back their historic names; it offered other forms of compensation to victimized teams, reorganized the endowment system, and, most important of all, gave the games more leeway to be just that: genuine games.

Traditional names such as MTK and Fradi, which had been discarded in an effort to ensure conformity to Communist policies after Liberation, were thus reestablished, compensating for the immense frustration (deliberate, to be sure) caused to the fans of these great historic teams. The new names were retained for more recent formations or for teams with less historical prestige. Honved survived, as did Ujpesti-Dozsa, still under the patronage of the police—so that two of the more important newer teams were still linked to security forces. Giving the teams back their names meant that traditional links could be reactivated—some local (for Ujpest, Csepel, or provincial teams), some "industrial" or exclusive (MTK or Vasas), some "national" (Fradi). The partial neutralization of names that had been artificially imposed as a result of the Communist wish for a tabula rasa was in any case a major concession to public opinion in general and to stadium audiences in particular, and the Kádár regime was willing to pay this price for acceptance, particularly as it did not involve directly political elements or high costs.

The relaxation of authoritarian measures originally introduced to enforce conformity was accompanied by a more flexible policy of manipulation and selective favors to particular teams. The new control system resembled a kind of "meritocratic" pluralism, with the authorities retaining the right to intervene in decisions about who could be at the top of the first-division championship lists—while admitting occasional exceptions to the rule that gave them supreme power in this matter. All indications were that top places in championships were the result of a careful dosing of concessions made to real team competitiveness and considerations that remained highly "political."

So, for instance, the joint prominence of Honved and the MTK came to

223

an end with the first year of the Kádár era (1957) in favor of Vasas, which won the championship for the first time in its history. Vasas repeated this feat several times in the following years—in 1960 and 1961, in 1965 and 1966, and again in 1977. While the MTK was still in second place in 1957, and even won the championship the following year, it then vanished from the top positions for twenty years and settled in the middle of the pack, indeed even at the bottom. Honved, already weakened by defections, did not win a championship until the 1980s, fluctuating between the second and the seventh place the rest of the time. The new (and old) top team was indisputably Ujpesti-Dozsa, which dominated championships between 1969 and 1975 and again in 1978–79 and won second or third place no fewer than nine times between 1960 and 1980.

As for Fradi, the fallen team of the Stalinist years, relaxed state control allowed it to reclaim its position among the better teams. In 1963, the year of a large-scale amnesty to political prisoners of the 1956–57 repression, the FTC won the championship—a feat it repeated several times thereafter (in 1964, 1965, 1968, 1976, and 1981).[8] Last among the great teams of the past, Csepel won only one championship (in 1959) and remained in the middle of the classification for the following decades.

The great innovation of the Kádár era was the historically unprecedented rise of a few provincial teams to the top of the first division. Before 1926, championships had been organized separately for the capital and for the rest of the country, and in the years after 1926, Budapest teams had systematically prevailed. This privilege was broken in 1963 with Vasas-Gyor in first place, a feat repeated many times in the 1980s. Other provincial teams now often achieved high positions just behind the Budapest top teams, sometimes even ahead of them: teams from mining towns, metalworking centers or big enterprises enriched by "Socialist industrialization," for instance Tatabanya, Dorog, Pecs, Salgotarjan, Diosgyor, and Videoton, which were now free to reach for the stars. Aside from the fact that these formerly fully marginalized sides could now work their way up to the top division, there were now intensified exchanges of players and coaches between the provinces and the capital—and not always to the advantage of the latter. The regime now seemed to allow a certain balancing of power structures at the expense of Budapest, an equilibrium maintained by the careful decentralization of the teams' winning chances. Nevertheless, the national team continued to be made up exclusively of players from the big Budapest teams— Fradi, Vasas, Ujpesti-Dozsa and Honved.

How Are We to Interpret This Rather Complex Evolution?

For a start, the political liberalization that followed the events of 1956 brought with it a decline in soccer's specific weight within the factors that gave the regime its internal legitimacy: the regime now had a more stable foundation as a consequence of the advancement of the "second economy" and of genuine results in efforts to improve the standard of living. Internationally, the Cold War was no longer the brutal confrontation between regimes that had justified the enormous efforts invested to show the superiority of Socialism at least in symbolic competitive areas such as international soccer. The relative liberalism now applied to Hungarian soccer followed the strategic principle of the Kádár regime: "Whoever is not against us is with us." The controlled pluralism allowed in this area was part of a greater policy granting an increasing degree of freedom for the expression of individual identities and special interests and accepting the existence of spontaneous sources of values and prestige that were not linked to manipulation or expropriation, such as the appeal of charismatic soccer personalities. A player like Florian Albert, winner of the Golden Ball award and unchallenged star of Hungarian soccer in the 1960s, could stay with Fradi and behave like a real "sport emperor" (the name given to him by his fans and by the sports press). The rise of formerly marginalized or victimized teams showed the will of the authorities to give more freedom of expression to local or new interests. One of the rare cases of major investment in sports facilities during the Kádár years was the modernization of the Fradi stadium in 1974, although the team's official status in the eyes of the regime was still somewhat ambiguous. A more open recruitment policy for the national team (which now included players from four different teams) also showed the desire for a greater consensual foundation for national soccer representation.

Nevertheless, these new freedoms remained closely guarded and clearly defined, especially in the years before the 1980s. The post-Stalinist regime also had its favorites. Kádár himself made a number of significant appearances at matches involving Vasas, one of the big winners of the post-1956 period. The powers that be now saw Vasas as being free of its old compromising relationship with Social Democracy, and its "proletarian" character was emphasized through its association with the workers of a big industrial combine in northern Budapest, Angyalfold. The other winner of this period, Ujpesti-Dozsa, also retained its position in the family of teams linked to the police forces of other "brother countries." The rising provincial teams, bearers of local identities, in fact owed their positions to the highly political promotion of "bastions of Socialist industrialization." At the same time, it was clear that teams with undesirable or uncontrollable symbolic conno-tations were condemned to languish in mediocrity—for instance the MTK, whose Jewish "frame of reference" was unpopular in a regime bent on prop-agating an image of Hungarian-style and "national" Socialism. Sidelining the MTK also countered the accusation of "Jewish power" that was still at-tached to Stalinism in the popular memory, a heritage that the regime was keen on repudiating.

Things began to change in the 1980s. With the growing "fin-de-règne" atmosphere spreading throughout the country, the position of soccer among possibilities of collective symbolic involvement and available op-tions for mobility and personal fulfillment weakened as the regime gradu-ally became more willing to grant sports a greater degree of autonomy. From this point on, competition in the stadiums depended more and more on lo-cal, indeed private interests. The system in the 1960s and '70s of merely sym-bolic competition among centrally controlled partners was transformed in the 1980s into a confrontation of local interests with a variety of financial, political, and administrative resources of their own. It was an utter novelty for teams sponsored by provincial factories embarked on a modernization course to beat squads belonging to a central authority such as the police or the army. On this fully new competitive chessboard, advanced technological enterprises such as automobile or television factories were clearly ahead of the old industrial giants in mining and metalworking. In any event, this evolution showed the rise to power of "red barons"—individuals with a solid regional base and highly placed Socialist connections who were now able to spend considerable amounts of money to support local teams, thus achieving additional influence and prestige through their teams' champi-onship results. The ineffectiveness of centralized control allowed special interests to blossom, and some of these involved corruption. These were the years of spectacular scandals (corruption of players, manipulation of the sports lotto, etc.). Under such conditions, the quality of the games was bound to suffer. The best players were bought by foreign teams, especially by teams in countries not known as leaders in international soccer. This brought the overall level of Hungarian soccer down to its historically lowest point.

"Fin de Règne" and Antisemitism in the Stadiums

In this new field of tension moving toward a pluralism subject to diminishing control, the old Fradi-MTK rivalry revived and gradually took on a new nature and meaning. It was no longer a contest between top teams, despite the fact that Fradi had had a few hours of glory in the recent past (winning six championships since 1956), and that the MTK had also managed to fight its way back to the top of the division—in 1987 and 1988—in an amazing comeback from as low as the second division in the early 1980s. In reality, the MTK had lost its original fan base over the years. The Holocaust had destroyed the mass of its fans, and their numbers had continued to decline as a consequence of emigration after 1947 and particularly after 1956, and as a result of aging or of the "natural assimilation" of those who remained. Some MTK fans switched over to Ujpesti-Dozsa, either because of an affinity with the team supported by the interior ministry (for former Communists) or because Ujpest had also originally had a few "Jewish references." Yet none of these gradual changes seemed to have diminished the "Jewish" character attributed to the MTK, though of course the club had not had a single Jewish player for years. In the early years of the Kádár era, the symbolic Fradi-MTK rivalry had still been expressed sharply in the antisemitic outbursts of Fradi fans. A Fradi victory after a match between the two rival teams in the early 1960s led to an outbreak of antisemitic excesses that had to be put down by police, with crowds chanting slogans such as "We have beaten Israel" and burning newspapers in front of the rabbinical training institute. Nevertheless, this discriminatory identification of the MTK sometimes had paradoxical manifestations. In 1967, after the Six-Day War, Fradi fans even cheered the MTK in a spontaneous effusion of opposition feeling and joy about the defeat of the Soviet regime's Arab protégés. But such exceptions did little more than confirm the rule. Since the 1980s the appearance of the MTK players had inevitably triggered anti-Jewish outcries of growing primitiveness among the supporters of the opposing team. These might have been fans from the famous Fradi "center-left section" as well as those of other major Budapest teams. Supporters of the police or army teams—Ujpesti-Dozsa or Honved—shared the same negative sentiments (see appendix 2). Fradi fans no longer had a monopoly on antisemitism in the stands: indeed, the stadium context gave rise to all sorts of resentments channeled in old patterns of populist antisemitism, especially vis-à-vis "the Jewish team" when it once again seemed to be headed for a dominant position (around 1987–88). Often enough, fans taunted the MTK players by smuggling a goose with a blue ribbon into their area, even during games played outside the capital.[9] For unsuspecting spectators, Hungarian stadiums during MTK matches in the 1980s seemed to have been transformed into gathering places for neo-fascists.

In order to understand such scenes of collective disorder and verbal violence that under other circumstances would presumably have been intolerable in a Communist country, we must remember the multiple dimensions they could have in this crisis-ridden twilight period of the regime.

Above all, this was a phase where the counter-violence that the authorities were capable of or willing to mobilize against all those viewed as troublemakers had clearly weakened, no matter whether the opponents were political dissidents or stadium hooligans. Initially strictly guarded by repressive security forces and kept in excessive check by party militants, Hungarian society found itself less and less policed as the 1980s progressed, and there was a hitherto unknown amount of liberty for collective, indeed public manifestations of letting off steam. But soccer audiences had also become younger over the previous decades. The decline in playing quality had turned older fans away from the stadiums, and supporters of the established teams—originally people from highly diverse social strata in local society (for the most part, higher-level administrative employees and members of more cultured milieus)—had also turned their backs on the sport. The younger generation of fans often belonged to the new *Lumpenproletariat* that had been spawned by the economic crisis of the regime's final years. The hooligans from the "center-left section" of the stadiums[10]—often abused in the local press—increasingly fit this description. In addition to the nearly ritual scenes of mockery and the invectives (addressed to the referee, to the opposing team or to its fans) that Hungarian stadiums had always witnessed, one now saw another kind of unruly behavior, more displays of aggression (gratuitous or targeted), more sheer vandalism, and more anti-police provocation than sporting emotion. These new patterns of collective behavior included antisemitic and xenophobic outbreaks in the stands (spectators hurling abuse at Gypsies, for example, but also at players who had transferred from Romanian, Yugoslav, or Soviet teams).

The analysis can be pursued further if we take into account the generic characteristics of Fradi fans and their relationship (especially that of newer fans) with the social and sporting establishment of these final years of the Communist regime. Fradi had always drawn part of its fan base from highly diverse areas outside the ninth district of Budapest. The local character of the reference to Franzstadt had long been replaced by a different kind of base with populist nationalist roots. Fradi's national legend rested on this great pool of heterogeneous fans, from totally different social classes and no longer geographically limited to one area. There were now out-of-town fans supporting Fradi, at times even to the detriment of their own regional teams. For this unfocused and dispersed group of people assembled in the center-left seats of the stadiums and representing the most organized and most articulate element of a specific identity, antisemitic slogans have at least three rather different meanings.

First of all, they are a code used to express negative attitudes—dissatisfaction, hostility, aggressiveness, or resentment. Codes of this sort operate in any society where the relationship to Jews (or to any other group seen as being foreign) is formulated in terms of separation between "us" and "them." Such codes can just as easily refer to Gypsies (this is the case in Hungary today) or to other groups (ethnic Germans in nineteenth-century Hungary under Austrian rule). They are not really directed at individual persons belonging to these groups. Young people questioned by police following one of the most severe antisemitic incidents, in 1987, did not seem to have ever known real Jews personally or even to have harbored concrete rancor against them.[11] The "structural constraint" of stadium stands can induce some fans to use such a code—in this case with nothing more than an "opportunistic value"—to rant against the opponent in the stadium, without "really meaning any harm."

The second meaning of such antisemitic behavior is linked to the image this Fradi public has of itself—the image of "ordinary people," of "real Hungarians," of "those down below," of "Mr. Everybody," of "good people," and so forth. This image inevitably has as its antithesis "those up there," the "establishment," the "people in power," "officialdom," and the "representatives of the regime"—the police in the stadiums, for instance. This dichotomized and intensely felt concept of social stratification is typical for people in totalitarian countries, where the regimes in power disregard most other usual social distinctions, distort their meaning, or flatten them with their management practices. The fact is that in the social balance of power of this popular imagery, Jews (or the collective image made of them) have always been seen as being associated with power. There are multiple reasons for this. In the prewar regime, Communism had often been depicted as a "universal Jewish conspiracy," a hypothesis hardly discredited by the Hungarian postwar experience of Stalinism, which was effectively led by a small coterie of leaders of Jewish origin. This view was subsequently reinforced by the fact that any antisemitic protest was carefully repressed by the Kádár regime, giving the impression that the regime continued to represent "Jewish power." In addition to all of this, we can perhaps add the idea inherited from prewar years that these Jews were wealthy, or at least people "who are not like us," making it easy for antisemitic discourse in the stadiums to become the medium for demonstrations of nonconformist attitudes or of antiregime sentiments.

Of course, such discourse also contains elements of a more traditional kind of political antisemitism. Some fans in the center-left section certainly have a clear memory of the Nazi regime, the so-called "revolution of assistant janitors." Young, disconnected stadium hooligans, seeking concrete targets for their destructive impulses, may have inherited from their parents a certain nostalgia for the "black years." If for many of the victims the color black has come to symbolize the loss of so many loved ones, and if for most Hungarians who lived through them these years were nothing but a moment of hateful collective folly, for the tormentors themselves they were above all an extraordinary moment of emancipation and a splendid form of self-assertion, as the constraints and rules of established society broke down and the balance of power and hierarchic relationships were reversed in favor of the *Lumpenproletariat* of "those down below," "us, the little people." The freedom to loot, to blackmail, to torment, and to kill that National Socialism gave its acolytes was indeed a moment of radical reversal of the social order and an unexpected chance for revenge for the most marginalized individuals or groups. From this point of view, uncontrolled and uncontrollable antisemitic abuse in the stadiums represents, for groups at the bottom of the intellectual, economic, or social ladder, the possibility of taking part and sharing in a hatred that vaguely touches everything that represents order—beyond the "Jews" whom they explicitly attack. Here again, the "black" hooligans—in Hungary, the uniform of local Nazis, the Arrow Cross members, was black—inevitably adopt the ideas and the color symbolism of the anti-order anarchism of the worst off.

And they do so with a clear conscience, with a sentiment of legitimacy that is all the more self-assured as this is, after all, only soccer and an essentially symbolic form of violence that, beyond the sporting opponent, is aimed at an abstract "enemy."

Translated from the French by Nicole Gentz

Appendix 1

Here are a few explanations by Hungarian specialists for this strange continuity (extracts of interviews). [12]

Sz. A.—There is something else about the MTK. Generally speaking, people don't like the fact that it is a Jewish team.

Question—What do you mean?

Sz. A.—Well, the circle of friends is made up of people of this religion.

Q.—In your opinion, why do people rant against the Jews during MTK matches?

B. D.—That's a funny question. I think that before, maybe, before the war, it was the Jews' team. I don't know. All I know is what everybody says, what I heard. I don't know why people say that. I don't understand why people don't like it. In any case, it's absurd nowadays to accuse the players of being Jewish. I don't know what's wrong with being Jewish. If I were, I wouldn't worry about it.

H. G.—It doesn't bother me at all. They could just as easily say "Dirty MTK!" There's even something about me—not that I am one [a Jew] by birth, but in my heart I am with them. In other words when they're ranting against the Jews, I often say to myself: "Come on! Let's show them that we [the MTK] are worth more than they are! . . ." And that happens often. When they curse us, when they send us to hell, there's no problem, we win.

Q.—Did you go to all the MTK matches during this period, when anti-Jewish abuse was taking place regularly?

K. L.—Of course! It was amazing. . . . At the next-to-last match, that was when we took first place. I stood up to see where I was. I looked around in the stadium, after about thirty minutes of play. It was staggering. . . . After that, the second time, we played at home against Franzstadt, and the same thing happened. What amazed me was that this was tolerated in Hungary, in the stadium of the team sponsored by the ministry of the interior. . . . In other words—since these are only kids—this meant that there had to be somebody there to tell them to shout these things! Those kids don't know what that was [the gas chambers]. Neither do I, thank God. But all of that during a soccer match! When two teams like that play each other, and one of them belongs to the police. . . . I don't think I'll ever forget that. As I stood up from the coaches' bench [facing the enraged fans], I was thinking that it couldn't be true. . . .

Sz. A.— . . . For the MTK, there were a lot of things happening at the same time. This anti-Jewish atmosphere comes on top of the excitement surrounding the team captain, but also a lot came from the fact that a team like that should win a championship so fast. With their excellent results, the team, the captain, and the players provoked more hostility than they made friends or fans.

Appendix 2

The following slogans were chanted by fans of certain teams competing for the national championship in various Budapest stadiums. They were recorded in the final years of the Communist regime (1987–88 season). [13]

Quack quack, poofter MTK!
Quack quack, poofter MTK!
Where is yellow?
Where is yellow?

Go Honved!
Olé olé olé,
Olé olé olé,
Shit on you,
Your mother's a whore!
Your mother's a whore!
Dirty Jews!
Dirty Jews!
That's what you are!
That's what you are!
We are better!
We are better!
Go Honved!

Here, my chick,
we have the habit
of not scoring
in the net of the Jews!

You, Vasas face,
playing with Jews!

Gypsy leading Jews!
Gypsy leading Jews!

Goose friends! Goose friends!
Dirty Jews! Dirty Jews!
Gas chambers! Gas chambers! [14]

Notes

This paper is based on five planned interviews with authorized informants. Its content was also drawn from many personal experiences and from data gathered informally (conversations at the table, in streetcars or in pubs, discussions between fans after matches, etc.). The article also includes a few explicitly quoted written sources. For the most part, the information presented in this essay is known to anyone interested in Hungarian soccer, but it has rarely been the subject of publication. It involves open secrets and non-events of Socialist society and its worthy successor, the "transitional" regime.

1. Nevertheless, the team was not as rich as has occasionally been suggested. After the shift to professional status in 1926, it seems to have paid its players less than the FTC, though it provided more substantial retirement benefits. One example worthy of mention is that of a player named Mandl who was given a fully equipped and fully stocked textile shop when he retired from the game.

2. Cf. Béla Nagy and András J. Gyenes, *Nyolcvan év. nyolcvan örökrangadó* (Eighty Years of Play for the Top of the List) (Budapest, 1983), pp. 3–6.

3. Cf. László Rejtö, *Kilenc klub kronikája* (Chronicle of Nine Clubs) (Budapest, 1969), p. 649. The colors of the opponent, the MTK, on the other hand, are white and blue—the colors of the flag of the Zionist movement and subsequently of the State of Israel. We have not been able to verify whether the MTK colors were chosen intentionally or not.

4. Cf. Lázló Hoppe, *Labdarugobajnokságaink, 1901–1969* (Our Soccer Championships, 1901–1969) (Budapest, 1970), pp. 278–79.

5. This true anecdote dates back to 1949. One Monday morning the all-powerful Secretary-General of the Politburo, Mátyás Rákosi, asked his secretary about the score of the Fradi-Vasas match of the previous day. The unfortunate secretary replied that he had no idea, and that he paid little attention to soccer, as he was in charge of important political matters. "Stalin's best pupil" then informed him that sports was an utterly political matter—especially if the match was between an old "right-wing" team and a "leftist" side.

6. Pál Kinizsi was a fifteenth-century Hungarian general reputed for his numerous victories against the Ottomans and frequently quoted in history books as an example of national bravery. School pupils in particular were expected to imagine him dancing for joy atop the bodies of his enemies and holding pieces of slain Turks in each hand and in his mouth(!).

7. In an effort to strengthen its "national" image, the Communist Party, soon after liberation, enforced the principle of Magyarization for the names of all important dignitaries, regardless of whether they were of Jewish, German, or other origin. Most of the influential members of the Politburo at the time adopted Magyarized names.

8. Fans' collective memory cannot fail to remember the rhythmic and rhymed slogan scrawled on the walls of Budapest after the decisive match that showed Fradi fans' gratitude to the regime: "The champion is Ferencváros, the top man is Kádár János" (Bajnok lett a Ferencváros / fasza gyerek Kádár János).

9. Geese remained associated with Jews as late as the nineteenth century. The association was by no means directly emblematic, but rural Jews were known for selling goose feathers, goose liver, and goose meat. It gave rise to a number of untranslatable anti-Jewish slurs in Hungarian.

10. Over the years, Fradi supporters took the habit of buying tickets in the center-left

section of the stands in order to be together. "Center-left" thus became a generic term in Hungarian soccer to describe unconditional and often violent Fradi fans.

11. The following is an extract from the police report following a serious antisemitic incident during a first-division match played in 1987. The speaker is a young engineer and the secretary of his company's Communist youth organization: "I went to the game with my girlfriend. The fans in question sat below the big clock. They never stopped shouting insults, particularly 'Dirty Jews,' throughout the whole match. After winning the match, the MTK players were hugging each other for joy and running to the coaches' bench. I was a bit excited, and I too shouted 'Dirty Jews! How much did you pay the referee?' I did this because during the match I had had the impression that they had purposely caused time to be lost over irregularities, and that the umpire had favored them, and because for ninety minutes I had had my ears full of the vituperations of the opposing side, below the clock. I was ashamed of myself for having used this expression, to the point that I apologized to a person who reproached me for it. Ultimately, what triggered my reaction was the joy shown by the MTK players." Cf. György Köbányai, "Korus a leláton" (Chorus in the stands), Uj tükör, (June 28, 1987).

12. Cf. Zsofia Mihancsik, HajráMTK! Hungária-körut (Go MTK! Hungaria Boulevard) (Budapest, 1988), pp. 35–36.

13. Quoted in one of the rare explicit reports on disorderly conduct in Hungarian stadiums, Mihancsik, Hajrá MTK!, pp. 26, 49, 105.

14. On June 13, 1988, the fans chanting these slogans—those of the Budapest Honved team—were awarded a prize for being the "most sporting public."

14. When Is a Yid Not a Jew?

The Strange Case of Supporter Identity at Tottenham Hotspur

John Efron

In November of 2000, along with thousands of other soccer supporters, I made my way down the High Road toward White Hart Lane in Tottenham, a depressed area of North London. We were on our way to watch the local team, Tottenham Hotspur, take on Manchester City. The atmosphere on that sunny but crisp Saturday afternoon was decidedly carnivalesque, the air full of enticing smells—curry, kebabs, and old staples like fish and chips and lager. They all wafted together to indicate that while it had not entirely disappeared, the old England now had grafted on to itself other cultures and tastes, one result being that it sported a new, exotic, olfactory identity.

Match day also provides a visual feast, with the streets surrounding the stadium a veritable sea of color, a marked contrast to the drabness that is midweek, N17. Everywhere, hawkers sell all kinds of clothing and memorabilia in team colors, while boisterous supporters in team jerseys spill out onto the sidewalks from pubs giving full voice to an array of songs and chants expressing their devotion to Tottenham Hotspur and their unbridled hatred for the enemy.

As I was peering in the window of the Spurs Super Store, a gigantic emporium replete with turnstiles where one can buy everything from replica kits worn by teams from the past to mouse pads and baby booties in team colors, my eye suddenly fixed on two young men in Spurs' team shirts. Where the number on the back normally appeared, these two had emblazoned on their outfits the expression, "Yid 4 Life." Then I saw other fans streaming toward the ground, some with the more simple word "Yids" on their garments, others with the same word but in the patois of North London—"Yiddo."

The game, which I had looked forward to for months, was now far from my thoughts. Instead, I could not shake the image of those inscriptions from my mind. What did they mean? Why had Tottenham Hotspur supporters adopted the word "Yids" (and variants thereof such as "Yiddo" and "Yid Army") as a term of self-designation? My curiosity only increased after entering the ground. Taking my seat, I settled in and began leafing through the match program. Among other things, I was desperately looking for some reference to what I had just seen. My search was in vain, for the club neither officially recognizes nor endorses the use of this racist epithet.[1] A mighty roar went up as the two teams emerged onto the pitch, and then suddenly, all around me, men, both young and old began chanting in unison, "Yids, Yids, Yids." Throughout the course of the match, the air was punctuated by the deafening cry of "Yids" as it spontaneously began in one grandstand, spread to the next, and then began to swirl around the stadium, thousands of males willing their team to victory with this most bizarre of battle-cries. Horrified, amused, but above all baffled, I set about deciphering what it was I had witnessed.

FOUNDED IN 1882, Tottenham Hotspur has long had a Jewish supporter base, one that grew considerably prior to and then again after World War II.[2] This is not so surprising when one considers that North London is home to the majority of London's Jewish population of approximately two hundred thousand.[3] However, Tottenham is, according to rough estimates, only the second team of choice among Jewish supporters, the majority of whom are now said to follow Arsenal. This is important to recognize, for Arsenal, despite its significant Jewish support and current Jewish chairman, David Dein, is not known as a "Jewish club." Only Tottenham sports that distinctive description within English football. Only Tottenham is recognized as "Jewish" by the soccer public at large. In this sense, Tottenham joins a number of continental clubs in also being designated as "Jewish." Most prominent among them are Ajax Amsterdam, Bayern Munich, Austria Vienna, MTK Budapest, and AS Roma, to name but a few.

But Jewish supporters play only a small part in the story of how Tottenham supporters came to refer to themselves as Yids, for what is most striking about the phenomenon is that the 1970s saw the widespread use of the term "Yid" and its variants, first adopted and incorporated into the fan culture at Tottenham by the club's non-Jewish supporters. In other words, what we have here are insiders, in this case Englishmen in the locus of that most English and working class of cultures, the soccer stadium, declaring their outsider status, namely that of the Jew or, more accurately, the hated Yid. While non-Jewish supporters who cultivate this identity would never claim that they are Jewish, they are nevertheless engaging in an act of parodic minstrelsy whereby they pretend, to varying degrees, to be Jewish (or their version of it) for the day. While it is less fully articulated than, say, performing black-face, it is, in its own way, performance. And as we shall see, it elicits responses that are performative themselves, for soccer stadiums provide attendees with a venue where they can publicly express and indeed act out deep feelings of loyalty, fickleness, adoration, hatred, despair, and ecstasy.[4]

By the late 1980s, the popularity of the term "Yid" was such that it was taken up by Tottenham's younger Jewish supporters. However, their ready use of the word to describe themselves as Tottenham fans is encoded differently from the way it is among non-Jewish users of the word. It is my sense that even when chanting in unison, Jewish and Gentile fans are not exactly saying the same things. Since Jewish supporters who chant "Yiddo, Yiddo," will indeed still be Jewish long after they leave the stadium, their performance is minstrelsy of an entirely different order. For one, they are imitating the antics and sentiments of Gentile supporters who themselves are engaged in an act of imitation and mimicry. While adopting the appellation "Yids," as a means of sharing the larger and more universal goal of supporting Tottenham, more parochial concerns are also in play. The willingness of Jews to chant "Yiddo" or declare that they are foot soldiers in the Yid Army is a liberating act of great license, marking a significant shift away from traditional Anglo-Jewish reticence about public proclamations about one's Jewish identity. This is a theme that will be addressed below.

Given the multiplicity of meanings, intents, goals, and rituals associated with the overall phenomenon, its heterogeneous nature makes it a valuable case study of what Umberto Eco has called "rhetorical code-switching."[5] As such, the songs, chants, sloganeering, and gestures of the various groups chanting "Yid" in the name of Tottenham and those responding to it with hostility can tell us much about each group's relation to and perception of the other, the semiotics of "interactional communicative behavior" or, to borrow again from Eco, this time from his ruminations on the connection between sports and society, what he refers to as "the deep area of the collective sensibility."[6] The different meanings that exist behind the chants are hidden from immediate view, obscured by the shared experience of either supporting or loathing Tottenham Hotspur. Hopefully, an analysis of this phenomenon will serve to shed light on the sometimes hidden, overlooked, or ignored properties and complexities of this somewhat strange and at times deeply disturbing manifestation of English soccer culture. It should be noted that even within the now vast scholarly literature on soccer and its cultures, much of it dealing with racism and soccer hooliganism, almost no mention is ever made of Tottenham's "Yid" phenomenon.[7] This paper represents, then, an initial attempt to highlight and come to terms with it.

How did the word "Yid" and its meaning in this particular context come into being? We must first recognize that there is, in a host of societies across a broad spectrum of cultural locations, an established social and cultural practice that sees traditionally pejorative terms undermined and given a positive valence. Ethnic, racial, and gender slurs are often turned upside down, subverting their normative and offensive linguistic orders and meanings. This process, which I would call value-switching, is one that entails the appropriation of a readily acknowledged term of abuse and the subsequent subversion of the word's generally accepted meaning. Not merely the word, but the entire cultural universe and deeper structures of meaning and cognition evoked by the word are also turned upside down when value-switching takes place. Value-switching can take several forms. To illustrate the point, two classic yet different contemporary examples of value-switching can take place with the words "queer" and "nigger."[8] The former was once a derogatory term for homosexuals, but has become redefined, having attained respectability through its use by homosexuals sometimes to describe themselves, their politics, and their culture. The word "queer" has become so accepted that an academic subfield of cultural studies is called "queer theory."

The other word that has undergone a change in meaning, though by no means has it become as accepted and indeed *salonfähig* as queer, is "nigger," which in some quarters of the black community in the United States is widely used. In his recent and deeply unsettling treatise, *Nigger: The Strange Career of a Troublesome Word*, Randall Kennedy observed that "for many blacks the N-word has constituted a major and menacing presence that has sometimes shifted the course of their lives," for it is, as the prosecuting attorney Christopher Darden observed, "the filthiest, dirtiest, nastiest word in the English language."[9] But despite the fact that large numbers, perhaps even a majority of people would concur with Kennedy and Darden, some African Americans have long employed the term "not in subjection to racial subordination but in defiance of it," and thus coming to terms with the revaluation of a word that is on its face simply noxious is an extremely complex epistemological undertaking.[10]

The word that I am concerned with here, whose value has also been switched, is of course, "Yid," which is Yiddish and literally means Jew. In Yiddish, it has no pejorative connotation whatsoever and, in fact, is a term of affection and familiarity. Upon greeting an acquaintance, a standard, informal salutation would be *"Vos macht a Yid?"* ("How is a Jew?"). This is considered warmer and more intimate than the mere use of the person's name to ask after their well-being. However, the word "Yid," when used in

English can easily become pejorative. The key change in meaning can be induced with a slight pronunciation shift. According to Leo Rosten, "when pronounced YEED, the way eastern European Jews say it, "yid" is an inoffensive term. Pronounced YID (rhyming with "did") the word becomes pejorative—a derogatory epithet used by antisemites."[11]

In British English, the word Yid is common currency (something, quite interestingly, that never happened in American English). When used by non-Jews, is a term of opprobrium and ridicule, akin to the derogatory Russian word "Zhid." Like the word "nigger," Yid too, to paraphrase Kennedy, has historically "constituted a major and menacing presence," serving as a battle-cry for those bent on doing violence to Jews. For example, in October 1936 the leader of the British Union of Fascists, Oswald Mosley, called on his shock troops to attack Jews. As they marched through the East End, London's most densely populated Jewish neighborhood, the "Battle of Cable Street" and shortly thereafter the pogrom along the Mile End Road erupted. As the crowd shouted "Down with the Yids," they did considerable damage to Jewish property and viciously assaulted Jews, including one young girl who was thrown through a plate-glass window.[12]

Unlike the case with words such as "queer" and "nigger," Jews have never appropriated antisemitic epithets such as kike, Jew-boy, or Ikey to describe themselves in order to subvert dominant racist structures. What makes the appropriation of the word "Yid" at Tottenham Hotspur so odd and so complicated is that it is perhaps the first time ever that members of a European Jewish community have ever taken on a slur in order to switch its meaning. More importantly, in the context of English soccer Yid is essentially a non-Jewish term and it is therefore non-Jews who have bestowed upon Tottenham an important part of its "Jewish" identity. This has been so successfully implanted that to supporters of rival clubs, the one word that is generally used to describe Tottenham's identity is "Jewish."

There is only one other contemporary example from the soccer world of this particular form of word-value reversal as it pertains to Jews, and it is to be found among the supporters of Ajax Amsterdam. This is a club with a significant Jewish history, in a city whose language is infused with Jewish words and whose colloquial name is "Mokum," the Yiddish word for place.[13] Since its founding in 1900, Ajax Amsterdam not only had Jewish players, Jewish presidents, and was located near what had once been Amsterdam's bustling Jewish quarter, but according to Salo Muller, the club physiotherapist from 1959 to 1973, even "the [non-Jewish] players liked to be Jewish." He explained it thus: During his tenure at the club, Muller recalled that "even the non-Jewish players would regularly pepper their speech with Jewish words and they greatly looked forward to the visitation of a local Jewish butcher who, prior to every European match, would bring the team a kosher salami."[14] Though seemingly trivial, this ritual added to the sense among the players that they shared a particular identity as Ajax players, an identity that was partly Jewish and uniquely Amsterdam.

During the 1980s, however, this historically deep and amiable association of Ajax with Jews changed when a group of Ajax's most boisterous and potentially violent supporters, known as the F-Side skinheads, responded to antisemitic slurs hurled at them by affirming their ersatz "Jewish identity." According to one of the leaders of the F-Side group:

> Calling ourselves Jews is normal now. Out-of-towners call us "Jews" as an insult. In the eighties we decided to take over the insult word as our own. We started carrying Israeli flags [this was after seeing fans of the English "Jewish" Club Spurs doing the same], calling ourselves Jews. . . . We are not Jewish, but I once heard that if you have just a drop of Jewish blood, you can call yourself Jewish. We have no relation to real Jews or feeling about Israel or anything like that.

Like members of the F-Side group, the Israeli media also does not appear to subscribe to the halakhic definition of Jewishness. When Ajax traveled to Israel in 1999 to play in a UEFA Cup match against Hapoel Haifa, the media described the game as a "Jewish derby."[15] And prior to their departure for Israel, Ajax's non-Jewish fans were interviewed on Israeli television, where they declared how happy they were to be "going home." According to David Winner, who has written on Dutch soccer, "F-Side members, accustomed to being treated like dangerous animals, were in Israel given VIP treatment and received like long-lost cousins."[16]

English football, whether in terms of the corporate structure of the game, fan culture, or even the phenomenon of hooliganism, exerts an enormous influence on global soccer culture. So too in the discussion at hand. It is quite clear from the testimony of the Ajax supporter that it was Tottenham supporters who led the way. It was they who first took on the derogatory terminology reserved for one group and appropriated it for themselves in myriad ways, completely subverting its meaning to such an extent that they then came to be seen by others as truly being members of the derided group.

Occasionally, there have been instances where soccer supporters of one team will adopt an alternate group identity or attribute an alternate identity to a particular group. For example, the Manchester United fanzine, *Red Issue*, takes pains to "other" rival supporters, ironically, vilifying them as English. Supporters of clubs in southern England such as Chelsea are routinely derided in the publication as swastika-tattooed skinhead racists from London, whether or not they are Londoners or racists. It is their Englishness that is seen to set them apart from true Manchester United supporters. Here, support for Manchester United becomes a cocooned act, withdrawn from the larger culture of British soccer, one where local patriotism gains primacy over integral nationalism. In Scotland after the mid-1980s, Rangers fans highlighted their English-Unionist identity, which in turn saw rival supporters oblige by challenging the club's authentically Scottish identity.[17] These expressions of "othering" differ from the case at Tottenham, where the traditionally despised ethnic underdog has been adopted as the symbol of the club. If, however, Rangers' support is expressive of different varieties of Scottishness, then Spurs supporters as Yids are expressing a non-English form of English identity.

Another consequence of calling themselves Yids and having a large Jewish supporter base is that Tottenham supporters have come to voice active opposition to racism in soccer. And unlike certain clubs that have developed nasty reputations for racism, Millwall, West Ham, Leeds, and Liverpool, to name but a few of the more notorious, Tottenham has largely been, in recent history at least, free of the ugliest manifestations of racism. Most recently, the 2001–2002 English Premier League season saw the transfer of Tottenham's Sol Campbell to arch-rivals Arsenal. The move evoked a deeply felt torrent of revulsion and betrayal by Tottenham supporters. It was suggested in some media circles, in particular by Ian Wooldridge writing in the *Daily Mail*, that the reaction of Tottenham fans was driven by racism, since Campbell is black. The Tottenham response to this charge was rapid, vehement, and indignant, precipitating a write-in campaign to the *Daily Mail*, intensive coverage of the saga on the Sky Sports television network, and enraged Tottenham fans airing their views in internet chat rooms. One of the strongest responses came from Danny Kelly, a featured columnist writing in the online journal *Football365.com*. Making the claim that it was Tottenham's status as a "Jewish club" that served to help it take a decided stance against racism, Kelly noted:

Let's be straight about this; there used to be racism at White Hart Lane. It was in the late Seventies and it was stamped out by an initiative between the club and the fans called "Spurs Against The Nazis." It was pointed out to the morons that there was something profoundly stupid in making Nazi salutes at a club traditionally aligned with North London's Jewish community and barracking opposition players when our own team contained black players (Crooks, Hughton) and a genius (Ardiles) who happened to be South American. Spurs Against The Nazis worked and while you will always get the odd idiot, the organised racial abuse of players has not been heard at White Hart Lane for the best part of 20 years. The country's most obviously Jewish club has even gone on to idolise an Arab player, Nayim.[18]

Tottenham supporters are duly proud of the relative absence of racism at White Hart Lane. And indeed, Kelly may well be right that, at the very least, those who sought to stamp it out were able to use instrumentally the club's affiliation with a large sector of North London Jewry and the fact that those who engaged in racist behavior thought nothing of referring to themselves as Yids.

How did Tottenham's supporters first come to refer to themselves as Yids, why do they do it, and how has this manifested itself over the years? The sources for much information on this issue are the responses I got to a set of questions I posed to a Tottenham Web site. I also conducted a number of phone and personal interviews. Two final sources of information have been fanzines and Web sites.

The origin of the term "Yid" in relation to Tottenham Hotspur is somewhat contested. Numerous interviews revealed differing theories. Some respondents were under the impression that the mere fact that Tottenham boasts a large Jewish supporter base led opposing fans in the 1960s to begin referring to the supporters and club alike as Yids.[19] Another theory has it that it emerged from a successful comedy program that ran on British television from 1965 to 1975, entitled *Till Death Us Do Part*. In this series about a right-wing English nationalist and racist who constantly laments Britain's postwar decline due to its loss of empire, mass non-white immigration, and the strength of the Labour Party and the trade union movement, the protagonist, Alf Garnett, was most often pictured sitting in his London living room, complaining bitterly about the state of the world. Draped around his neck was the scarf of his beloved soccer team, West Ham United. He would often launch into tirades about soccer and on several occasions declared that the upcoming match against Tottenham would see his team "go off to play the Yids."[20]

Another respondent recalled that it all began when Alf Garnett began one of his "inane monologues where he referred to Spurs as 'The Jews' and stated that the Blitz was primarily Hitler's attempt to bomb White Hart Lane. 'Third set of floodlights past Southend!' His screen stepson pointed out that floodlights didn't appear until after the war, but the connection was made."[21]

Those who subscribe to the Alf Garnett theory, and it is the majority, believe that upon hearing this term of opprobrium, Tottenham supporters adopted it as their own. Yet another theory has it that it did not come from *Till Death Us Do Part*, but that the protagonist's use of the word "Yid" to refer to Tottenham exacerbated and encouraged use of the pejorative.[22]

An interesting interpretation from a Chelsea supporter's Web site offers an unlikely explanation of the origin of the word "Yids" as it pertains to Tottenham. At the very least it says something about a half-informed English view of London Jewry:

> Tottenham have a large following in the Stamford Hill area of London. Stamford Hill is heavily populated by Hassidic, Orthodox Jews, who wear the typical Orthodox black robes etc. The Orthodox Jews speak Yiddish, which is a Germanic dialect. They are also very disapproving of non-Orthodox Jews. Chelsea probably have more Jewish fans than Tottenham do, but as the Tottenham Jewish supporters were more liable to speak Yiddish and also disparaged non-Orthodox Jews, the latter responded by calling them Yids. This was then taken on to mean Spurs fans in general.[23]

The first manifestations of the particular semiotic space that saw the creation of what I would call "Yiddo culture" made themselves apparent by the mid 1970s. By Yiddo culture I mean both the specific act of self-designation by Spurs supporters and the response to it by rival fans. It is no accident that this was a time of heightened National Front activity in stadiums throughout the United Kingdom. Extremist right-wing groups sold or gave away their literature to a soccer-going public they saw as ideal and receptive targets for their racist worldviews. The combination of racist agitation and the increasing presence of black players who were beginning to enter the English game at this time also saw the rise (though as yet un-documented) of antisemitic chanting whenever Spurs played.[24]

So, despite the fact that Tottenham (and Ajax) had long been associated with Jews, the modern phenomenon that I am describing here has less to do with traditional associations and the specific sociology of Jewish life, especially the proximity of Jewish neighborhoods to soccer stadiums of teams supported by Jews than with the rise of racist hooliganism in the 1970s.

By the late 1970s and early 1980s, Gentile Tottenham supporters rose to the challenge of antisemitism directed at Tottenham's hooligan element (the irony of this alone is noteworthy) in a most interesting and disarming way. They responded to the incessant, abusive chant of "Yiddos, Yiddos" by chanting back, "Yiddos, Yiddos."[25] This served to blunt the edge of the taunt, as Tottenham supporters celebrated and embraced the racist epithet. According to one respondent:

> The chants from opposition supporters "Yiddos Yiddos, does your Rabbi know you're here?" etc. really became prevalent from around '74–'75 onwards. Even then it was mostly during local games against West Ham, Chelsea and especially Arsenal. I did not actually hear a Northern team chanting these songs until the relegation match v Man City 1977 by which time the Tottenham lads had taken on the persona themselves. . . . After this it went nationwide, even international. . . . If I had to put a date on when these chants were adopted by Spurs fans (the vast majority of whom are not of the Jewish faith) I would say April 3rd, 1976. On this day the Tottenham hooligan element invaded the Arsenal North Bank. . . . The Spurs yobbos got the better of their Arsenal counterparts this day taking over virtually the whole of the Arsenal terracing, reducing the Arsenal fans to the outer terracing behind the obligatory line of police attempting to keep the two gangs apart. From there the Arsenal fans started chanting "Yiddos Yiddos" at the Spurs boys, [who] retorted "Yiddos took the North Bank, Yiddos took the North Bank." From this day whenever opposition fans tried to insult the Spurs fans with insults or anti-Jewish chants they were met with Spurs fans' chants of "Yiddos Yiddos" which negated the effect of their chanting.[26]

One interviewee, a Jewish Tottenham supporter from North London, recalled his first encounter thus: "It was 1980 or 1981. We were playing away at Manchester United. That was always a nasty place to go. We entered the ground and suddenly I saw a bunch of big blokes, *shtarkers* [Yiddish for bruisers]. Spurs supporters were wearing filter masks, not over their mouths but on the top of their heads, as kippot. Then the chanting starts—Yiddos, Yiddos, Yiddos." When asked about the origin of the word Yids at Tottenham, the respondent added, "the chanting of Yiddos doesn't start en masse till 1980–1981."[27]

Another observer noted that "around this time, 1980–81, the Spurs fans adoption of their Yiddo character was at its height. In those days the flag of Israel was a common sight bedecking the Spurs area . . . to indicate away fans' areas. Today the Star of David is less often seen, replaced by the Union Flag or Flag of St George marked with lettering of [the] area where [the] fan lives: typically Dagenham Yids would appear."[28]

According to a Manchester City fan who was interviewed by the scholar of soccer Les Back, "Yes, I mean Tottenham do flaunt this Jewish thing, don't they, they have flags don't they with the Star of David and stuff like that. This thing, the Yiddo Army and all that sort of thing."[29] Not only do they flaunt it but they commodify it as well, with vendors selling T-shirts outside White Hart Lane on match day, the garments bearing the words "Yid-O" and "Yid 4 Life."

Ritualized abuse of players, referees, and opposing fans is commonplace in British soccer culture. Sometimes it is characterized by what has been aptly called "scallawag terrace banter," which itself is taken as a source of humor.[30] Another respondent added the following story, this time centered at Manchester City, where humor was employed to undermine the abuse:

> Away at Man City in the mid-eighties—half time behind the away end. There is only a thin wire fence separating us from the City supporters and a large group of them are singing the "We've got foreskins, we've got foreskins, you ain't" song. Nothing nasty, just some mild abuse. Large group of well-known Jewish Spurs supporters comes along, drop their trousers en masse and then wave their circumcised members at the City supporters. Supporters on both sides of the fence collapse into laughter—the City fans even applaud.[31]

What of course needs to be noted here is that the Manchester City supporters who first taunted the Spurs fans had absolutely no idea that the latter were in fact Jewish. Yet in their minds, the identification of all Tottenham supporters as Jews was complete and indisputable, a ringing testament to the strength of "Yiddo culture." The perception of Tottenham as Jewish and flaunting it has been taken up by John King in his novel, *The Football Factory*. In this fictional account of a Chelsea hooligan, the protagonist completely blurs the line between Jews and non-Jews as all Tottenham supporters become Jewish and even entire neighborhoods of London become similarly metamorphosed:

> Tottenham away is a cracker. There's always been a healthy hatred for Spurs. They're yids and they wear skullcaps. They wave the Star of David and wind us up. We're Chelsea boys from the Anglo-Saxon estates of West London. Your average Chelsea fan coming up to Tottenham from Hayes and Hounslow is used to Pakis and niggers, but go up Seven Sisters Road and it's all bagels and kebab houses. . . . Tottenham have always had a reputation for being flash. Silver Town yids. They're rich spivs to West Ham's poor dockers. At least that's how the story goes. You go through Stamford Hill and Tottenham and you wouldn't think you're in the same city as Hammersmith and Acton. We've got Paddies in West London, but none of these yid ghettoes. I'm no Christian myself, but still Church of Fucking England.[32]

Chants by rival fans directed at Spurs supporters often make reference to circumcision or Jewish dietary practices, further reinforcing the idea that all Spurs supporters celebrate such rituals. At Chelsea, a commonly heard song went like this, the details of which belie a total ignorance of Judaism but confirm the view that to support Tottenham is to be a Jew (the specific reference is to a Spurs hooligan):

> Now Big Jim is their leader,
> He's got a heart of gold.
> But he hasn't had a foreskin,
> Since he was one day old.
> And as you walk in the Park Lane End,
> You'll hear a mighty wail.
> Big Jim is our leader,
> The King of Israel.[33]

Another commonly heard rhyme that has all Tottenham supporters observing kashrut goes, "Tottenham boys, Tottenham boys—no pork pies or saveloys." Similarly, at Chelsea, the following ditty could be heard, "Tiptoe, Past the Tottenham, With some roast pork and a bacon sandwich."[34] Again, with no regard for the fact that the majority of people at whom such songs are directed are Christian, one can, to a certain extent, claim that in the minds of their rivals, all "Yids" are Jews. Such relatively mild and possibly playful banter did not last long, for the more Spurs fans tended to embrace the idea of the Yid, the nastier became the response.

The lines of identity—Jewish/Gentile, outsider/insider—become totally blurred when one considers one of the most disturbing aspects of "Yiddo culture": the invocation of the Holocaust. The most vicious manifestation of this is the hissing directed at Spurs supporters, the sound of which is intended to evoke the sound of gas in the extermination camps. One Tottenham supporter recalled: "I remember a trip to Old Trafford in 1987 . . . when the entire Stretford End was hissing." Another fan recalled that "a couple of visits to Pride Park [the home of Derby County] have been marred by some appalling abuse, the hissing and Nazi salutes being just two examples." [35] Other fans remembered Leeds and Chelsea as being grounds where this happened frequently. The hissing was also accompanied by a host of songs, chants, and rhymes. While they could be heard at any number of grounds, not only were they perhaps most frequently heard at Chelsea, the songs sung by certain Chelsea supporters have been documented and posted on a Web site entitled "Sing Something Sinful: 30 years of Chelsea Verbal Aggro." The vitriol is remarkable for its intensity, the sentiments entirely without irony or ambiguity:

> Spurs are on their way to Auschwitz,
> Hitler's gonna gas 'em again,
> We can't stop them,
> The yids from Tottenham,
> The yids from White Hart Lane. [36]

Likewise at Chelsea, the following was sung directly at Tottenham supporters:

> Good old Adolf Hitler,
> He was a Chelsea fan,
> One day he went to White Hart Lane,
> And all the Jew Boys ran.
> At last he got a few of them,
> Up against a wall,
> At first he laughed a little bit,
> And then he gassed them all.
> hahhahahahhaahhhhh,

hohhohohohhoohoho,
hahhahahhhahha etc, etc.[37]

By all accounts such songs, especially the hissing, cut Spurs supporters to the quick. In such situations, Tottenham fans were deliberately taunted in the most vile and hurtful way. And it was a way that was designed to inflict maximum emotional and psychological distress to a Jew. What is notable is that non-Jewish Tottenham supporters also reacted to these manifestations with great rage and anger, as one would expect of decent people anywhere. But the outrage that Holocaust references conjured up only confirmed the provocateurs' misguided sense that Tottenham's Yids *really* are Jewish and hence it only encouraged the singing of hurtful songs celebrating the extermination of the European Jewry.

As the philosopher Jean Baudrillard has observed, "there is an increasingly definitive lack of differentiation between image and reality which no longer leaves room for representation as such."[38] This is precisely what happens when Spurs supporters are subject to taunts containing references to Belsen or Auschwitz, or to the hissing itself. The reality of most of the fans being non-Jews is entirely blurred, as they are considered no longer to be merely "Yids," that is, supporters of Tottenham, but, rather, Jews who are likely to be hurt by such references. One of the most interesting responses to the hissing that has been documented came from a Tottenham fan who was deeply upset by the hissing because he is black: "I mean I'm always contending that the two scariest chants that I've ever heard in a football match have been the sound of monkey grunts, which you don't hear at all now, and a gassing sound . . . which you do hear all the time, and it's just incredibly frightening . . . that is the one thing that makes the Tottenham fans flip."[39]

In response to such vile abuse, Spurs fans have sometimes deliberately chosen to be as callous and cruel as their rivals. One respondent observed that when the above mentioned hissing began at Manchester United in 1987, "the reaction from Spurs fans was to take out a paper insert in the program, fold it into a paper airplane, throw them in the air and spin a version of 'Magnificent Men in their Flying Machines . . .' followed by 'Munich' songs, a reference to the Munich air disaster that claimed much of the Manchester United team in 1958."[40]

But the hissing also provokes violent responses, as another Tottenham supporter informed me:

I have heard this at a number of grounds. The worst fans for this are Nottingham Forest. At every game I went to at the City Ground this started up and I think on all bar one occasion it resulted in pretty serious trouble and skirmishing on the terraces. I even know of people who complained to the stewards and police at the time but they showed no interest. The next worst fans for starting this are Manchester United. I've also heard it at West Ham and Chelsea on similar scales. These four are probably the worst grounds for receiving this treatment.[41]

The adoption of the Yid identity constitutes what anthropologists term a symbolic practice, one that provides structure and meaning to supporter culture.[42] This is best exemplified by the testimony of an Ajax fan who directly addresses the function played by the adoption of an ersatz Jewish identity. Speaking of the Star of David as the team symbol, he remarks: "We like to provoke a little bit with this symbol."[43] I would suggest that something very similar motivates some Tottenham supporters, and it is the desire to be hated for it, reifies and strengthens the tribal nature of supporter groups. This recently became an issue of rare public comment at the highest levels of English soccer. In a somewhat self-serving vein, the respective club chairmen of Tottenham's London arch-rivals Chelsea and Arsenal, Ken Bates and David Dein, implored Spurs to prevent their supporters from referring to themselves as "Yids." According to Bates and Dein, who aired their views at UEFA's Unite against Racism conference held at Stamford Bridge on March 5, 2003, by tolerating the use of the word and practices associated with it, Tottenham Hotspur Football Club was inadvertently fostering a culture of racism. Dein charged: "We see very little racism in domestic soccer but antisemitic racism is an issue, particularly where Spurs fans are known colloquially as 'yiddos.' I find that offensive as I am sure most people would. But as I understand it, there is a certain section of Spurs fans who like to be known themselves that way." Indeed, the latter claim is true, but the overall charge, namely, that it was entirely the fault of Tottenham and that Chelsea and Arsenal bear no responsibility for reining in the antisemitic sentiments of their own supporters, undermines the exaggerated piousness of Bates and Dein, though not the accurate charge that those chanting "Yids!" do so, in part, to provoke antisemitism.[44]

The great Tottenham player and captain Danny Blanchflower once observed, "The noise of the crowd, the singing and chanting, is the oxygen we players breathe." Indeed, the chanting of the word "Yids" is onomatopoeic and threatening and, while traditionally shouted in a pogrom, at Tottenham its use as a means to spur the team on constitutes not just a literal but a sonic inversion of the word's traditional invocation. Used by Spurs fans, the word is intended to encourage both the team and the supporters.[45] "You're a Yid and you know you are," shout Tottenham supporters at players rumored to be coming to the club or who have left but retain the affections of the fans. Certain superstars like David Ginola were treated to chants of endearment such as:

> Plays down the wing
> (Plays down the wing)
> Crosses it over (ahhh, ahhh, ahhh)
> His name's Ginola (ahhh, ahhh)
> He's our French Jew[46]

Les Back has noted that "the songs and rituals of football support provide a means to represent locality and social life in the realm of metaphor and symbolism."[47] The non-Jewish invention and celebration of Yiddo culture at Tottenham—one that entails imagining Jewishness (expressing rage at Holocaust taunts and accepting with humor rituals such as circumcision and dietary laws)—sees the supporters (and their rivals) accept the exaggerated and untrue notion that Spurs is a "Jewish" club, taking that on as part of their collective tribal identity. In so doing, they emulate or map, in a cultural act of ontogeny recapitulating phylogeny, Jewish tribal identity.

When the term "Yid" first came into vogue, it bespoke a desire of those Tottenham fans who used the word to be seen as marginal, for paradoxically, this was considered empowering. In his treatise of 1946, *Antisemite and Jew*, Jean-Paul Sartre observed that "it is not the Jewish character that provokes antisemitism but, rather, that it is the antisemite who creates the Jew."[48] In the case of Tottenham's Gentile Yids, it is they who contribute to the creation of the antisemite, but for the purposes of rallying the troops of the Yid Army. Being marginalized gives a deeper layer of meaning to their support for Tottenham. This characteristic has led to what Spurs supporters proudly proclaim as a special Tottenham trait—namely, taking the side of the "other." According to one supporter: "I've always thought that there is something about Spurs supporters that really likes putting two fingers up to the rest of the world. As well as the Stars of David which were always well represented at away games, during the mid-eighties we also continued (post-Falklands) the tradition of having a few Argentinean flags among the away support."⁴⁹ At any rate, the desire for outsider status is, of course, a complete misreading of Jewish sentiments. What ethnic group wants to be vilified? But in the fantasy world of the Yid, being the target of abuse and hatred helps forge bonds of togetherness and kinship, constituting, for them, the probable source of an imagined and ill-informed sense of Jewish solidarity. Moreover, all soccer fans see being a supporter of their club as a form of chosenness. But in the case of Tottenham, it permits, however unconsciously, a reinforcement of a pseudo-Jewish identity wherein the "Yid" and the club enter into a covenantal relationship with one another, thereby recapitulating a version of the Biblical narrative.

As for Jewish supporters who also see themselves as "Yids," Jews are included in the "cultural capital," to borrow Bourdieu's term, of what it means to be a soccer fan. With soccer one of the most important leisure venues for the expression of Englishness among Jews, especially today when most are middle class, soccer allows for the creation of a "horizontal alliance" wherein Jews participate in the ritualized behavior that makes up the largely working-class culture of soccer fandom. At the same time, the younger generation's proud appropriation of Yiddo identity has an internal logic, for it mitigates the impact of their parents' assimilationist tendencies. That is to say, the younger generation of Jews accepts the term "Yid" because of its efficacy in reasserting a strong sense of Jewish identity in the face of several developments in modern Anglo-Jewish history. These include the successful and near total acculturation of Jews into British society, their near total ascent from the working into the middle class, and the relatively recent rejection of the general passivity and quiet anonymity of British Jewry. Chanting "Yids!" at the top of one's lungs within a deeply British institutional and cultural setting is an expression of pride and marks an abandonment of the reticence of British Jews to publicly proclaim their Jewishness. Interestingly enough, this is a "top down" phenomenon wherein the term comes from the typical English racist soccer supporter—Alf Garnett—and was appropriated by Tottenham's non-Jewish supporters. It is their sanctioning of the identity that allowed Jewish supporters to ride the coattails of this unusual act of self-identification by Tottenham's Gentile supporters.

As studies of soccer songs, hooliganism, and racism in British soccer have demonstrated, the tropes and culture of soccer fandom are not static, but change in accordance with the times.⁵⁰ It would, therefore, be mistaken to assume that Yiddo culture has remained unchanged in meaning over time. Hence, I would speculate that a further impetus to recent Jewish use of the term "Yids" may indeed be related to the perception among Anglo-Jewry that antisemitism is on the rise in British society. Of late, this has been made most manifest in the media, where the anti-Israel biases of the BBC, *The Independent*, and *The Guardian*, for example, are often couched in terms that are sometimes less obviously and sometimes more blatantly antisemitic.[51] A recent cover of the *New Statesman*, which bore a Union Jack being pierced by a Star of David, with the caption "A Kosher Conspiracy?" was the most thoroughly antisemitic sentiment to be expressed in the mainstream media for a very long time.[52]

In conclusion, this study of Yiddo culture supports the idea that identity boundaries are porous, and reinforces the notion of the contingent nature of group and individual identity, even if only in ways that require pantomime and parody to help bring them to the fore. I would also venture to suggest that the appropriation of the term "Yid" by Tottenham's non-Jewish supporters also owes much to the self-deprecatory strain that runs throughout English humor, for in Yiddo culture's complete reversal of values and in its undermining of traditional structures, acts that elevate the traditional outsider and bestows upon him insider status, we have a Pythonesque celebration of the absurd. Nothing better illustrates this supposition than the song that Tottenham supporters directed at their hero, the German star Jürgen Klinsmann, who transferred to Tottenham from Monaco in 1994. In what is surely one of the most ironic and absurd of all chants, Tottenham supporters used to express their affection for Klinsmann by singing the following song to him:

> Chim chiminee, chim chiminee
> Chim Chim churoo
> Jürgen was a German
> But now he's a Jew!

Notes

1. Here it is worth noting the difference between this situation and the one that obtains in the United States with the Atlanta Braves baseball team, whose official symbol, regarded as racist by many, is a cartoon caricature of an American Indian.
2. On Tottenham Hotspur's first seventy years, see Roy Brazier, *Images of Sport: Tottenham Hotspur Football Club 1882–1952* (Stroud, 2000).
3. Jewish Virtual Library, "The Jewish Population of the World," http://www.jewishvirtuallibrary.org/jsource/Judaism/jewpop.html. On the Jewish population of Britain as a whole, taken from 1937 to 1994, see Bernard Wasserstein, *Vanishing Diaspora: The Jews in Europe Since 1945* (Cambridge MA, 1996), p. viii. Todd Endelman, *The Jews of Britain, 1650–2000* (Berkeley CA, 2002), pp. 94–96, 196, 230–31.

More generally on British Jewry, see Eugene C. Black, *The Social Politics of Anglo-Jewry*, 1880–1920 (Oxford, 1988).

4. See David Canter, et al., *Football in its Place: An Environmental Psychology of Football Grounds* (London, 1989).

5. Umberto Eco, *A Theory of Semiotics* (Bloomington IN, 1979), pp. 286–298.

6. Umberto Eco, *Travels in Hyper Reality* (New York, 1986), p. 160.

7. A number of academic disciplines have recently turned their methodologies toward an analysis of soccer. For a history of British soccer see James Walvin, *The People's Game* (London, 1975); James Walvin, *Football and the Decline of Britain* (Hampshire, 1986); Tony Mason, *Association Football and English Society* (Brighton, 1980); Stephen Wagg, *The Football World: A Contemporary Social History* (Brighton, 1984); Nicholas Fishwick, *English Football and Society, 1910–1950* (Manchester, 1989). For an analysis that draws on cultural studies, see Chas Critcher, "Football Since the War," in John Clarke, et al., eds., *Working Class Culture: Studies in History and Theory* (London, 1979), pp. 161–84. The studies of John Williams constitute some of the leading sociological analyses of English football. See, for example, his *British Football and Social Change—Getting into Europe* (Leicester, 1991). Also see the Web site of the Sir Norman Chester Centre for Football Research, University of Leicester, http://www.le.ac.uk/snccfr/. The work at the Centre is largely sociological in orientation.

8. The latter is sometimes written as "nigga" or "niggah" (pl. niggaz) to distinguish it from the normative and thus pejorative "nigger."

9. Randall Kennedy, *Nigger: The Strange Career of a Troublesome Word* (New York, 2002), pp. 12, 28.

10. Kennedy, *Nigger*, pp. 34–55: the quotation appears on pp. 46–47.

11. Kim Pearson, "Yid," The Writer's Den, http://kpearson.faculty.tcnj.edu/Dictionary/yid.htm. See also Leo Rosten, *The Joys of Yiddish* (New York, 1968), p. 445.

12. Endelman, *The Jews of Britain*, pp. 202–3. See also Tony Kushner and Nadia Valman, eds., *Remembering Cable Street: Fascism and Anti-Fascism in British Society* (London, 1999).

13. See Simon Kuper's compelling history of Ajax and the Jews: "Ajax, de Joden, Nederland," AJAX-USA, http://www.ajax-usa.com/history/kuper/. This is an online version of his book, *Ajax, the Jews, the War* (London, 2003). More generally, see the official history of Ajax Amsterdam at the club's Web site: "1900–1915: The Ancient Ajax," AJAX-USA, http://www.ajax-usa.com/history/ajax/the_ancient_ajax.html.

14. David Winner, *Brilliant Orange: The Neurotic Genius of Dutch Football* (London, 2001), p. 217.

15. The game took place at the Kiryat Eliezer Stadium on October 21, 1999. Ajax won 3–0.

16. Winner, *Brilliant Orange*, p. 218. Numerous Web sites carry message boards with endless declarations of mutual admiration from Ajax and Hapoel Haifa supporters. For example, see the Hebrew language Web site for Hapoel Haifa, http://www.hapoel-haifa.org.il/europe/uefa/2000/uefamain2000.html. See also this Dutch Web page from an Ajax fan who waxed rhapsodic about his trip to Israel: Rob van Vliet, "Reisverslag Hapoel Haifa (21-10-1999)," www.f-side.nl, http://www.f-side.nl/verslagen/9900hap_aja.html.

17. Gary Armstrong and Richard Giulianotti, eds., *Fear and Loathing in World Football* (Oxford, 2001), pp. 17–18, 40.

18. Danny Kelly, "Sol Abuse Has Nothing to Do with Colour of His Skin," *Topspurs: Jim Duggan's Spurs Site*, http://www.topspurs.com/thfc-article25.htm.

19. According to the "Frequently Asked Questions" page of the Web site of the online fanzine *My Eyes Have Seen the Glory*, " 'Yids' or 'Yiddoes' began to be used in the 1980s, mainly by rival Arsenal fans, because of the large Jewish population in the Haringey area. The Spurs fans made the nickname a badge of honor by calling themselves the 'Yids' or 'Yiddoes,' " (http://www.mehstg.com/faqs.htm).

20. Phone interview: Norman Fenton (December 6, 2001). The character of Alf Garnett was played by veteran actor Warren Mitchell, publicly proud and outspoken about his Jewish identity and an avid Tottenham supporter who attends nearly every home game. It would seem to me that this is the likely origin of the association of Tottenham as Yids.

21. Email from Les Wilson to the author (April 21, 2002).

22. Phone interview: Ivan Cohen (March 31, 2002).

23. Nicholas Harrison, "Tottenham," "Sing Something Sinful: 30 Years of Chelsea Verbal Aggro," http://www.nicholas.harrison.mcmail.com/cfcsong3.htm.

24. See C. Waters, "Racial Chanting and the Ultra Right at Football Matches," BA Dissertation, Leeds Polytechnic, 1988; Richard Turner, *In Your Blood: Football Culture in the Late 1980s and Early 1990s* (London, 1990); Bill Buford, *Amongst the Thugs* (London, 1991), p. 147; and Les Back, et al., ed., *The Changing Face of Football* (Oxford, 2001), pp. 21–38.

25. A somewhat analogous situation, though having nothing to do with Jews, is to be found at the Scottish club Aberdeen, whose fans are taunted with the vulgarity, "Sheep-shagging bastards, you're only." Their response to this is to affirm the characterization of their predilection for bestiality by chanting in retort, "Sheepshagging bastards, we're only." Quoted in Peter Pericles Trifonas, *Umberto Eco and Football* (Cambridge, 2001), pp. 19–20.

26. Email from Jim O'Neill to the author (April 16, 2002).

27. Phone interview: Ivan Cohen (March 31, 2002).

28. Email from Jim O'Neill to the author (April 16, 2002).

29. Les Back, et al., ed., *The Changing Face of Football*, p. 109.

30. The term is taken from Scott Fleming and Alan Tomlinson, "Football, Racism and Xenophobia in England (I): Europe and the Old England," in *Racism and Xenophobia in European Football*, Udo Merkel and Walter Tokarski, eds. (Aachen, 1996), p. 82.

31. The same song was also sung by Chelsea supporters as they waited to go through the metal detectors at Tottenham on August 22, 1987: Harrison, "Tottenham," http://www.nicholas.harrison.mcmail.com/cfcsong3.htm.

32. John King, *The Football Factory* (London, 1997), pp. 22–23.

33. Harrison, "Tottenham," http://www.nicholas.harrison.mcmail.com/cfcsong3.htm.

34. Harrison, "Tottenham," http://www.nicholas.harrison.mcmail.com/cfcsong3.htm.

35. Email from Jonathan Adelman to the author (April 17, 2002).

36. Harrison, "Tottenham," http://www.nicholas.harrison.mcmail.com/cfcsong3.htm.

37. Harrison, "Tottenham," http://www.nicholas.harrison.mcmail.com/cfcsong3.htm.

38. Quoted in Steve Redhead, ed., *The Passion and the Fashion: Football Fandom in the New Europe* (Aldershot), 1993, p. 14.

39. Les Back, et al., ed., *The Changing Face of Football*, p. 110.

40. Email from Steff to the author (April 17, 2002).

41. Email from Andy Gardner to the author (April 17, 2002).

42. Les Back., ed., et al., *The Changing Face of Football: Racism, Identity and Multiculturalism in the English Game* (Oxford, 2001), p. 37.

43. Winner, *Brilliant Orange*, p. 218.

44. *Daily Mirror* (March 6, 2003).
45. See http://www.glennhoddlesblueandwhitearmeeee.co.uk/WhyAreWeCalled.html (cached version available at http://72.14.203.104/search?q=cache:48-yMvc5ANEJ: www.qontour.com/HTML/2002_2003/QFriendlymatches/qstory_yids_ftho40802 .html+%22ever+wondered+why+tottenham+fans%22&hl=en&client=firefox-a). At this Web site, the page entitled "Ever Wondered Why Tottenham Fans Are Called 'Yids'?" stated that "One song or chant! that you won't fail to hear starts before the game as you walk down Tottenham high road. You'll hear it in pubs for your pre match drink up, You'll also hear it at five minutes to three when the team comes out onto the pitch and it will more than likely continue throughout the game . . . within the stands of the stadium no one means it in an insulting or derogatory way but as a way to encourage our team to victory."
46. Glen's Hjemmeside, "Sanger til Tottenham," http://home.no.net/glenside/sanger_til _tottenham.htm.
47. Les Back., ed., et al., *The Changing Face of Football*, p. 73.
48. Jean-Paul Sartre, *Antisemite and Jew* (New York, 1987), p. 143.
49. Email from Bill Leask to the author (April 23, 2002).
50. Redhead, ed., *The Passion and the Fashion*. On hooliganism, see the recent study by Gary Armstrong, *Football Hooligans: Knowing the Score* (Oxford, 2000); Garry Robson, "No One Likes Us and We Don't Care": The Myth and Reality of Millwall Fandom* (Oxford, 2000).
51. See the detailed report prepared by the London solicitor Trevor Asserson, "The BBC and the Middle East: A Critical Study," BBCWATCH.COM (March 2002), http://www .bbcwatch.co.uk. See also the January 26, 2002, report in *The Guardian* on the perception of rising antisemitism in Britain and its relationship to the Palestinian-Israeli conflict, "A New Anti-Semitism?" at http://www.guardian.co.uk/leaders/story/0,3604, 639688,00.html. Finally, see the September 30, 2002, article by Saron Sandeh titled "U.K. Jews up in Arms over Media's Israel Coverage" in the Israeli liberal daily *Ha'aretz* on reactions to three anti-Israel documentaries shown on British television: http:// www.haaretzdaily.com/hasen/pages/ShArt.jhtml?itemNo=214129&contrassID=2& subContrassID=11&sbSubContrassID=0&listSrc=Y&itemNo=214129.
52. The issue was dated January 14, 2002. The editor, Peter Wilby, later offered an apology for the inflammatory cover, though tellingly, not the contents of the article. For a picture of the cover and a story of the apology it sparked, see Charlotte Halle, "New Statesman Apologizes for 'Anti-Semitic' Cover—Not Story," at http://www.haaretzdaily.com /hasen/pages/ShArt.jhtml?itemNo=128266&contrassID=2&subContrassID=1&sbSub ContrassID=0&listSrc=Y. More recently, it was reported that on September 10, 2002, the Israel Football Association (IFA) had approached Tottenham Hotspur, seeking permission for the national team to play its home games for the Euro 2004 championship at White Hart Lane, given that FIFA will not permit Israel to play its home games in Israel due to the risky security situation. While Tottenham's Jewish chairman, Daniel Levy, declined to permit the staging of Israel's home matches at White Hart Lane, what is of note here is that the IFA did not approach any other London club—Arsenal, for example, or any so-called "Jewish" club on the continent—for similar assistance. For the IFA, anticipating a goodwill gesture from North London's "Jewish" club, not to mention a stadium full of Jewish (and Yiddo) supporters, Tottenham appeared the most obvious, indeed, only choice for an Israeli national team seeking support for its cause. Tottenham fans' reactions in an internet chat room to the decision by Tottenham

to not support the IFA's request were mixed, though largely sympathetic responses. Typical of such was this one, dated September 25, 2002: "Initially I thought this [an opportunity lost]. But my guess is that the Board were [sic] considering the worst case scenario. Say a Palestinian terrorist or sympathiser decided to use the opportunity of the game to perform an act of atrocity such as a suicide bomber, not only would it be bad for the club, but there could be structural damage to the ground, which would then be subsequently closed until fit to be reopened. Maybe the club were [sic] thinking of the increased costs for policing such a game. What would the club's responsibilities be with regard to hosting this game in terms of policing etc? Or if nothing were to happen at an Israel game, who's to say a terrorist would not perform an atrocity at a Spurs game because the club had been associated with Israel. It's a sad state of affairs when you have to think like this, but that's my guess what has happened." This response drew a most angry reply from one subscriber to the chat list, one which went to the heart of Anglo-Jewish sensibilities regarding Israel and antisemitism. On September 25, 2002, he responded vehemently to the person responsible for the above: "A [the initial letter of the man's name], I had hoped that this kind of meek, mild-mannered keep your head down Jewish thinking had disappeared. . . . Personally, if the scenario you describe is the case, then like Zola (not Gianfranco!): J'accuse. I accuse the Board of being gutless wonders who kowtow to a veiled threat which has no basis thus far in any kind of reality. My personal guess is that such a scenario has occurred, probably due to the influence of the Met Police, who have a long and unfettered history of latent antisemitism."

List of Contributors

Jacob Borut is a research fellow at the Yad Vashem archives. He is the author of *A New Spirit among Our Brethren in Ashkenaz* (1999) and is currently completing a book on everyday antisemitism during the Weimar Republic.

Michael Brenner is Professor of Jewish History and Culture at the University of Munich. His books include *The Renaissance of Jewish Culture in Weimar Germany* (1996); *After the Holocaust: Rebuilding Jewish Lives in Postwar Germany* (1997); *Zionism: A Brief History* (2003).

John Bunzl is a member of the Austrian Institute for International Affairs. His books include *Gewalt ohne Grenzen: Nahostterror und Österreich* (1991) and *Between Vienna and Jerusalem: Reflections and Polemics on Austria, Israel and Palestine* (1997).

Tony Collins is a research fellow in the International Centre for Sports History and Culture at De Montfort University, Leicester. He is the author of *Rugby's Great Split: Class, Culture and the Origins of Rugby League Football* (1998), and coeditor of the journal *Sport in History*.

John Efron is Koret Professor of History and Jewish Studies at the University of California, Berkeley. He is the author of *Defenders of the Race: Jewish Doctors and Race Science in fin-de-siècle Europe* (1994) and *Medicine and the German Jews: A History* (2001).

Sharon Gillerman is Associate Professor of Jewish History at the Hebrew Union College in Los Angeles. She is currently completing a book on the Jewish family, welfare and reproduction in the Weimar Republic entitled *Germans into Jews: Remaking the Jewish Social Body in the Weimar Republic*.

Philipp Grammes is a journalist for *Bayerischer Rundfunk* and *Jüdische Allgemeine Zeitung*. He wrote his master's thesis at the University of Munich in 2004 on the Yiddish newspaper *Undzer Wort*, published 1946–47 in Bamberg (Bavaria). He is the author of a forthcoming book, *Ein Beweis, dass wir da sind: Die jiddische Wochenzeitung 'Undzer Wort'—Kommunikationsstrukturen und -interesse von Displaced Persons*.

Miklós Hadas is Professor of Sociology at the Corvinus University of Budapest. His primary research concerns elite training, the social history of cultural performance (especially music), the sociology of sports, and the study of gender, particularly the social history of manhood. His major book on the subject was published in Hungarian under the title *Birth of the Modern Man* (Budapest, 2003).

Jack Jacobs is Deputy Executive Officer of the Ph.D. program in political science at the Graduate Center of the City University of New York and Professor of Government at John Jay College, CUNY. He is the author of *On Socialists and "the Jewish Question" after Marx* (1992) and the editor of *Jewish Politics in Eastern Europe: The Bund at 100* (2001).

Michael John is Professor of Social and Economic History at the University of Linz. He is the author of *Wohnverhältnisse sozialer Unterschichten im Wien Kaiser Franz Josephs* (1984) and *Bevölkerung in der Stadt: "Einheimische" und "Fremde" in Linz* (2000).

Victor Karady is Senior Research Director Emeritus in Sociology at the French National Center for Scientific Research (CNRS) and, at present, Recurrent Professor in the Department of History at the Central European University (CEU) in Budapest. His main research interests include the institutionalization of the social sciences, the social history of academia, elite selection and elite training, patterns of cultural assimilation of minorities in modern nation states, and Jewish social history (which he teaches at CEU). His latest books in English are *The Jews of Europe in the Modern Era, A Socio-Historical Outline* (2004), and, with Lucian Nastasa, *The University of Kolozsvar and the Students of the Medical Faculty (1872–1918)* (2004).

Albert Lichtblau is Professor of Jewish history at the University of Salzburg. He is the author of *Antisemitismus und soziale Spannung in Berlin und Wien 1867–1914* (1994) and *Als hätten wir dazugehört* (1999).

Rudolf Oswald is currently completing his dissertation, "Volksgemeinschaftendiskurs im deutschen Fussballsport," at the University of Munich.

Gideon Reuveni is a research fellow at the Department of Jewish History and Culture at the University of Munich. He is the author of *Reading Germany: Literature and Consumer Culture in Germany before 1933* (2006) and coeditor of *Jüdische Geschichte lesen: Texte der jüdischen Geschichtsschreibung im 19. und 20. Jahrhundert* (2003).

Daniel Wildmann is Deputy Director of the Leo Baeck Institute in London. He is the author of *Begehrte Körper* (1998) and *Arisierungen in Österreich und ihre Bezüge zur Schweiz* (2002). He is currently completing a book tentatively titled "Sports, the Body, and Identity."

Moshe Zimmermann is Professor of German History and director of the Richard Koebner Center for German History at the Hebrew University, Jerusalem. He is the author of *Wilhelm Marr: The Patriarch of Antisemitism* (1986) *Die deutschen Juden, 1914–1945* (1997), and *Deutsch-Jüdische Vergangenheit: Der Judenhaß als Herausforderung* (2005).

Index